The WAR that TIME FORGOT ★★★★★

VOL ★ TWO

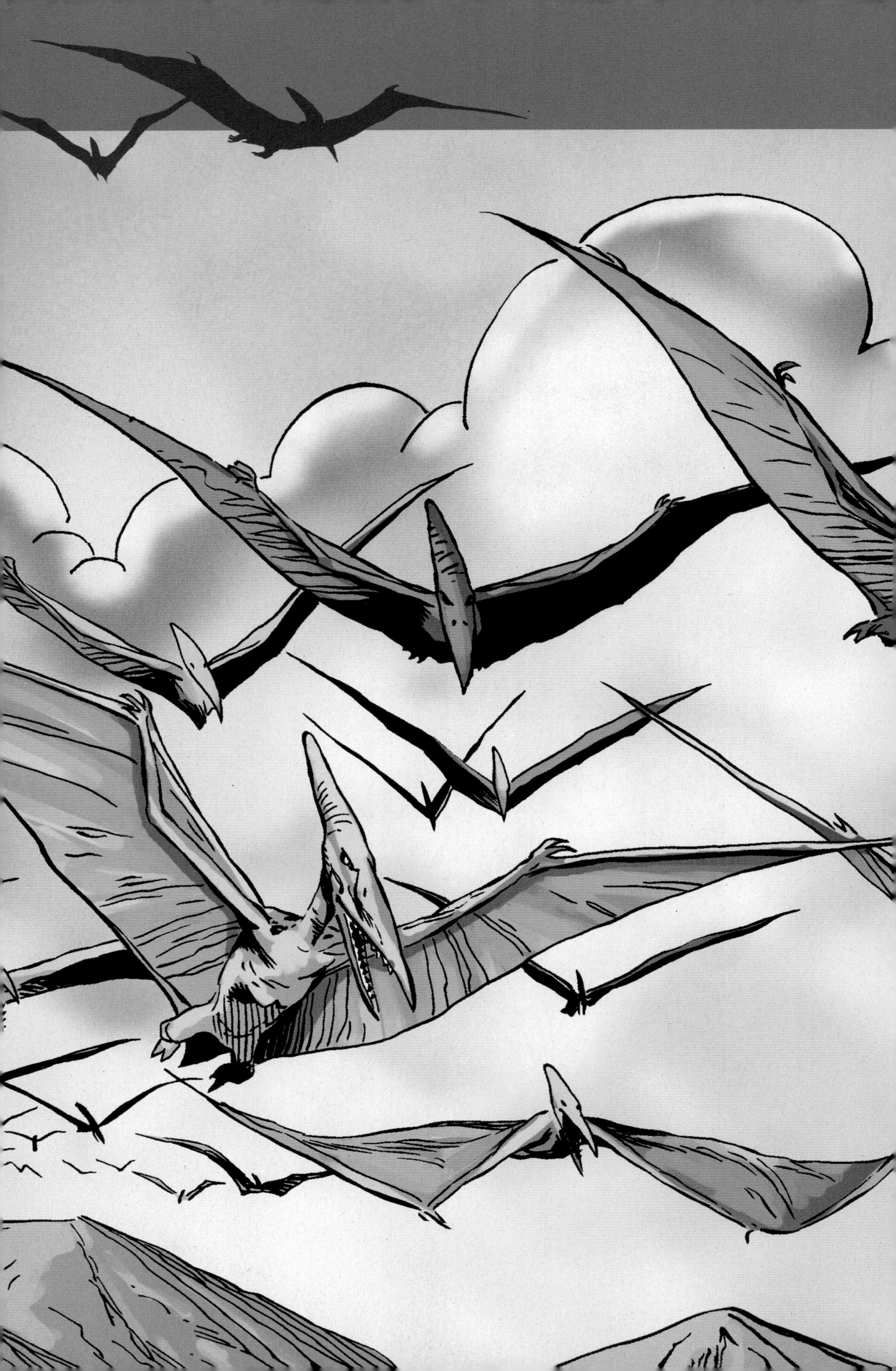

The WAR that TIME FORGOT

VOLUME TWO

BRUCE
JONES
writer

AL BARRIONUEVO
chapters 7, 8 & 12

SCOTT KOLINS
chapter 9

GRAHAM NOLAN
chapters 10 & 11
pencillers

DAN GREEN
chapters 7, 8, 10, 11 & 12

SCOTT KOLINS
chapter 9
inkers

WAYNE FAUCHER
co-inker, chapter 8

SAL CIPRIANO
letterer

MIKE ATIYEH
colorist

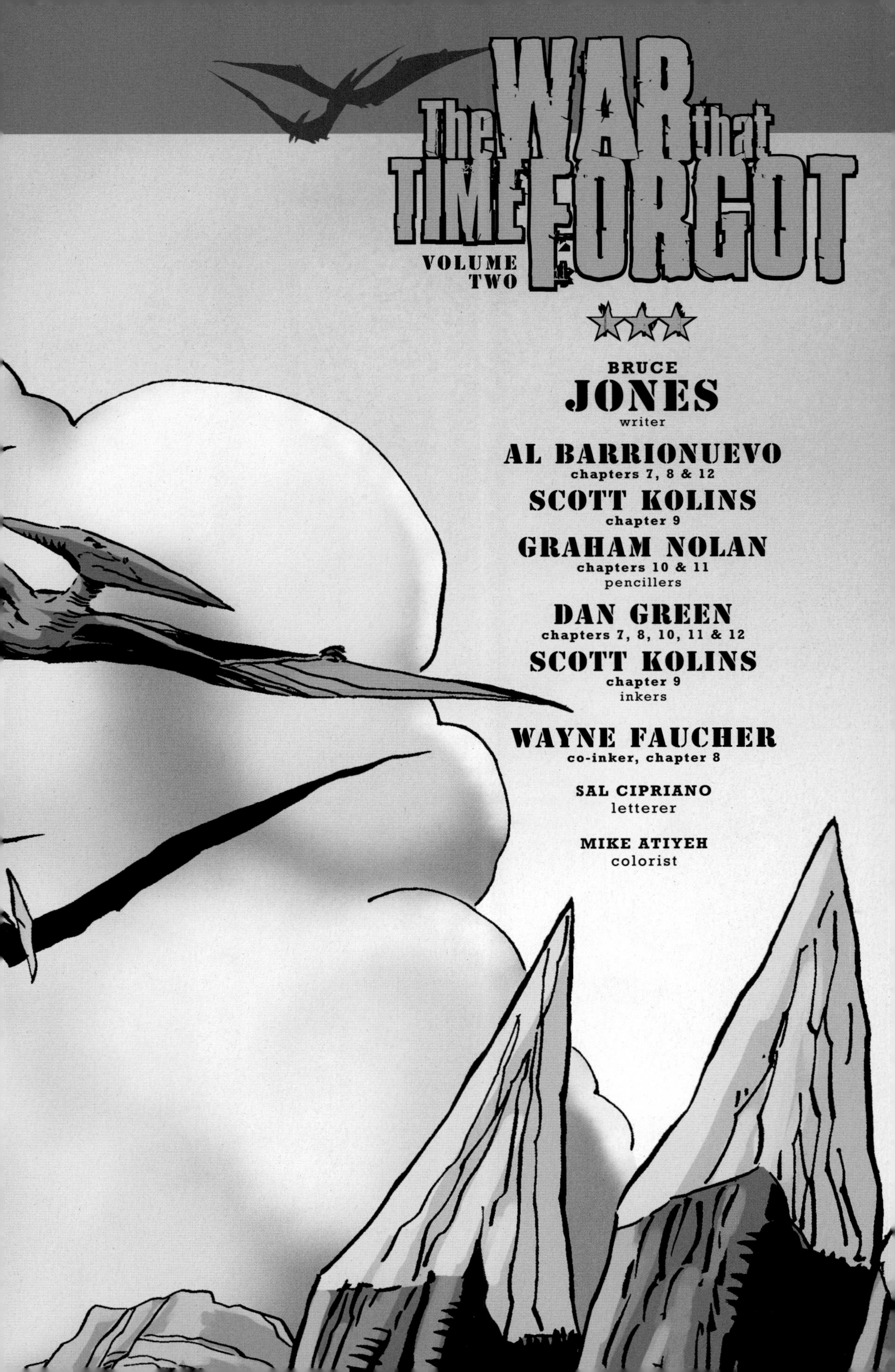

DAN DIDIO SVP – Executive Editor
JOEY CAVALIERI Editor – Original Series
CHRIS CONROY Assistant Editor – Original Series
GEORG BREWER VP – Design & DC Direct Creative
BOB HARRAS Group Editor – Collected Editions
PETER HAMBOUSSI Editor
ROBBIN BROSTERMAN Design Director – Books

DC Comics
PAUL LEVITZ President & Publisher
RICHARD BRUNING SVP – Creative Director
PATRICK CALDON EVP – Finance & Operations
AMY GENKINS SVP – Business & Legal Affairs
JIM LEE Editorial Director – WildStorm
GREGORY NOVECK SVP – Creative Affairs
STEVE ROTTERDAM SVP – Sales & Marketing
CHERYL RUBIN SVP – Brand Management

Cover by Justiniano with Mike Atiyeh
Publication design by Robbie Biederman

THE WAR THAT TIME FORGOT Volume Two
Published by DC Comics.
Cover, text and compilation Copyright © 2009 DC Comics.
All Rights Reserved.

DC Comics, 1700 Broadway, New York, NY 10019
A Warner Bros. Entertainment Company
Printed in Canada. First Printing.
ISBN: 978-1-4012-2475-2

SFI
CERTIFIED
SOURCING

Fiber used in this product line meets the
sourcing requirements of the SFI program.
www.sfiprogram.org
PWC-SFICOC-260

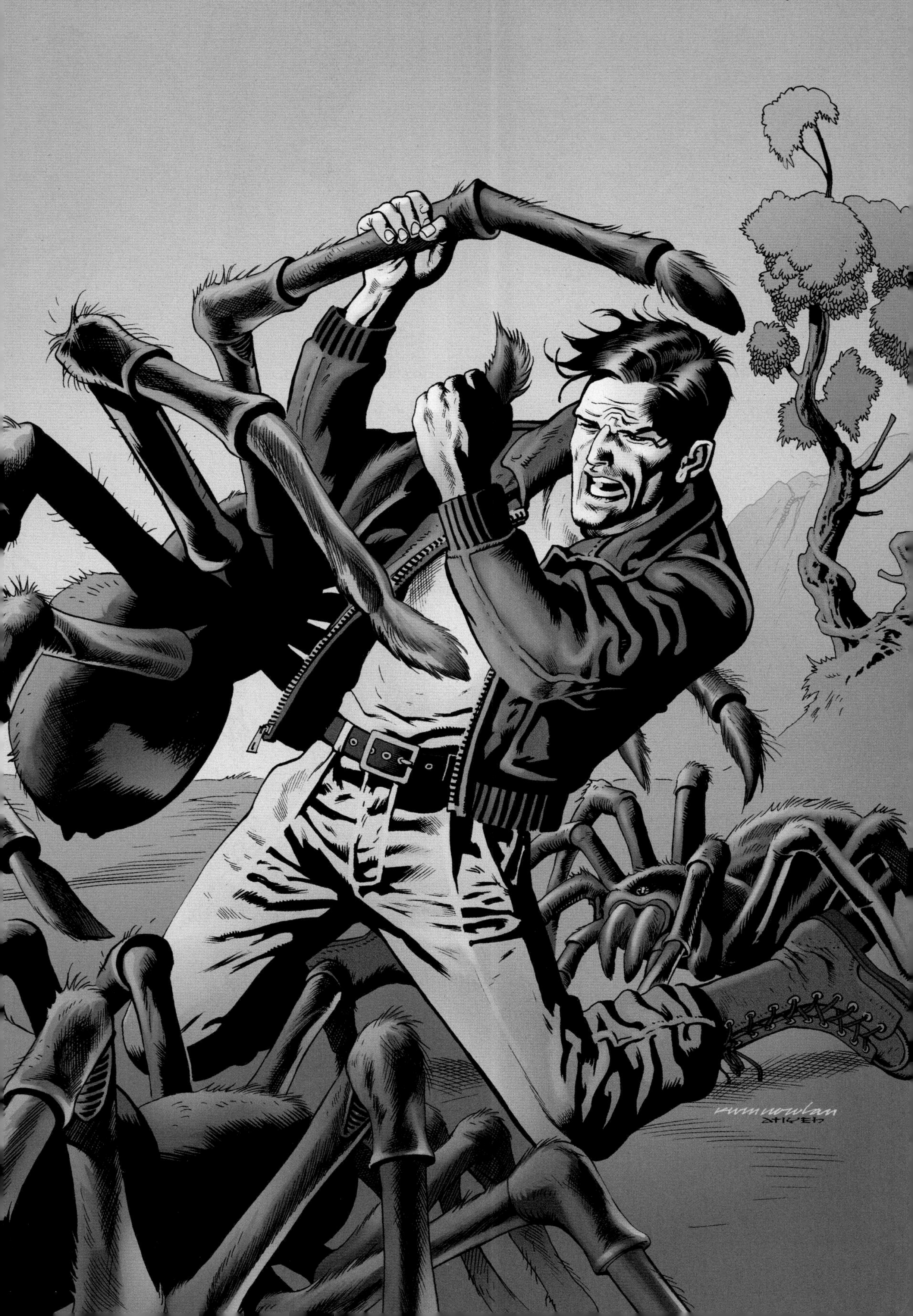
kevin nowlan
atiyeh

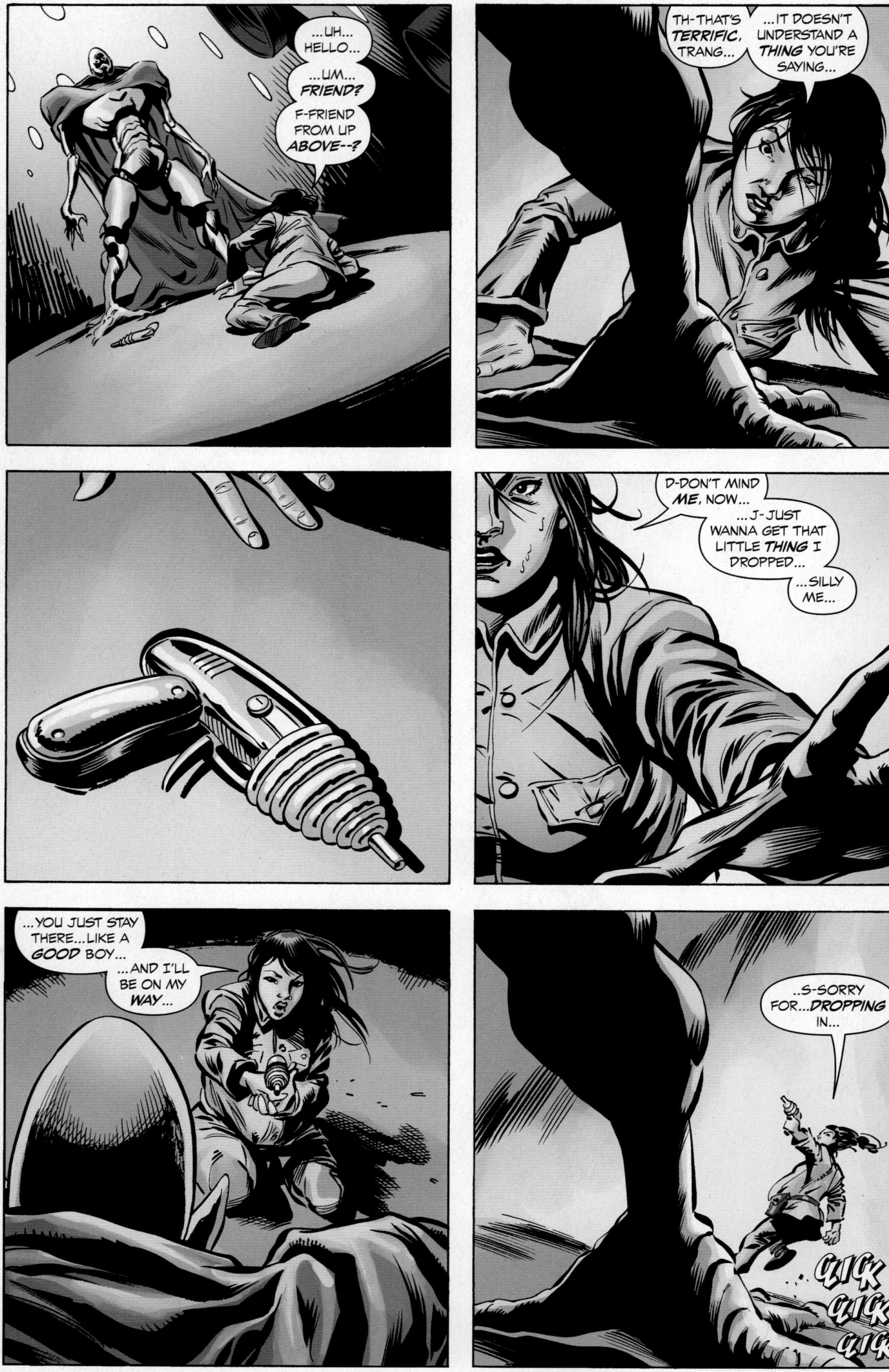
...UH... HELLO...
...UM... FRIEND?
F-FRIEND FROM UP ABOVE--?
TH-THAT'S TERRIFIC, TRANG...
...IT DOESN'T UNDERSTAND A THING YOU'RE SAYING...
D-DON'T MIND ME, NOW...
...J-JUST WANNA GET THAT LITTLE THING I DROPPED...
...SILLY ME...
...YOU JUST STAY THERE...LIKE A GOOD BOY...
...AND I'LL BE ON MY WAY...
..S-SORRY FOR...DROPPING IN...
CLICK
CLICK
CLICK

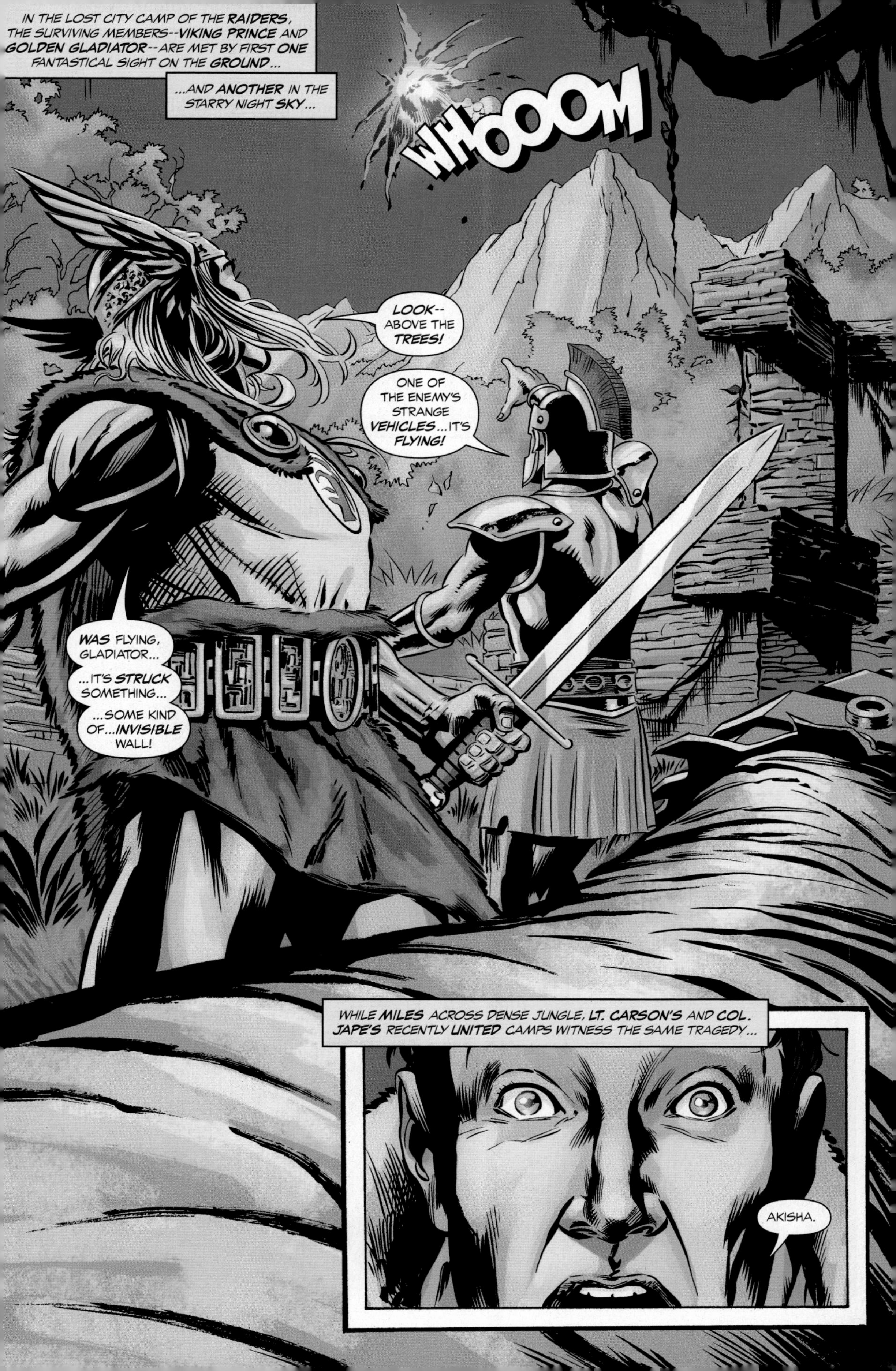
IN THE LOST CITY CAMP OF THE RAIDERS, THE SURVIVING MEMBERS--VIKING PRINCE AND GOLDEN GLADIATOR--ARE MET BY FIRST ONE FANTASTICAL SIGHT ON THE GROUND...
...AND ANOTHER IN THE STARRY NIGHT SKY...
WHOOOOM
LOOK-- ABOVE THE TREES!
ONE OF THE ENEMY'S STRANGE VEHICLES...IT'S FLYING!
WAS FLYING, GLADIATOR...
...IT'S STRUCK SOMETHING...
...SOME KIND OF...INVISIBLE WALL!
WHILE MILES ACROSS DENSE JUNGLE, LT. CARSON'S AND COL. JAPE'S RECENTLY UNITED CAMPS WITNESS THE SAME TRAGEDY...
AKISHA.

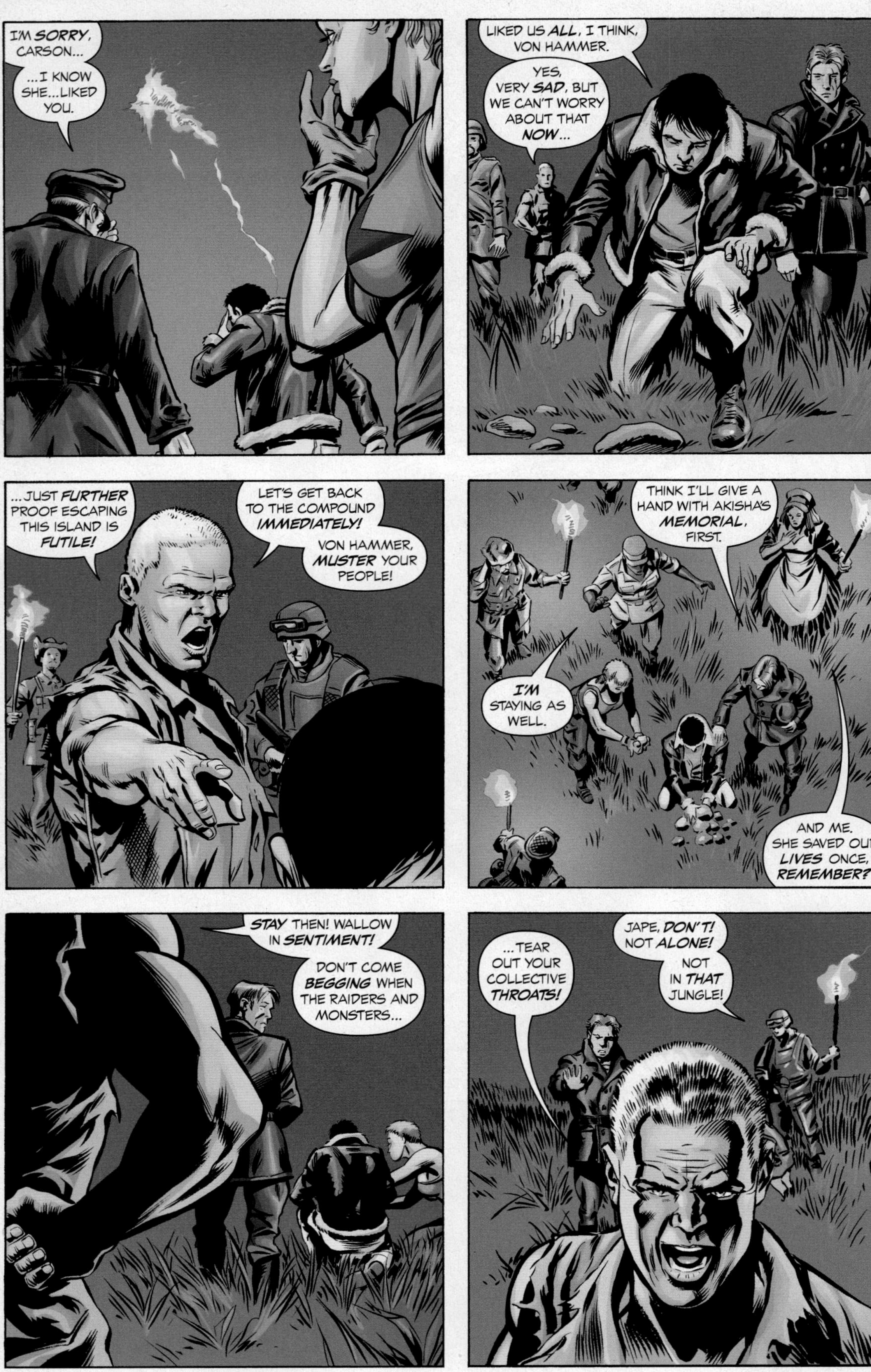
I'M SORRY, CARSON...
...I KNOW SHE...LIKED YOU.
LIKED US ALL, I THINK, VON HAMMER.
YES, VERY SAD, BUT WE CAN'T WORRY ABOUT THAT NOW...
...JUST FURTHER PROOF ESCAPING THIS ISLAND IS FUTILE!
LET'S GET BACK TO THE COMPOUND IMMEDIATELY!
VON HAMMER, MUSTER YOUR PEOPLE!
THINK I'LL GIVE A HAND WITH AKISHA'S MEMORIAL, FIRST.
I'M STAYING AS WELL.
AND ME. SHE SAVED OUR LIVES ONCE, REMEMBER?
STAY THEN! WALLOW IN SENTIMENT!
DON'T COME BEGGING WHEN THE RAIDERS AND MONSTERS...
...TEAR OUT YOUR COLLECTIVE THROATS!
JAPE, DON'T! NOT ALONE!
NOT IN THAT JUNGLE!

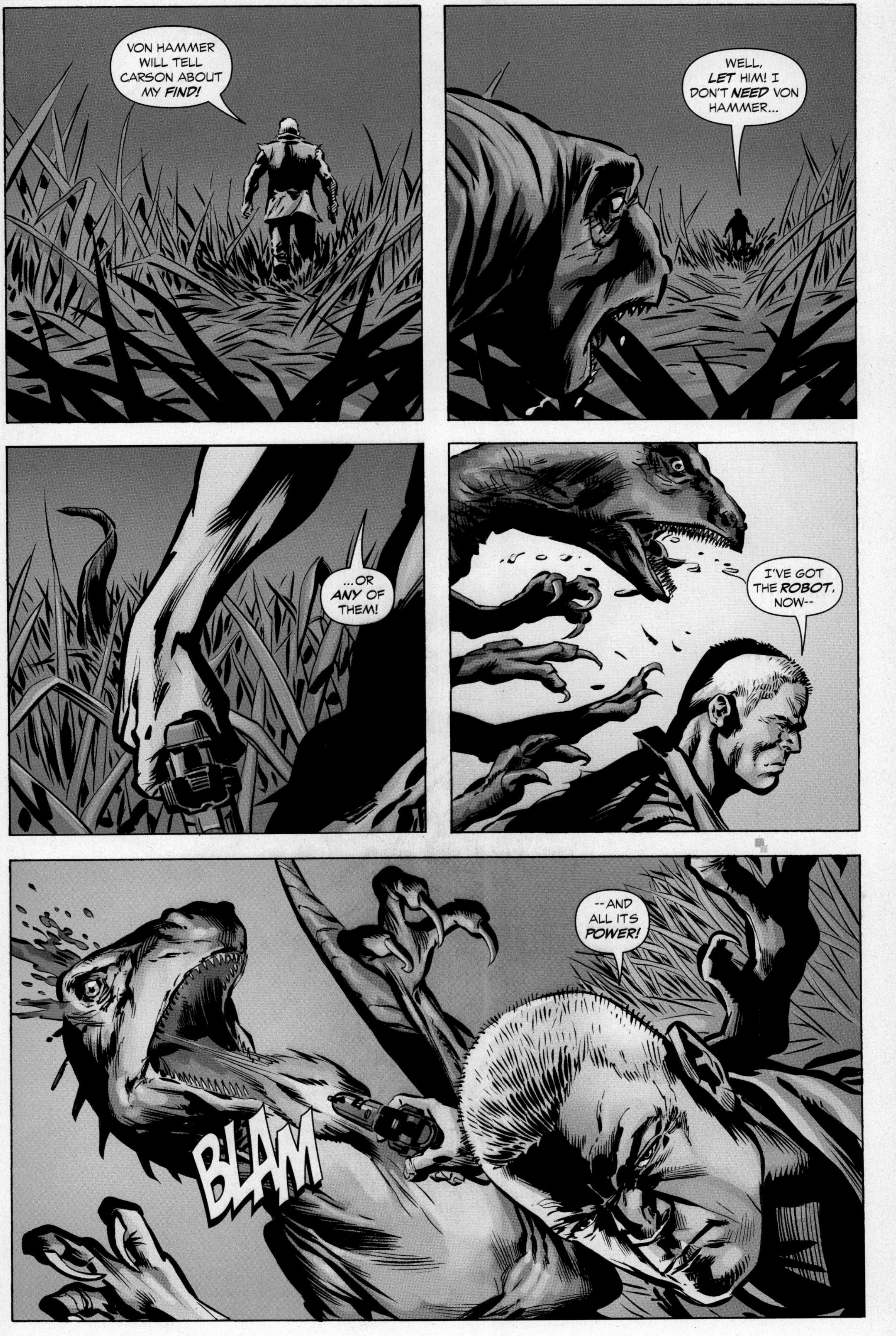
VON HAMMER WILL TELL CARSON ABOUT MY FIND!
WELL, LET HIM! I DON'T NEED VON HAMMER...
...OR ANY OF THEM!
I'VE GOT THE ROBOT, NOW--
--AND ALL ITS POWER!
BLAM

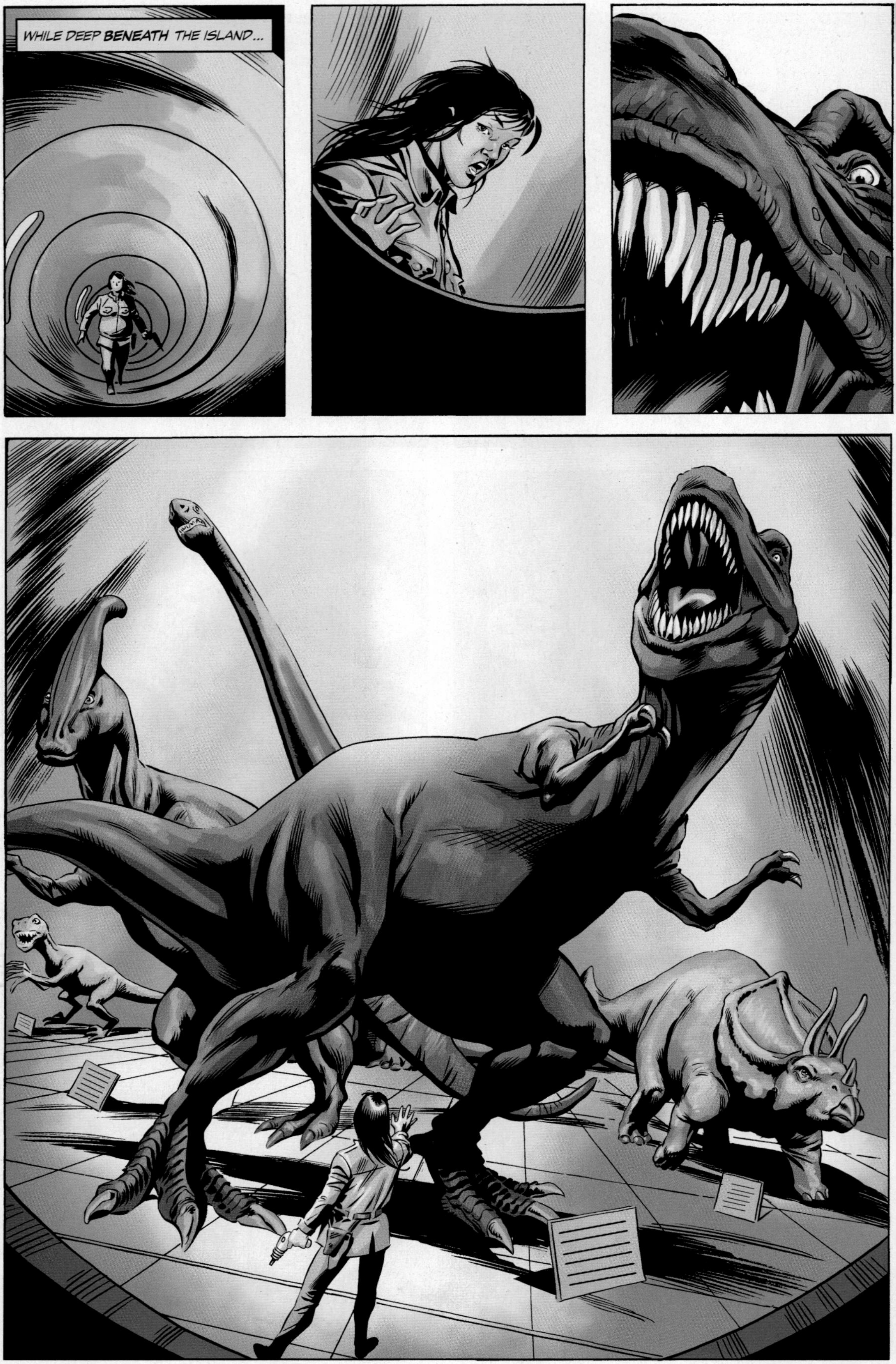
WHILE DEEP BENEATH THE ISLAND...

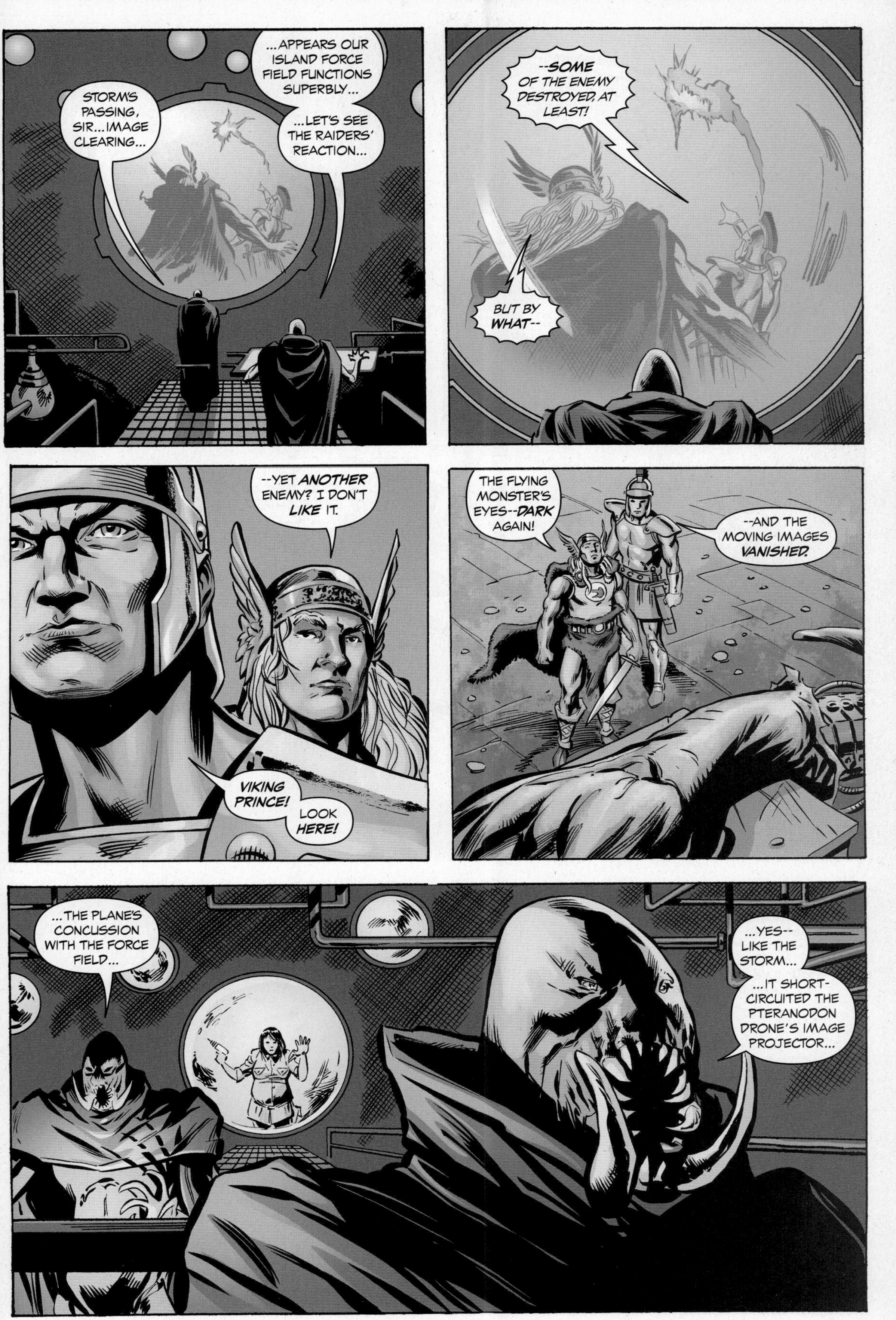
STORM'S PASSING, SIR...IMAGE CLEARING...
...APPEARS OUR ISLAND FORCE FIELD FUNCTIONS SUPERBLY...
...LET'S SEE THE RAIDERS' REACTION...
--SOME OF THE ENEMY DESTROYED, AT LEAST!
BUT BY WHAT--
--YET ANOTHER ENEMY? I DON'T LIKE IT.
VIKING PRINCE!
LOOK HERE!
THE FLYING MONSTER'S EYES--DARK AGAIN!
--AND THE MOVING IMAGES VANISHED.
...THE PLANE'S CONCUSSION WITH THE FORCE FIELD...
...YES--LIKE THE STORM...
...IT SHORT-CIRCUITED THE PTERANODON DRONE'S IMAGE PROJECTOR...

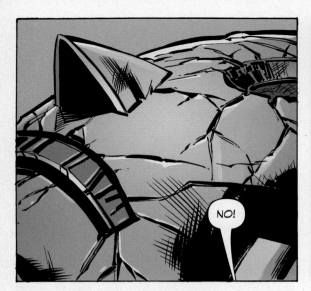

NO!

HIS *EYE LENSES* ARE *DEAD!*

SOMEONE'S *BEEN* HERE--

--*SEEN* HIM!

OR PERHAPS *NOT*...

APPEARS TO BE JUST AN *OVERLOADED* CIRCUIT.

I CAN FIX THIS!

THAAAT'S BETTER!

AH...THE *EVER* AMBITIOUS *LT. CARSON!*

AND WHAT *IMPORTANT* ROLE DID *YOU* PLAY IN WORLD *HISTORY,* LIEUTENANT...

...THAT *SOMEONE* FINDS SO *VITALLY* INTRIGUING?

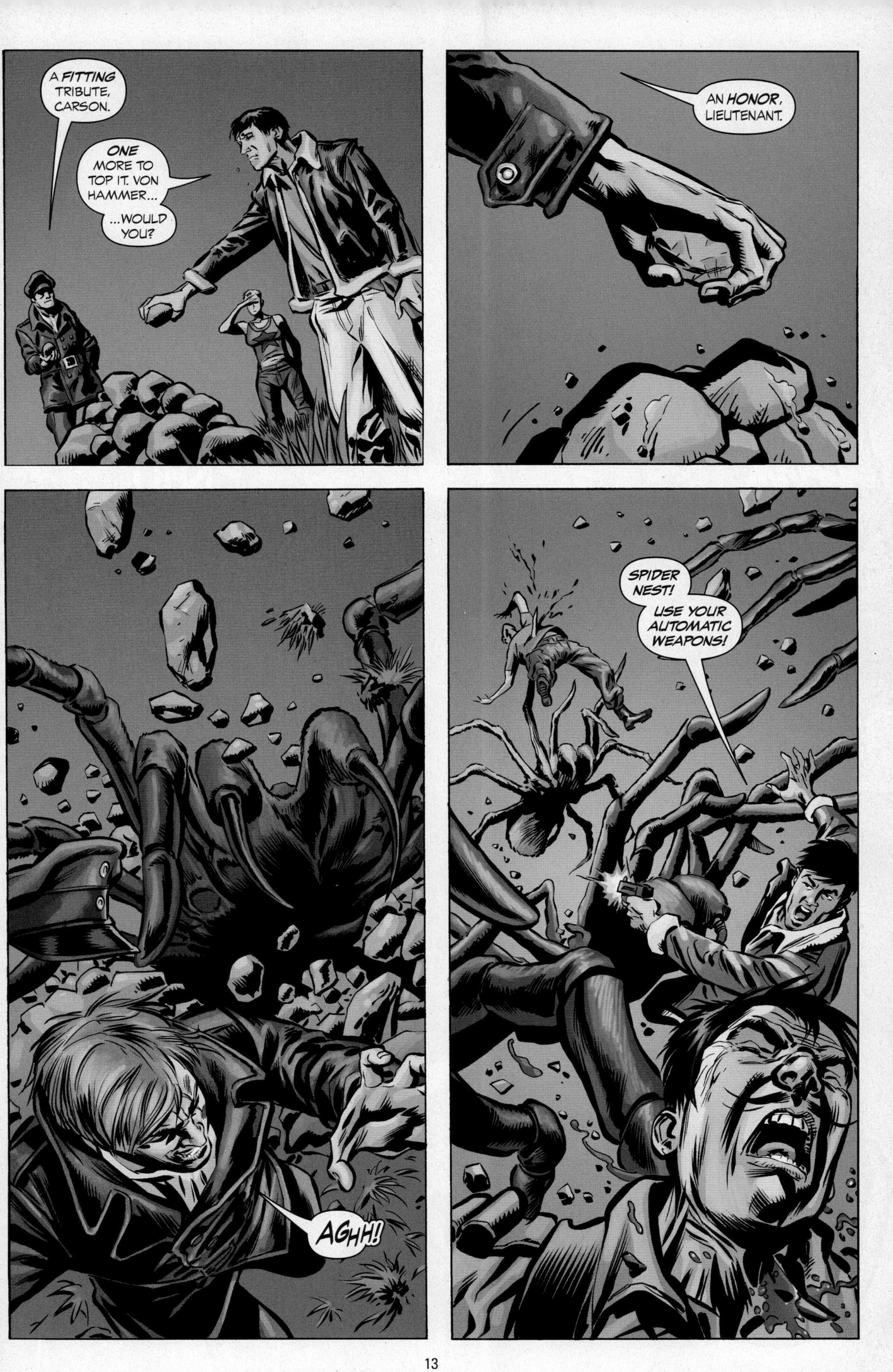

A *FITTING* TRIBUTE, CARSON.
ONE MORE TO TOP IT. VON HAMMER...
...WOULD YOU?
AN *HONOR*, LIEUTENANT.
AGHH!
SPIDER NEST! USE YOUR AUTOMATIC WEAPONS!

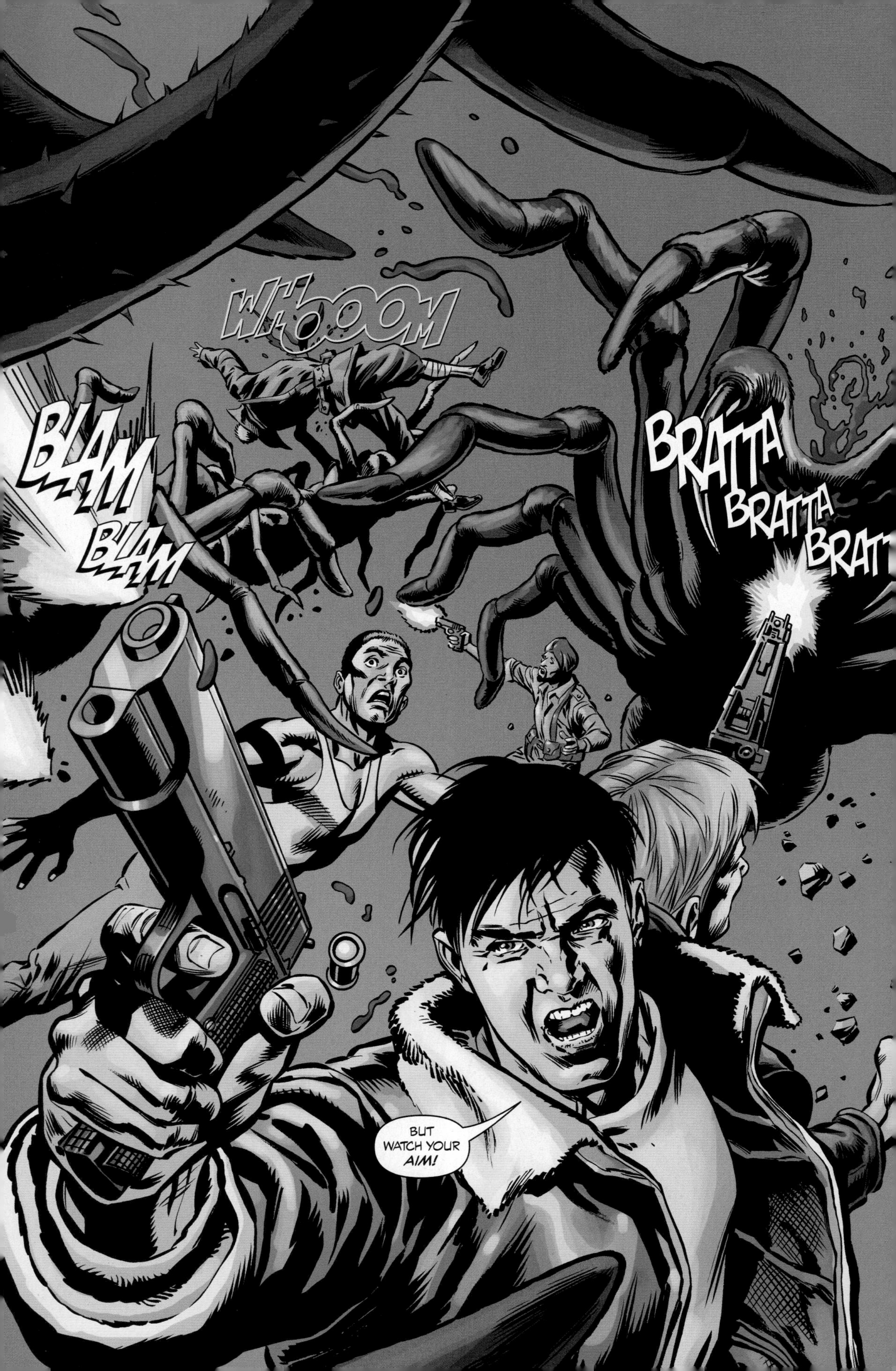
WHOOOM
BLAM
BLAM
BRATTA
BRATTA
BRATT
BUT WATCH YOUR AIM!

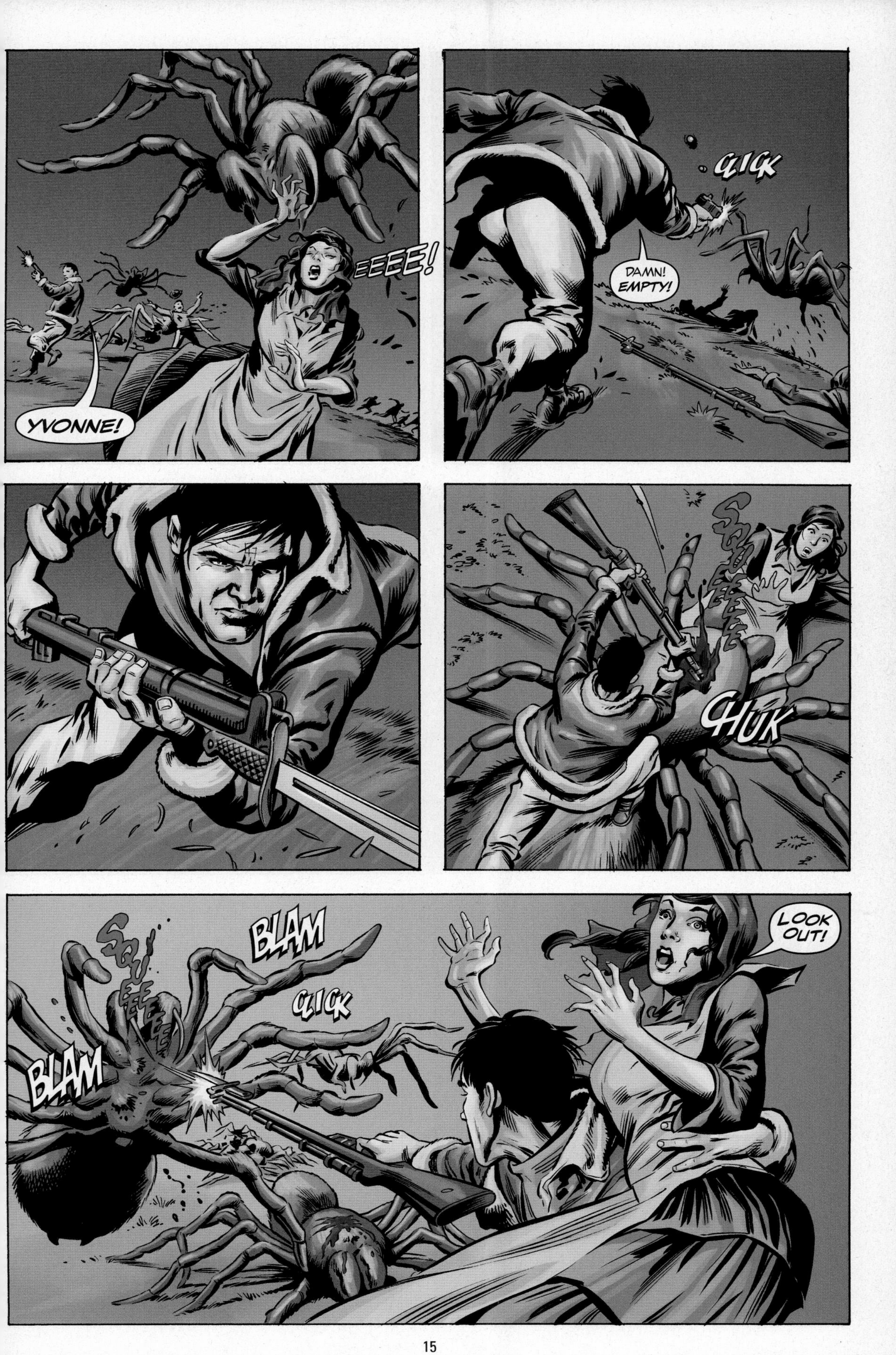
EEEEE!
YVONNE!
CLICK
DAMN! EMPTY!
SQUEEEEE
CHUK
BLAM
SQUEEEEEE
CLICK
BLAM
LOOK OUT!

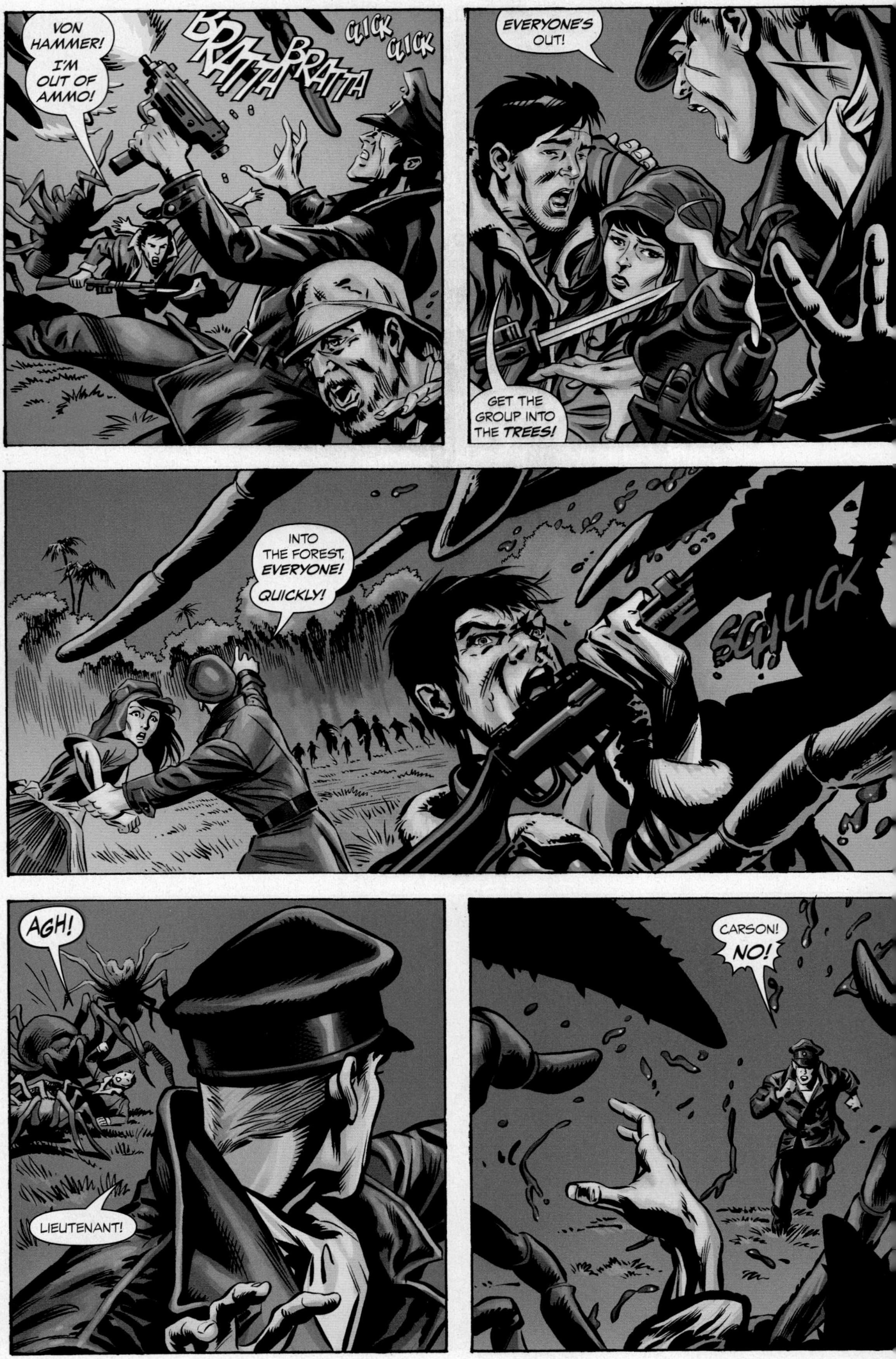
VON HAMMER!
I'M OUT OF AMMO!
BRATTA BRATTA
CLICK CLICK
EVERYONE'S OUT!
GET THE GROUP INTO THE TREES!
INTO THE FOREST, EVERYONE!
QUICKLY!
SCHLICK
AGH!
LIEUTENANT!
CARSON! NO!

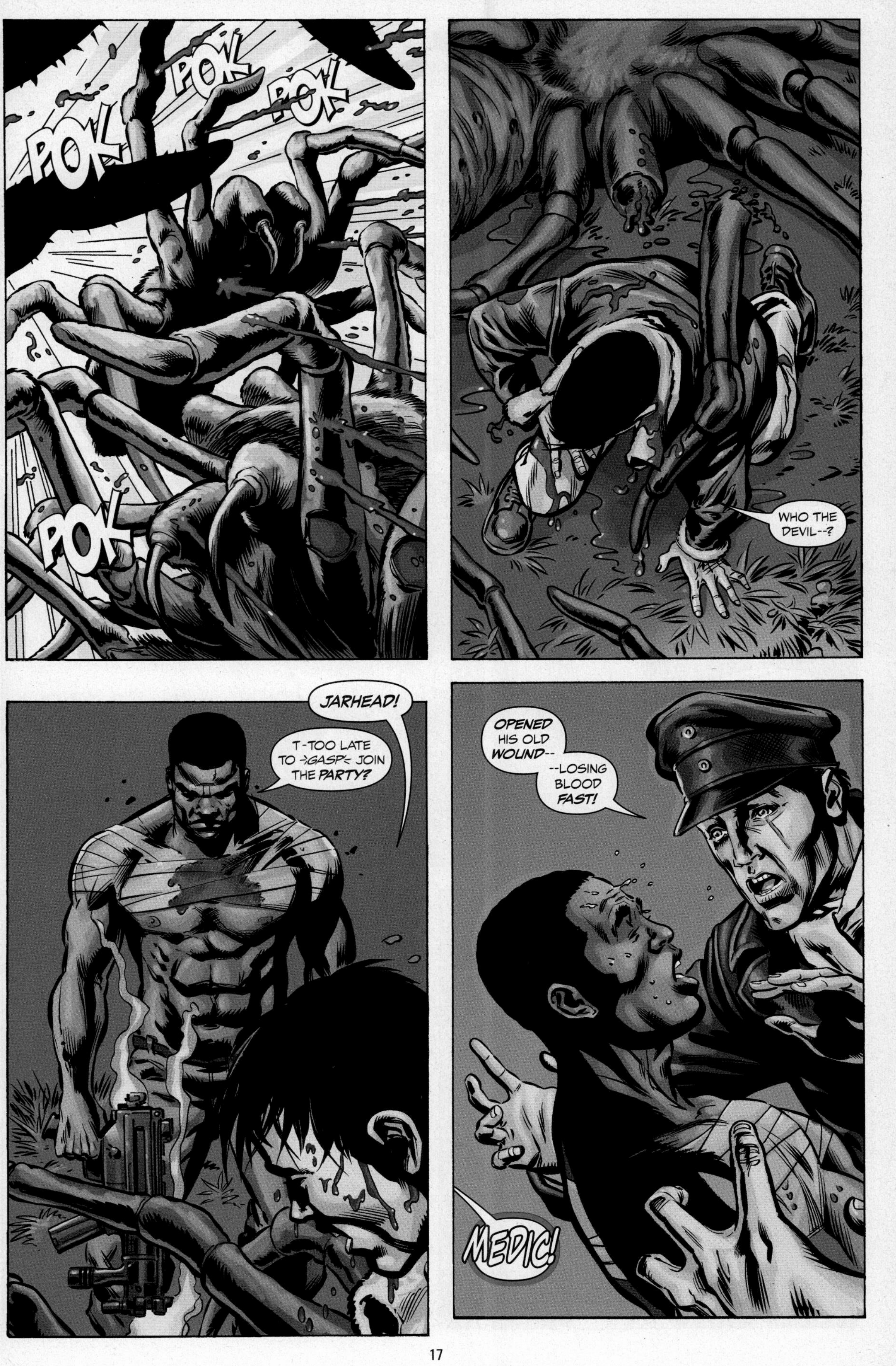
POK
POK
POK
POK
WHO THE DEVIL--?
JARHEAD!
T-TOO LATE TO -GASP- JOIN THE PARTY?
OPENED HIS OLD WOUND--
--LOSING BLOOD FAST!
MEDIC!

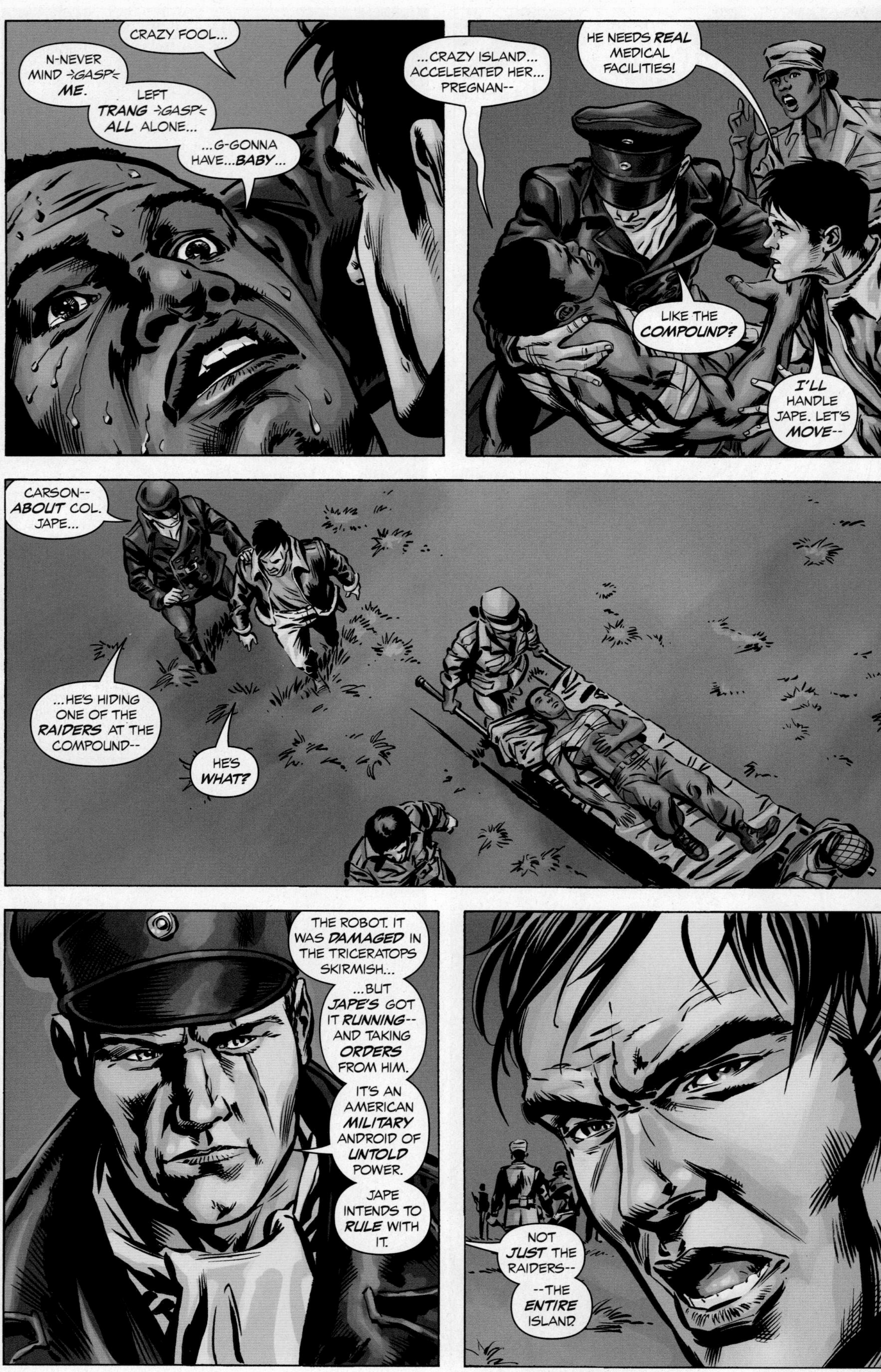
CRAZY FOOL...
N-NEVER MIND ~GASP~ ME.
LEFT TRANG ~GASP~ ALL ALONE...
...G-GONNA HAVE...BABY...
...CRAZY ISLAND... ACCELERATED HER... PREGNAN--
HE NEEDS REAL MEDICAL FACILITIES!
LIKE THE COMPOUND?
I'LL HANDLE JAPE. LET'S MOVE--
CARSON-- ABOUT COL. JAPE...
...HE'S HIDING ONE OF THE RAIDERS AT THE COMPOUND--
HE'S WHAT?
THE ROBOT. IT WAS DAMAGED IN THE TRICERATOPS SKIRMISH...
...BUT JAPE'S GOT IT RUNNING-- AND TAKING ORDERS FROM HIM.
IT'S AN AMERICAN MILITARY ANDROID OF UNTOLD POWER.
JAPE INTENDS TO RULE WITH IT.
NOT JUST THE RAIDERS--
--THE ENTIRE ISLAND.

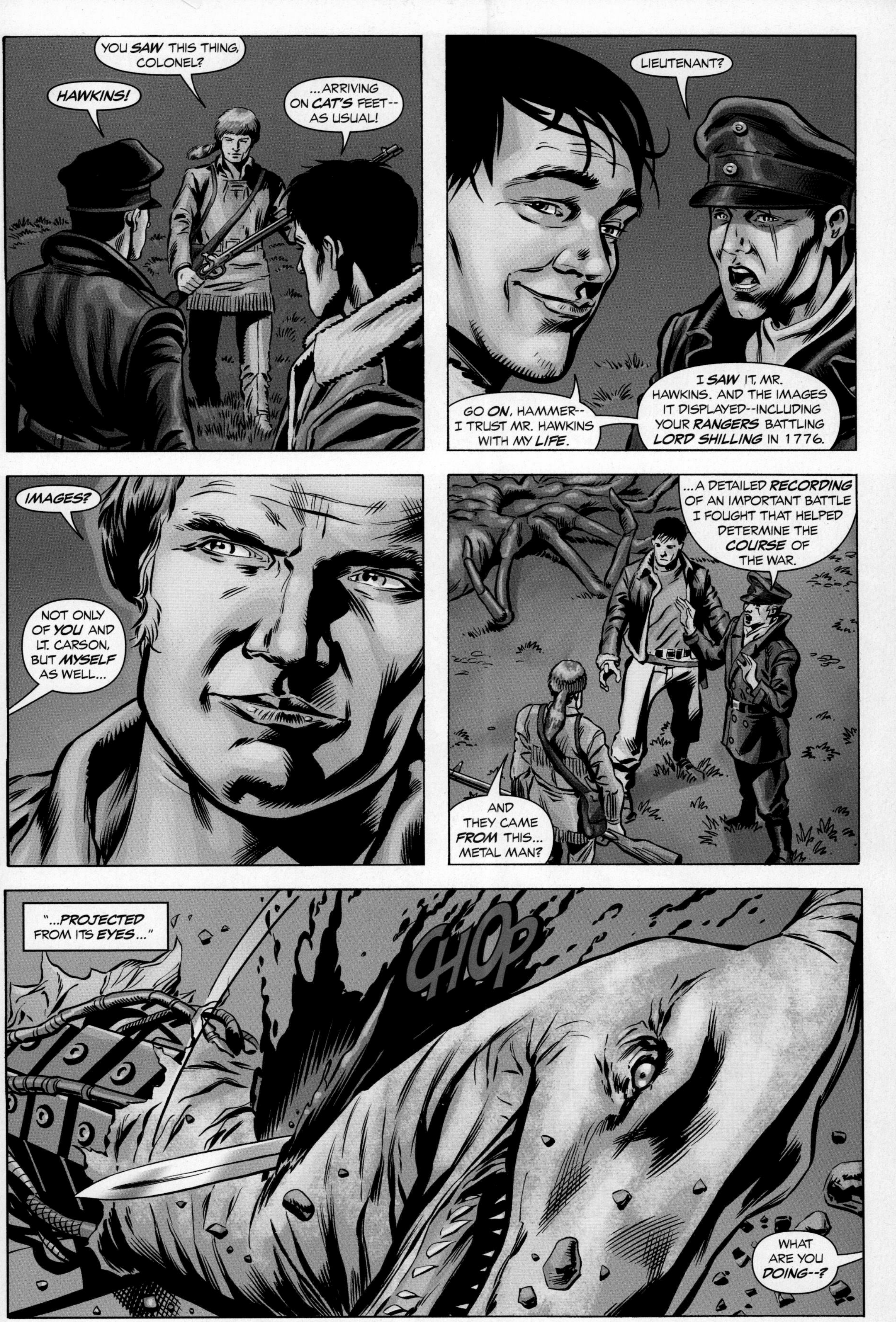
YOU SAW THIS THING, COLONEL?
HAWKINS!
...ARRIVING ON CAT'S FEET-- AS USUAL!
LIEUTENANT?
GO ON, HAMMER-- I TRUST MR. HAWKINS WITH MY LIFE.
I SAW IT, MR. HAWKINS. AND THE IMAGES IT DISPLAYED--INCLUDING YOUR RANGERS BATTLING LORD SHILLING IN 1776.
IMAGES?
NOT ONLY OF YOU AND LT. CARSON, BUT MYSELF AS WELL...
...A DETAILED RECORDING OF AN IMPORTANT BATTLE I FOUGHT THAT HELPED DETERMINE THE COURSE OF THE WAR.
AND THEY CAME FROM THIS... METAL MAN?
"...PROJECTED FROM ITS EYES..."
CHOP
WHAT ARE YOU DOING--?

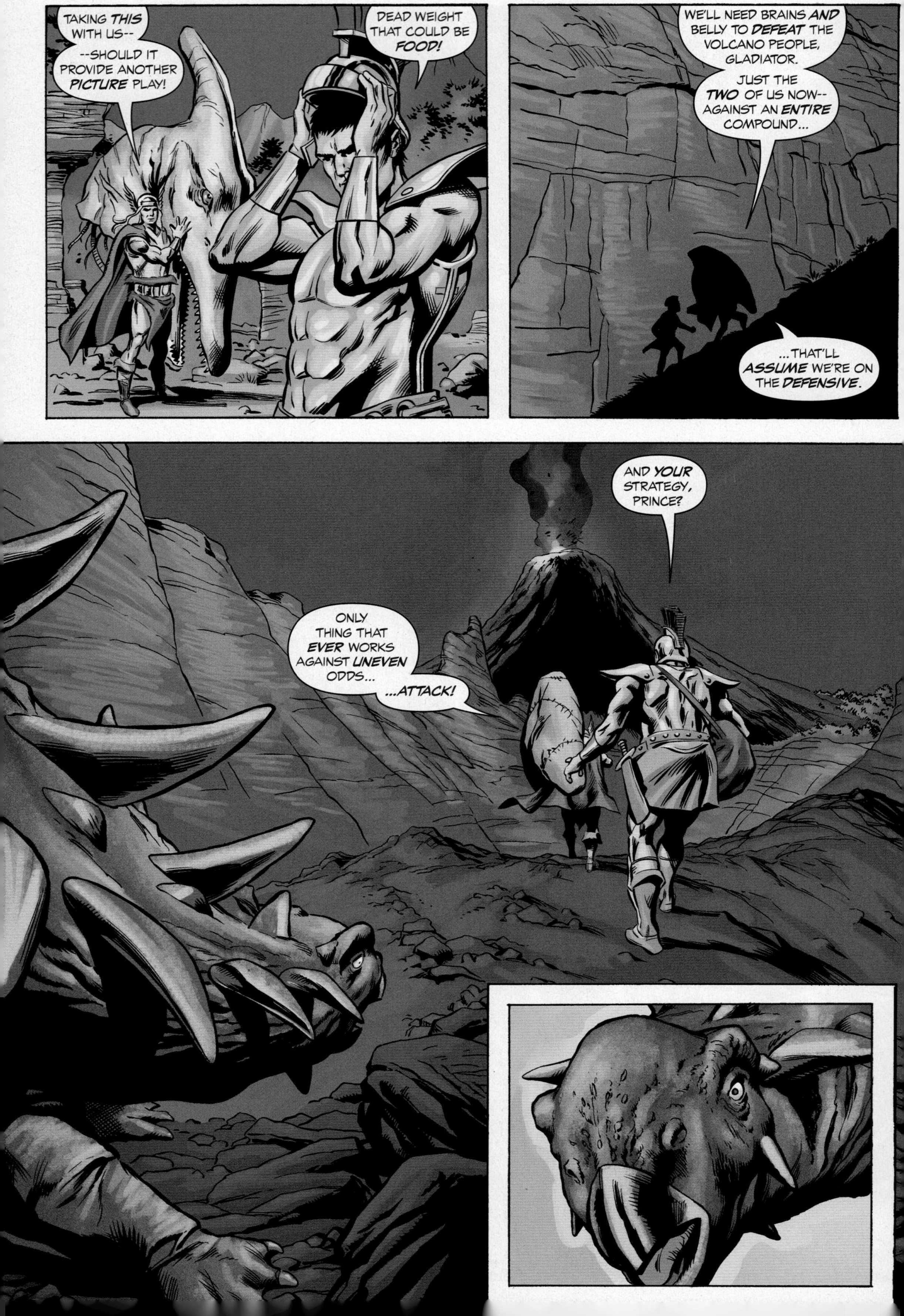
TAKING THIS WITH US--
--SHOULD IT PROVIDE ANOTHER PICTURE PLAY!
DEAD WEIGHT THAT COULD BE FOOD!
WE'LL NEED BRAINS AND BELLY TO DEFEAT THE VOLCANO PEOPLE, GLADIATOR.
JUST THE TWO OF US NOW-- AGAINST AN ENTIRE COMPOUND...
...THAT'LL ASSUME WE'RE ON THE DEFENSIVE.
AND YOUR STRATEGY, PRINCE?
ONLY THING THAT EVER WORKS AGAINST UNEVEN ODDS...
...ATTACK!

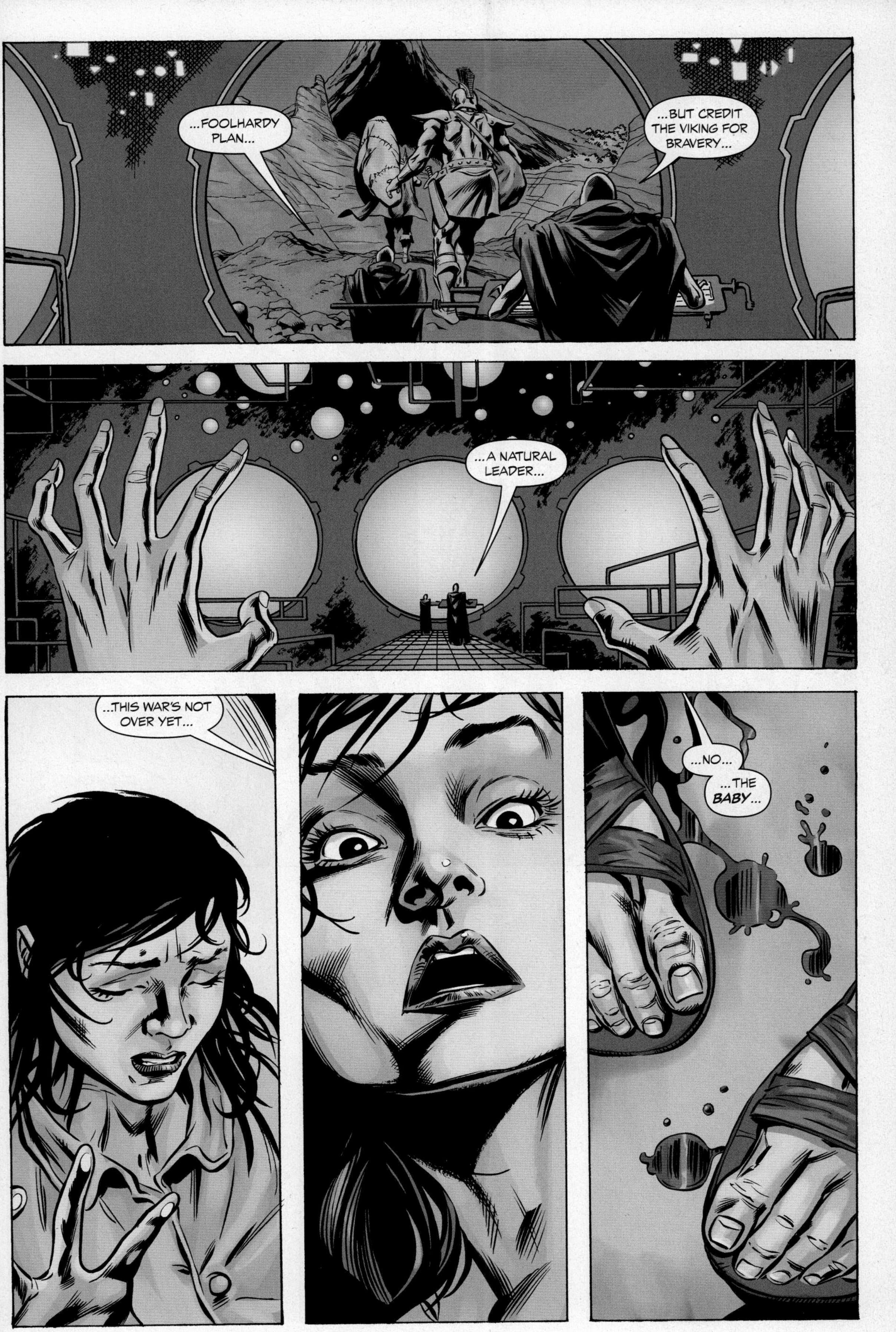
...FOOLHARDY PLAN...
...BUT CREDIT THE VIKING FOR BRAVERY...
...A NATURAL LEADER...
...THIS WAR'S NOT OVER YET...
...NO...
...THE *BABY*...

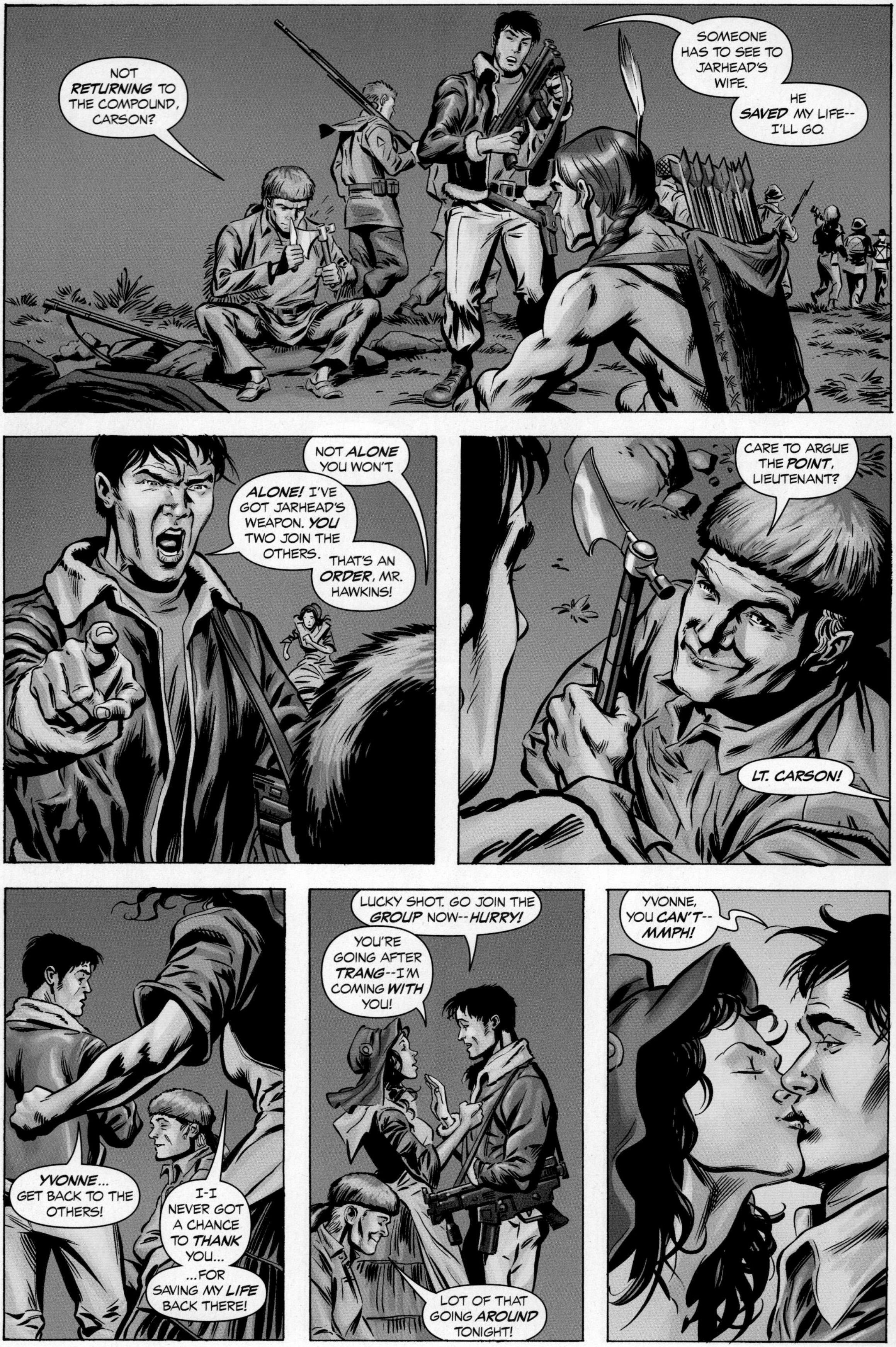
NOT RETURNING TO THE COMPOUND, CARSON?
SOMEONE HAS TO SEE TO JARHEAD'S WIFE.
HE SAVED MY LIFE-- I'LL GO.
NOT ALONE YOU WON'T.
ALONE! I'VE GOT JARHEAD'S WEAPON. YOU TWO JOIN THE OTHERS.
THAT'S AN ORDER, MR. HAWKINS!
CARE TO ARGUE THE POINT, LIEUTENANT?
LT. CARSON!
YVONNE... GET BACK TO THE OTHERS!
I-I NEVER GOT A CHANCE TO THANK YOU...
...FOR SAVING MY LIFE BACK THERE!
LUCKY SHOT. GO JOIN THE GROUP NOW--HURRY!
YOU'RE GOING AFTER TRANG--I'M COMING WITH YOU!
LOT OF THAT GOING AROUND TONIGHT!
YVONNE, YOU CAN'T-- MMPH!

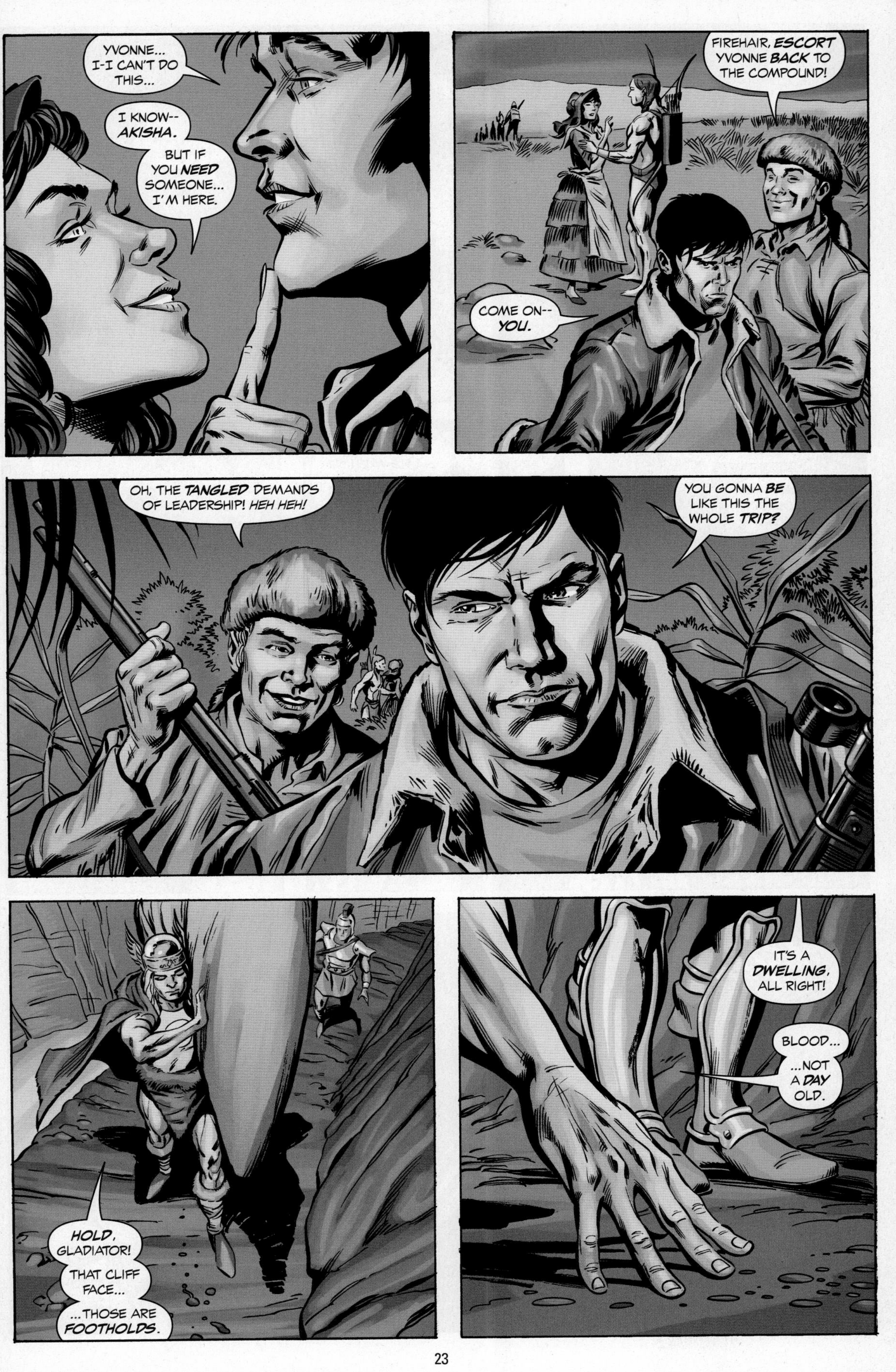
YVONNE... I-I CAN'T DO THIS...
I KNOW-- AKISHA.
BUT IF YOU NEED SOMEONE... I'M HERE.
FIREHAIR, ESCORT YVONNE BACK TO THE COMPOUND!
COME ON-- YOU.
OH, THE TANGLED DEMANDS OF LEADERSHIP! HEH HEH!
YOU GONNA BE LIKE THIS THE WHOLE TRIP?
HOLD, GLADIATOR!
THAT CLIFF FACE...
...THOSE ARE FOOTHOLDS.
IT'S A DWELLING, ALL RIGHT!
BLOOD...
...NOT A DAY OLD.

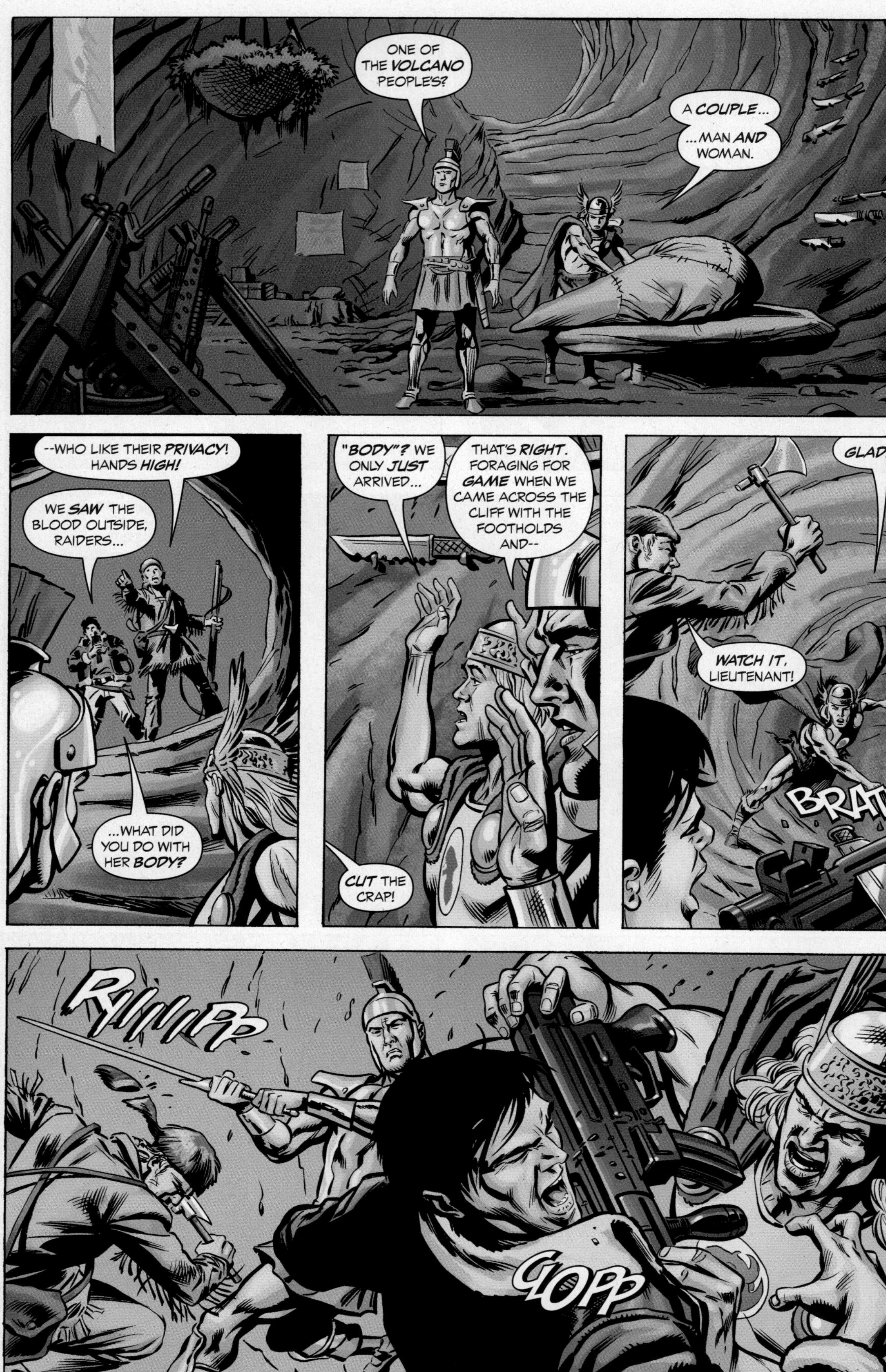
ONE OF THE VOLCANO PEOPLE'S?
A COUPLE...
...MAN AND WOMAN.
--WHO LIKE THEIR PRIVACY! HANDS HIGH!
WE SAW THE BLOOD OUTSIDE, RAIDERS...
...WHAT DID YOU DO WITH HER BODY?
"BODY"? WE ONLY JUST ARRIVED...
THAT'S RIGHT. FORAGING FOR GAME WHEN WE CAME ACROSS THE CLIFF WITH THE FOOTHOLDS AND--
CUT THE CRAP!
GLADLY!
WATCH IT, LIEUTENANT!
BRATTA
RYIIIPP
CLOPP

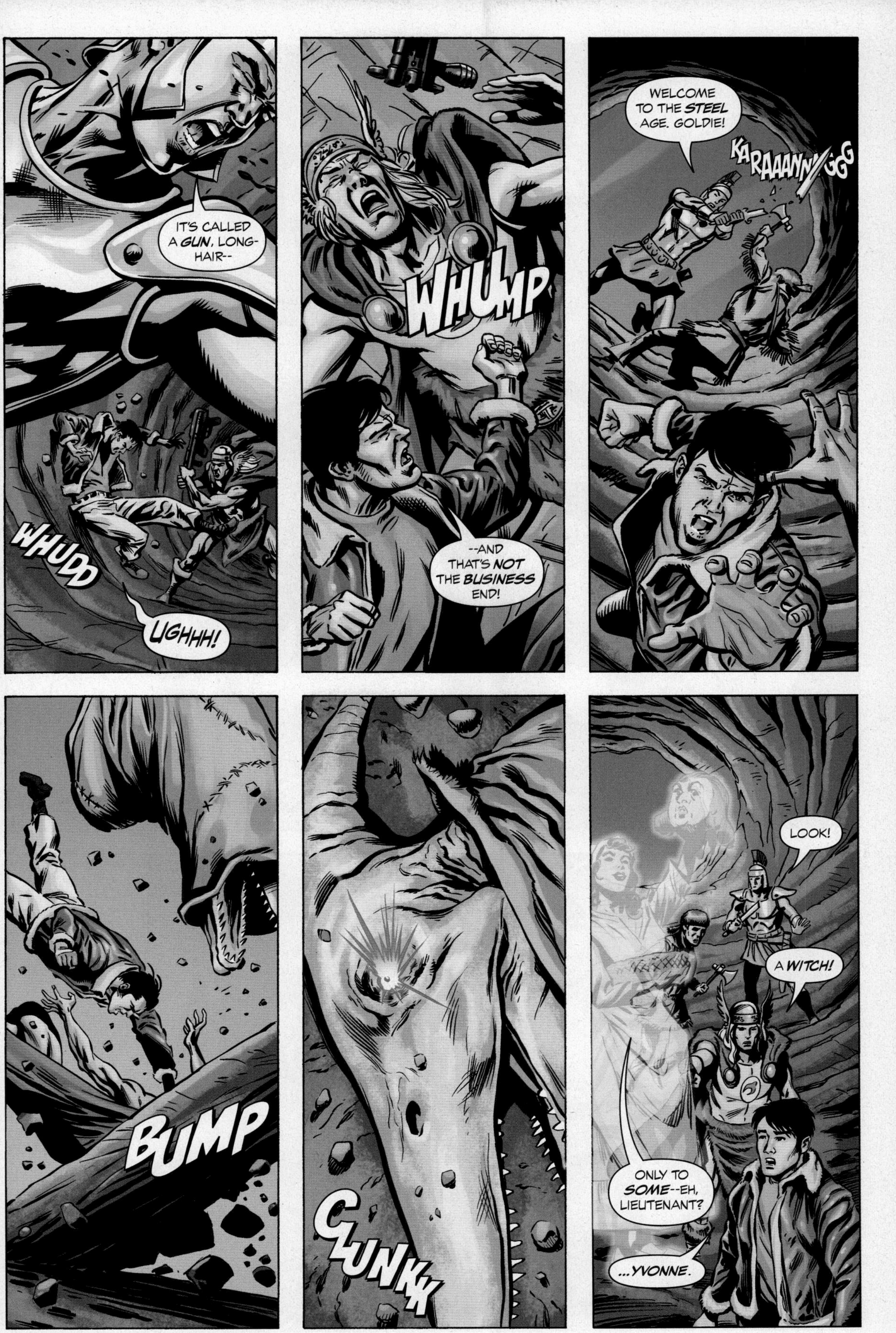
IT'S CALLED A GUN, LONG-HAIR--
WHUDD
UGHHH!
WHUMP
--AND THAT'S NOT THE BUSINESS END!
WELCOME TO THE STEEL AGE, GOLDIE!
KARAAANNNGGG
BUMP
CLUNKK
LOOK!
A WITCH!
ONLY TO SOME--EH, LIEUTENANT?
...YVONNE.

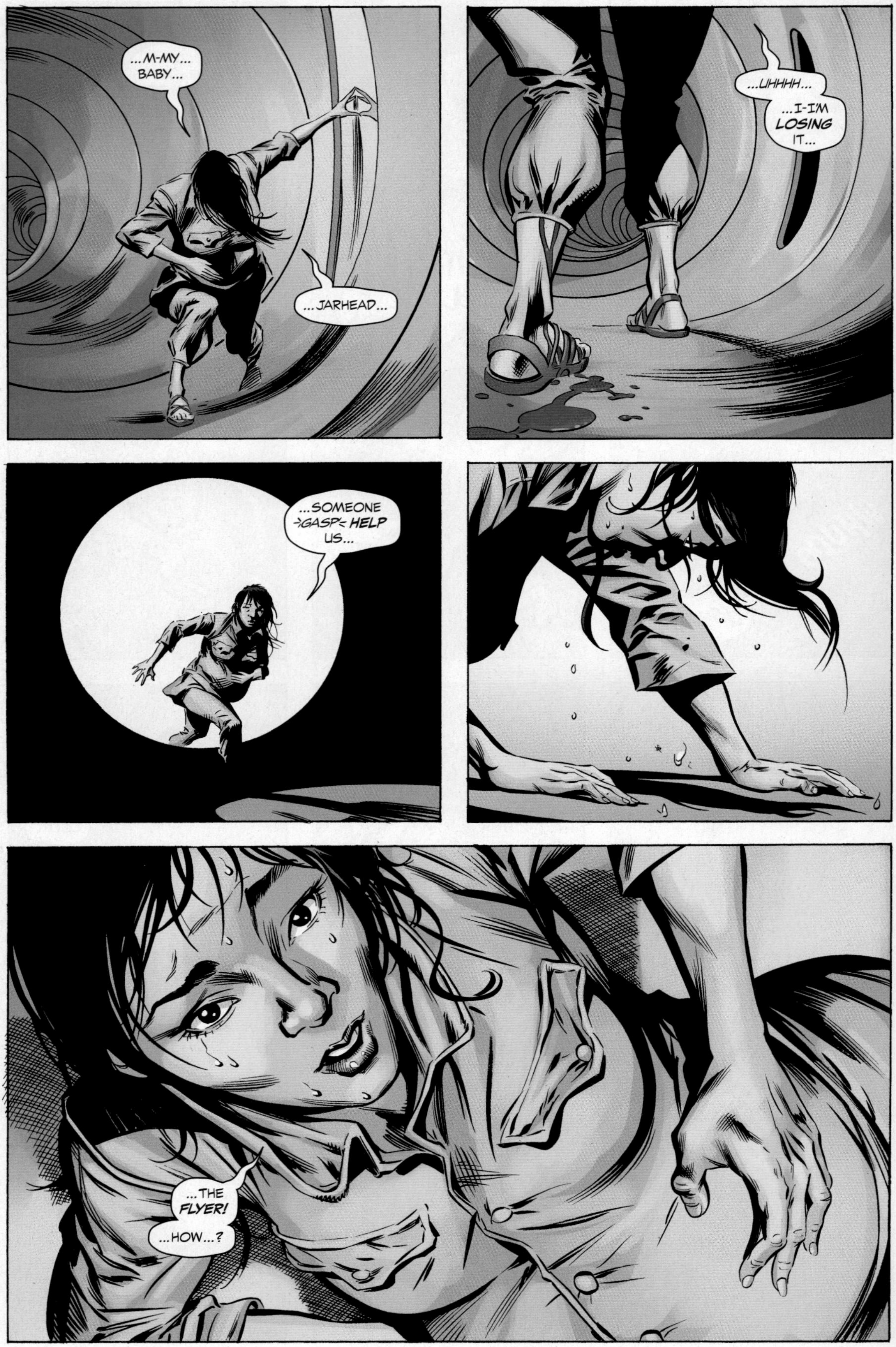
...M-MY... BABY...
...JARHEAD...
...UHHHH...
...I-I'M LOSING IT...
...SOMEONE >GASP< HELP US...
...THE FLYER!
...HOW...?

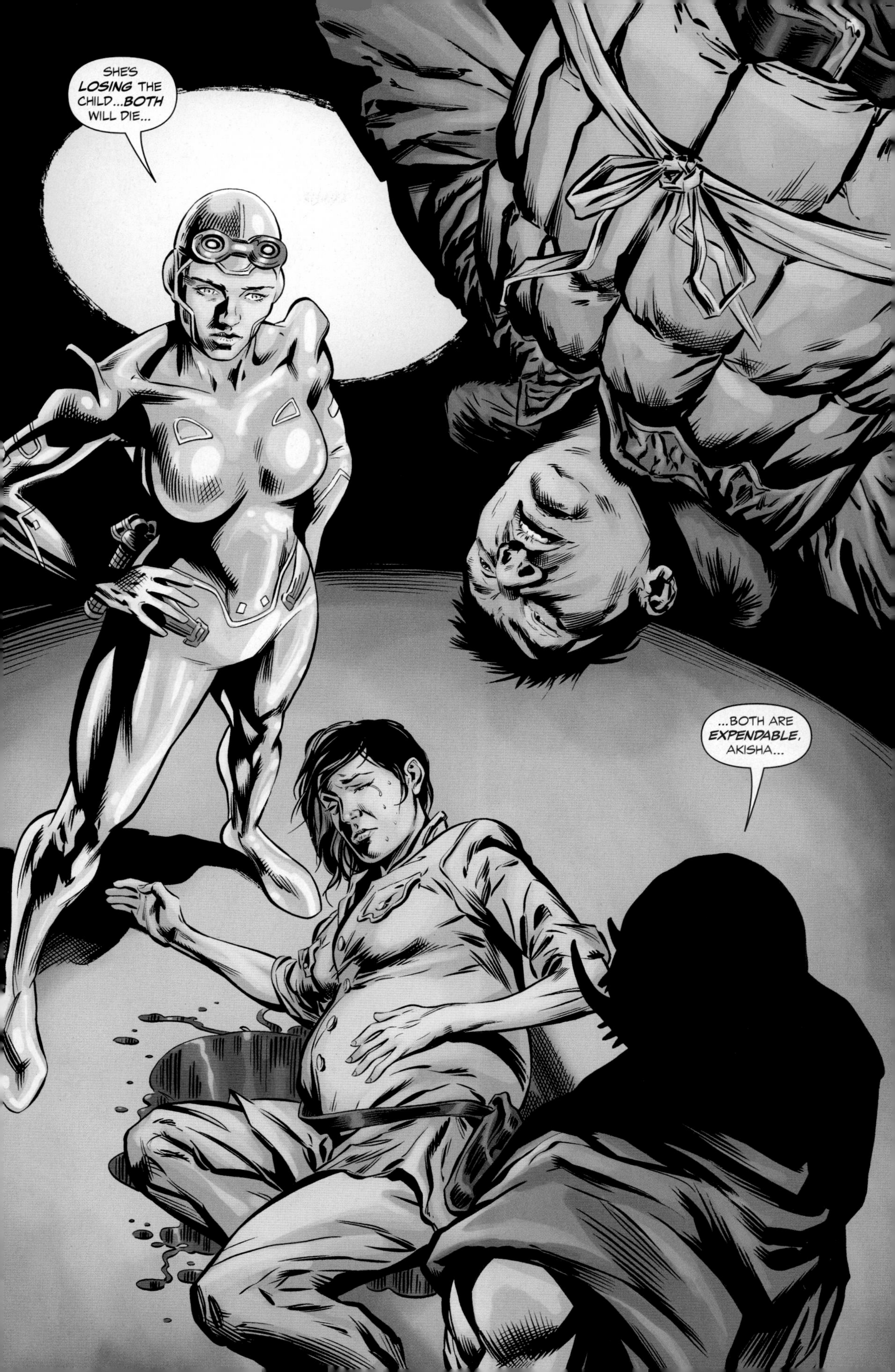
SHE'S LOSING THE CHILD...BOTH WILL DIE...
...BOTH ARE EXPENDABLE, AKISHA...

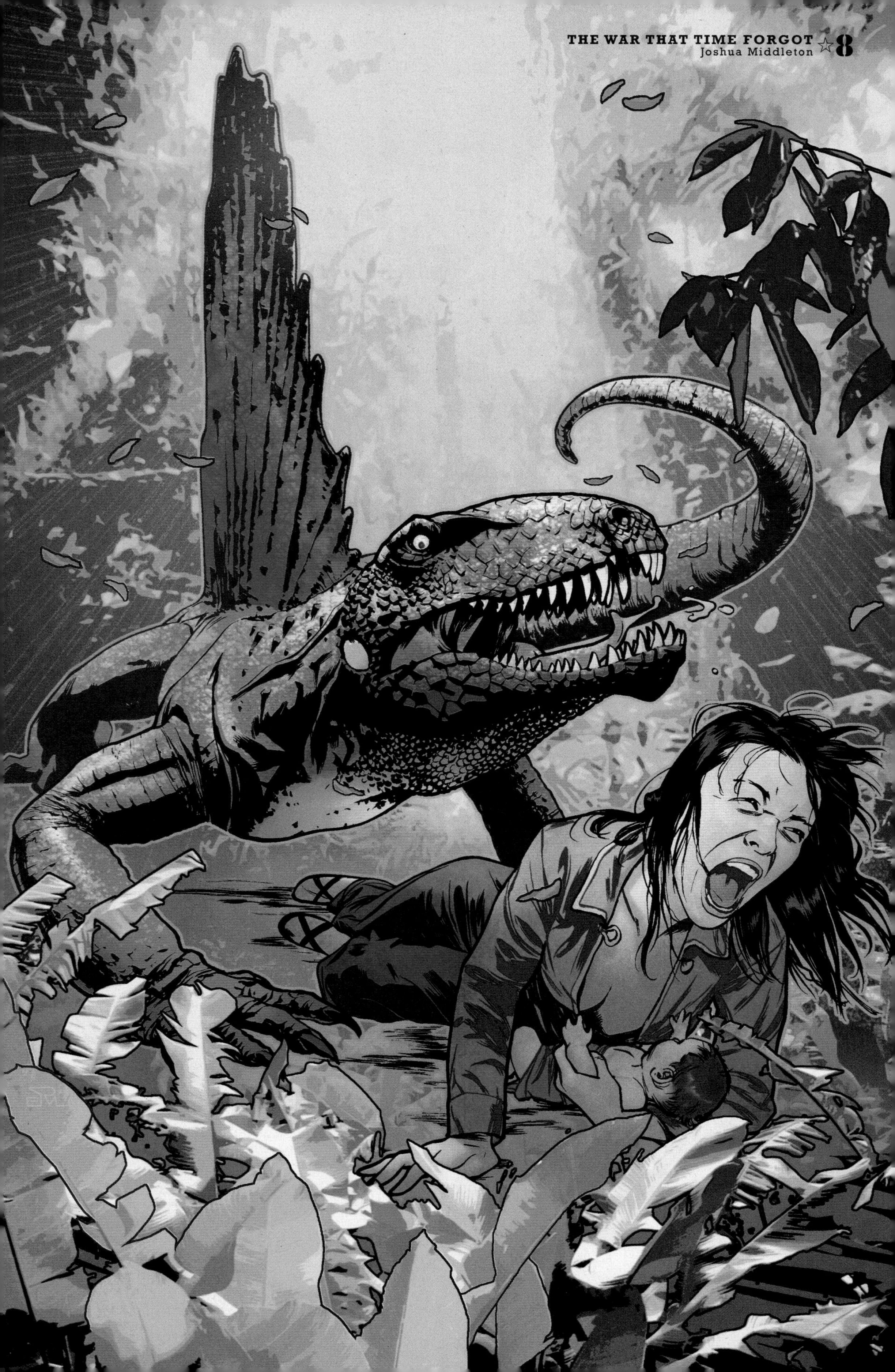

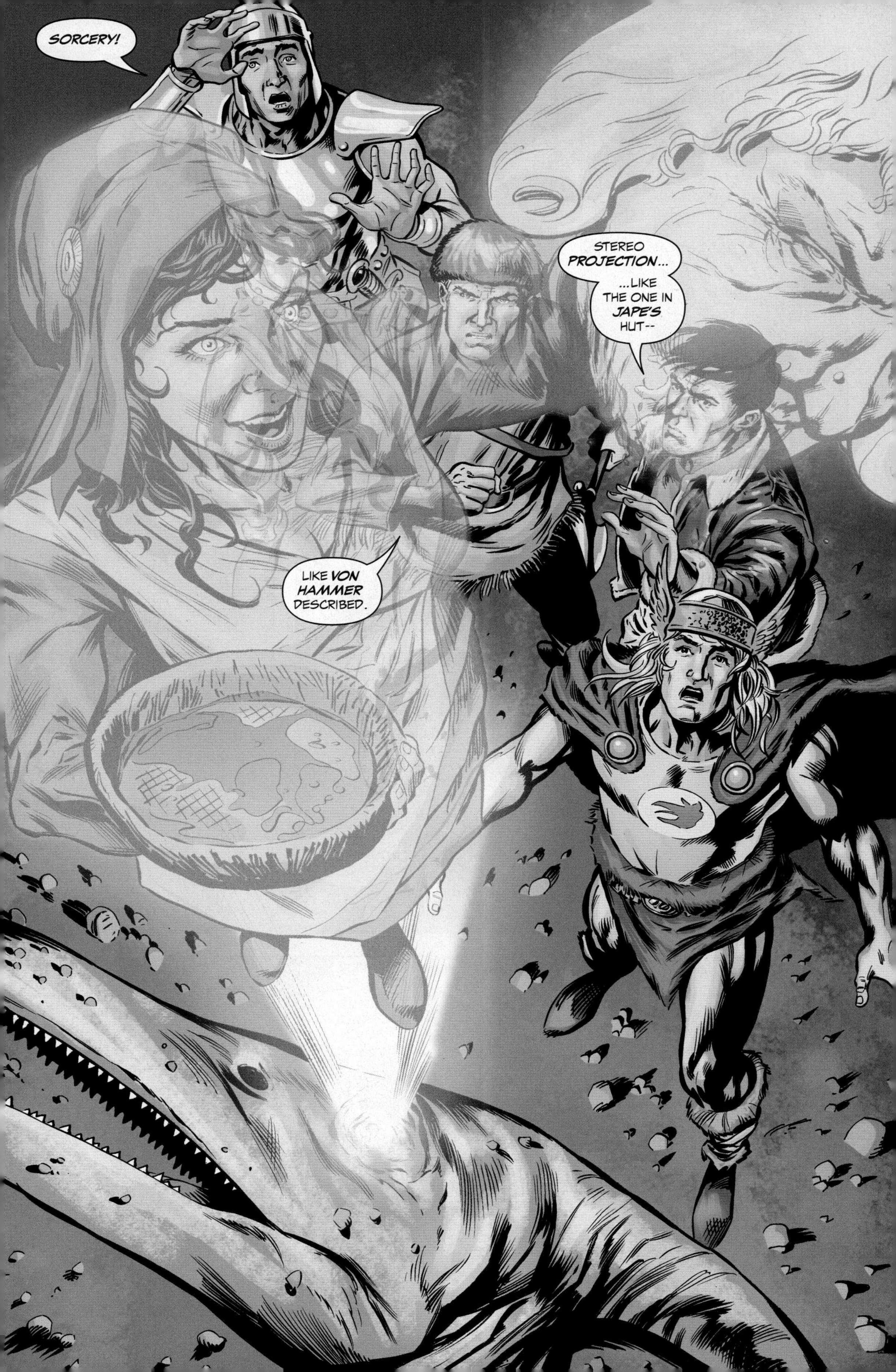
SORCERY!
STEREO PROJECTION...
...LIKE THE ONE IN JAPE'S HUT--
LIKE VON HAMMER DESCRIBED.

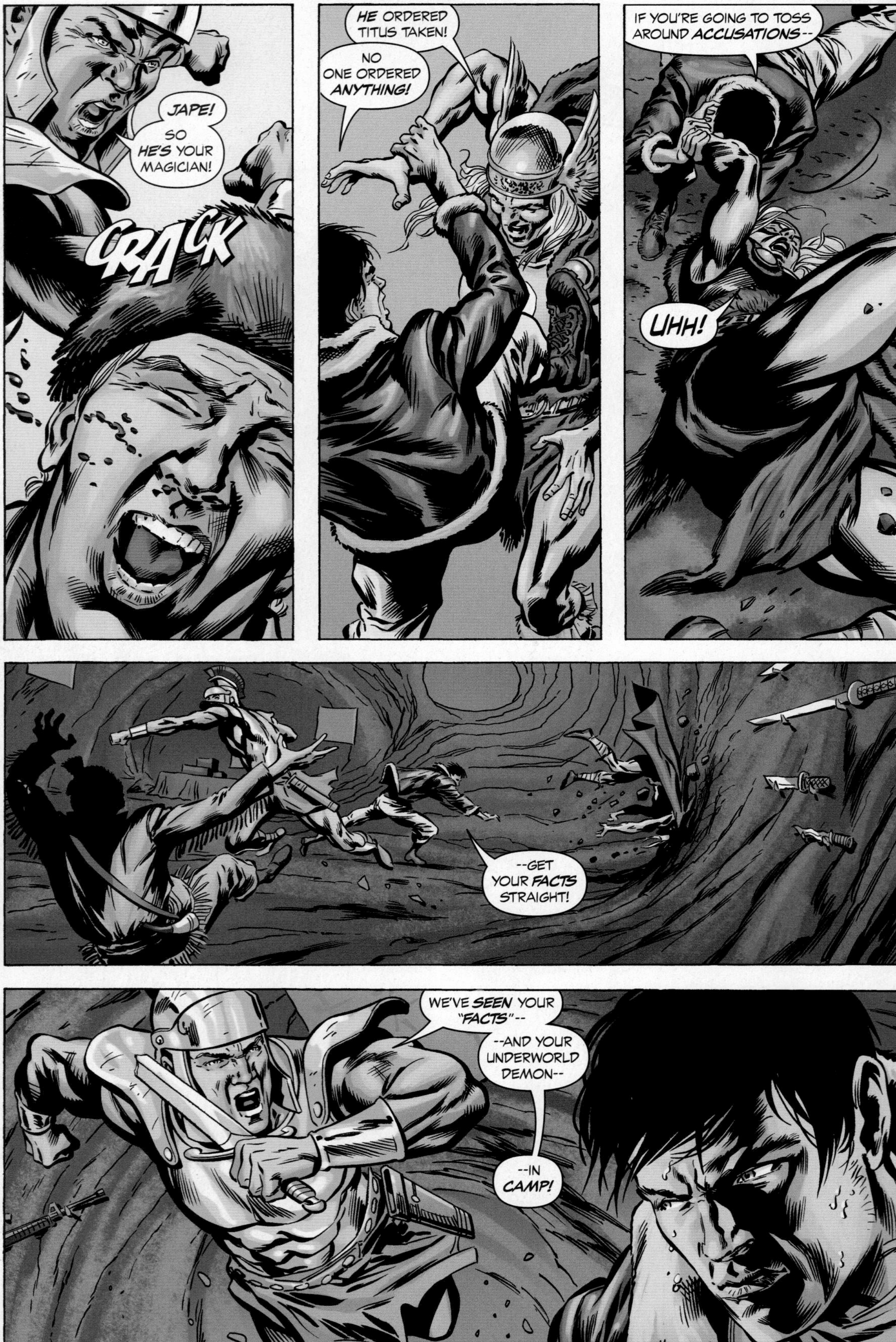
JAPE!
SO HE'S YOUR MAGICIAN!
CRACK
HE ORDERED TITUS TAKEN!
NO ONE ORDERED ANYTHING!
IF YOU'RE GOING TO TOSS AROUND ACCUSATIONS--
UHH!
--GET YOUR FACTS STRAIGHT!
WE'VE SEEN YOUR "FACTS"--
--AND YOUR UNDERWORLD DEMON--
--IN CAMP!

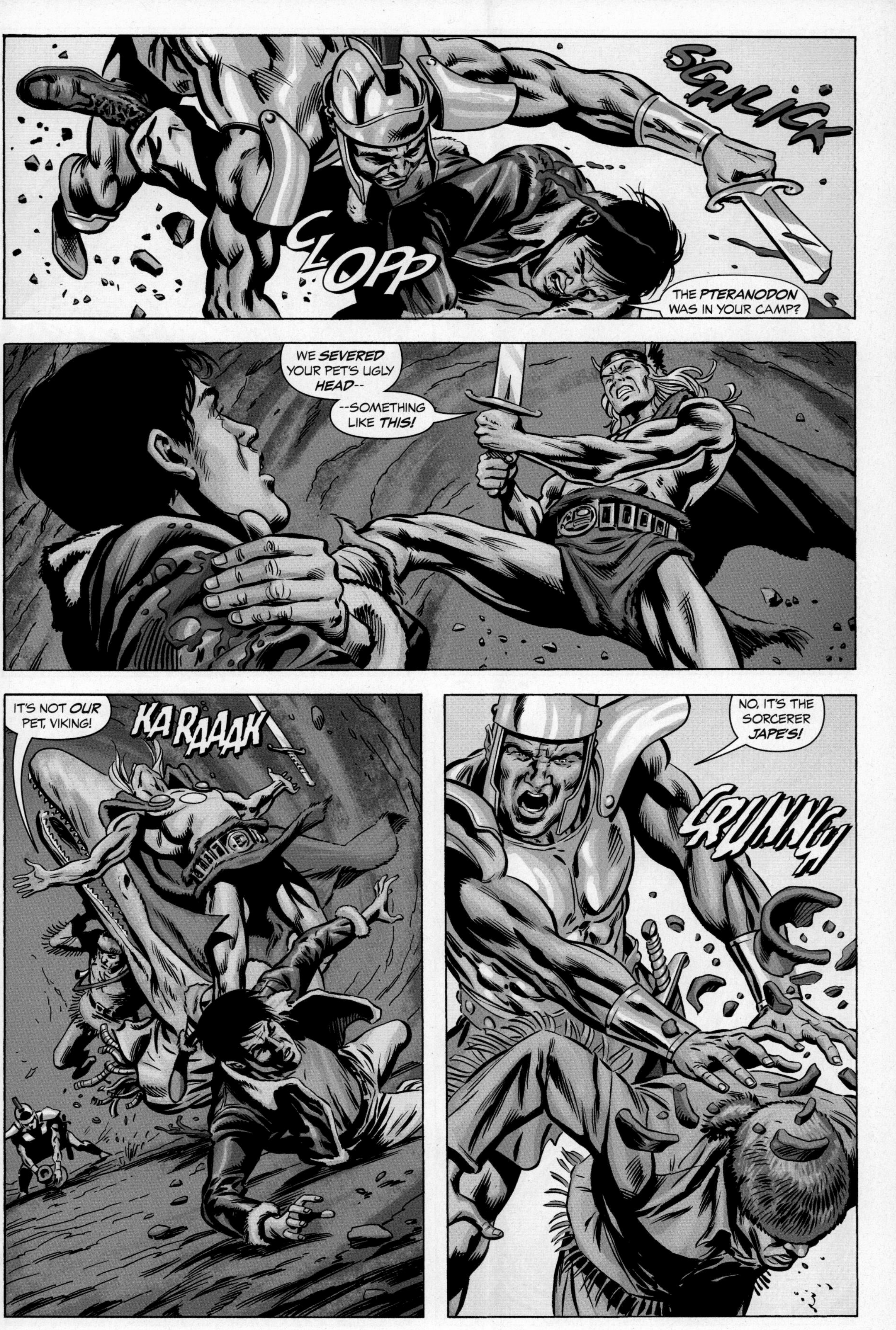
SCHLICK
CLOPP
THE PTERANODON WAS IN YOUR CAMP?
WE SEVERED YOUR PET'S UGLY HEAD--
--SOMETHING LIKE THIS!
IT'S NOT OUR PET, VIKING!
KARAAAK
NO, IT'S THE SORCERER JAPE'S!
CRUNNCH

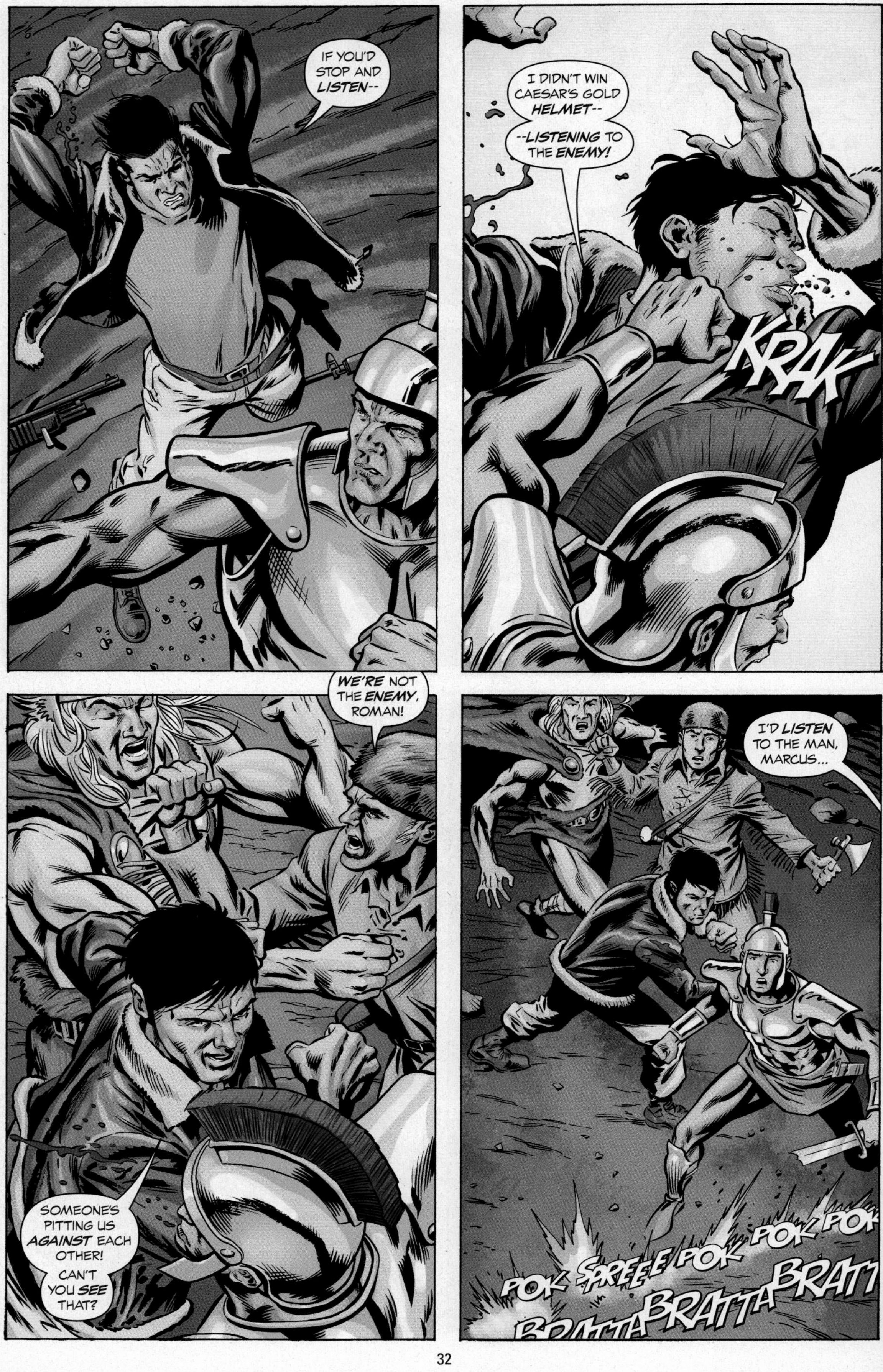
IF YOU'D STOP AND LISTEN--
I DIDN'T WIN CAESAR'S GOLD HELMET--
--LISTENING TO THE ENEMY!
KRAK
WE'RE NOT THE ENEMY, ROMAN!
SOMEONE'S PITTING US AGAINST EACH OTHER!
CAN'T YOU SEE THAT?
I'D LISTEN TO THE MAN, MARCUS...
POK SPREEEE POK POK POK
BRATTA BRATTA BRATTA BRATT

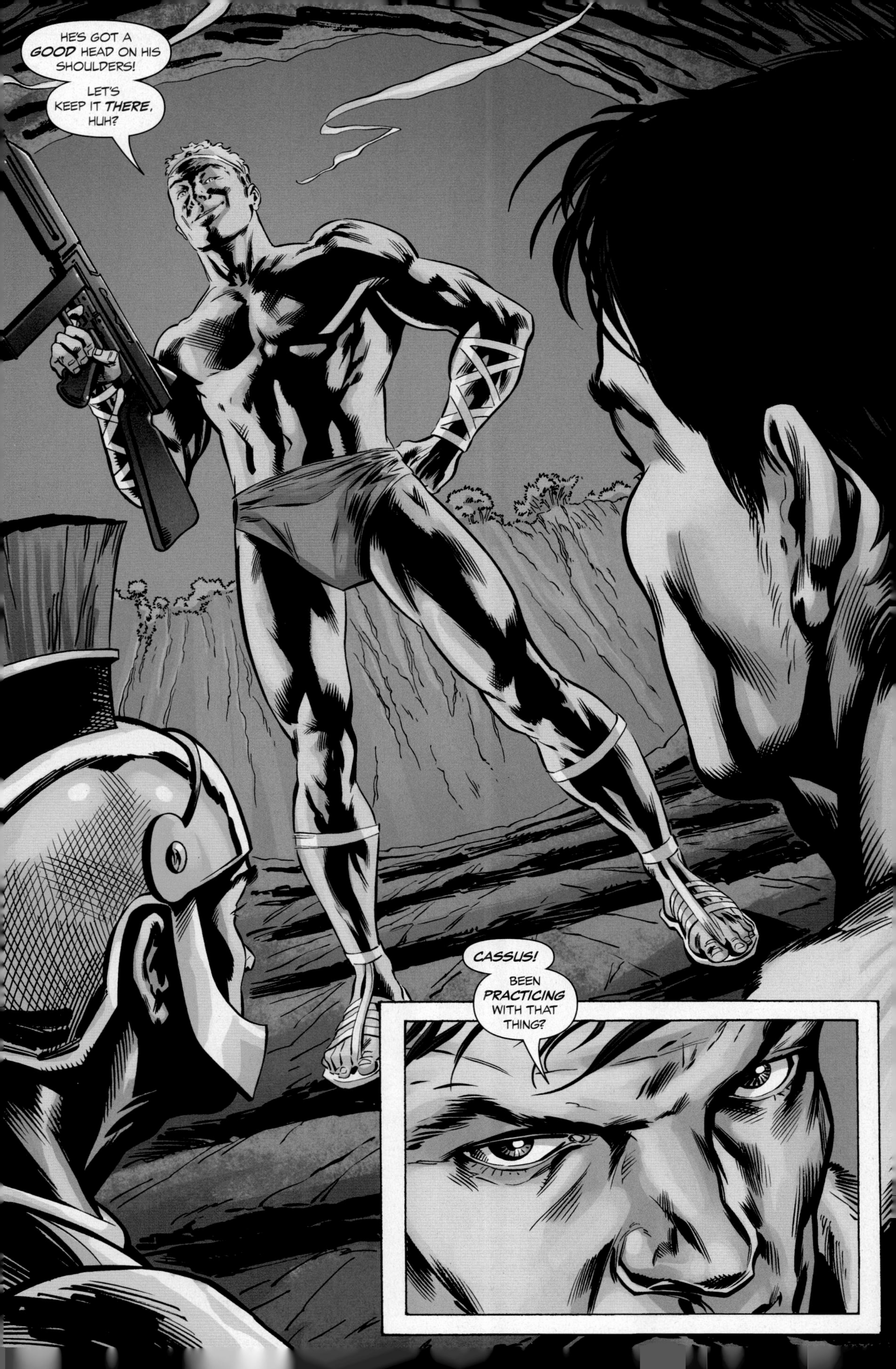
HE'S GOT A GOOD HEAD ON HIS SHOULDERS!
LET'S KEEP IT THERE, HUH?
CASSUS!
BEEN PRACTICING WITH THAT THING?

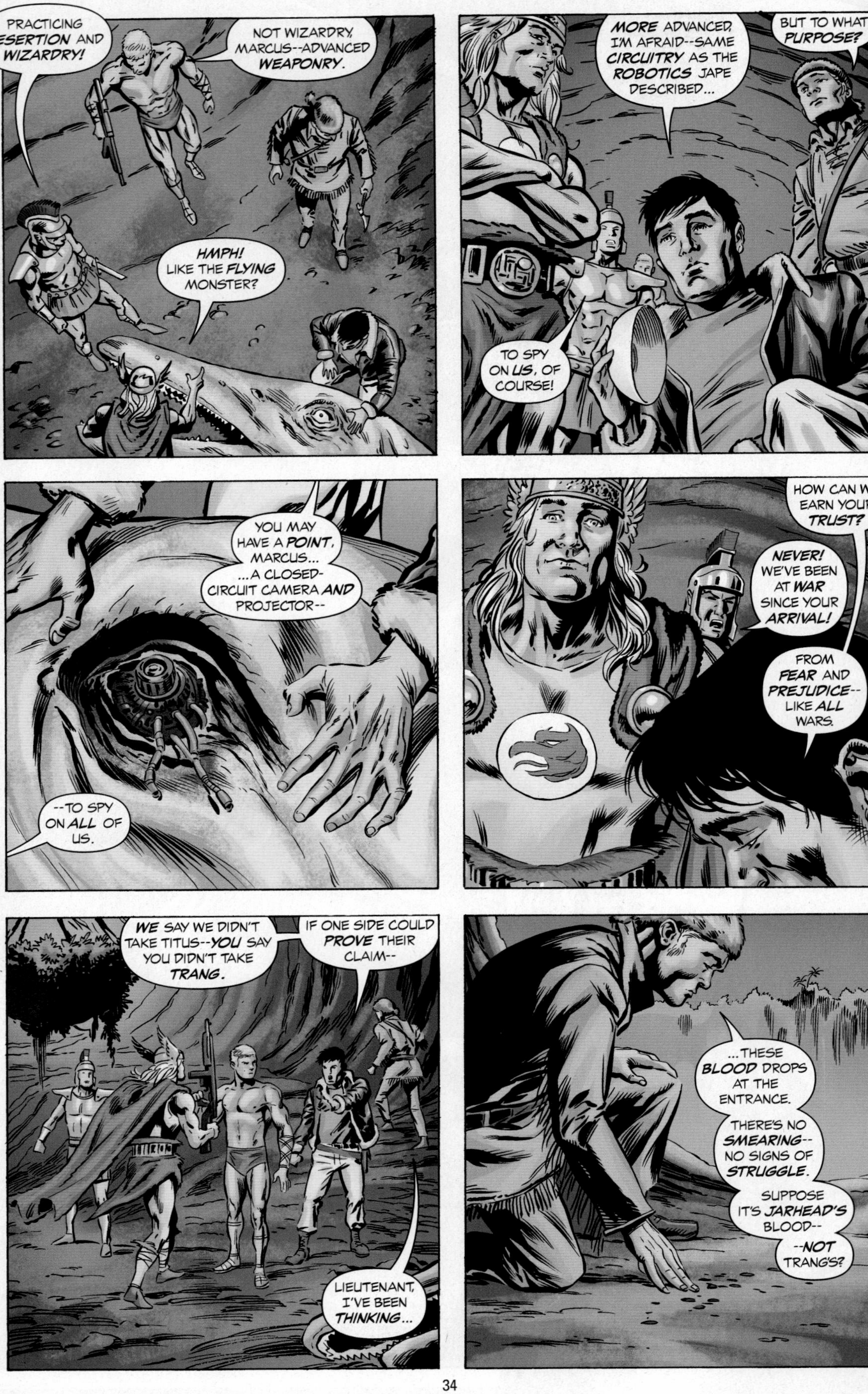
PRACTICING DESERTION AND WIZARDRY!
NOT WIZARDRY, MARCUS--ADVANCED WEAPONRY.
HMPH! LIKE THE FLYING MONSTER?
MORE ADVANCED, I'M AFRAID--SAME CIRCUITRY AS THE ROBOTICS JAPE DESCRIBED...
BUT TO WHAT PURPOSE?
TO SPY ON US, OF COURSE!
YOU MAY HAVE A POINT, MARCUS...
...A CLOSED-CIRCUIT CAMERA AND PROJECTOR--
--TO SPY ON ALL OF US.
HOW CAN WE EARN YOUR TRUST?
NEVER! WE'VE BEEN AT WAR SINCE YOUR ARRIVAL!
FROM FEAR AND PREJUDICE--LIKE ALL WARS.
WE SAY WE DIDN'T TAKE TITUS--YOU SAY YOU DIDN'T TAKE TRANG.
IF ONE SIDE COULD PROVE THEIR CLAIM--
LIEUTENANT, I'VE BEEN THINKING...
...THESE BLOOD DROPS AT THE ENTRANCE.
THERE'S NO SMEARING--NO SIGNS OF STRUGGLE.
SUPPOSE IT'S JARHEAD'S BLOOD--
--NOT TRANG'S?

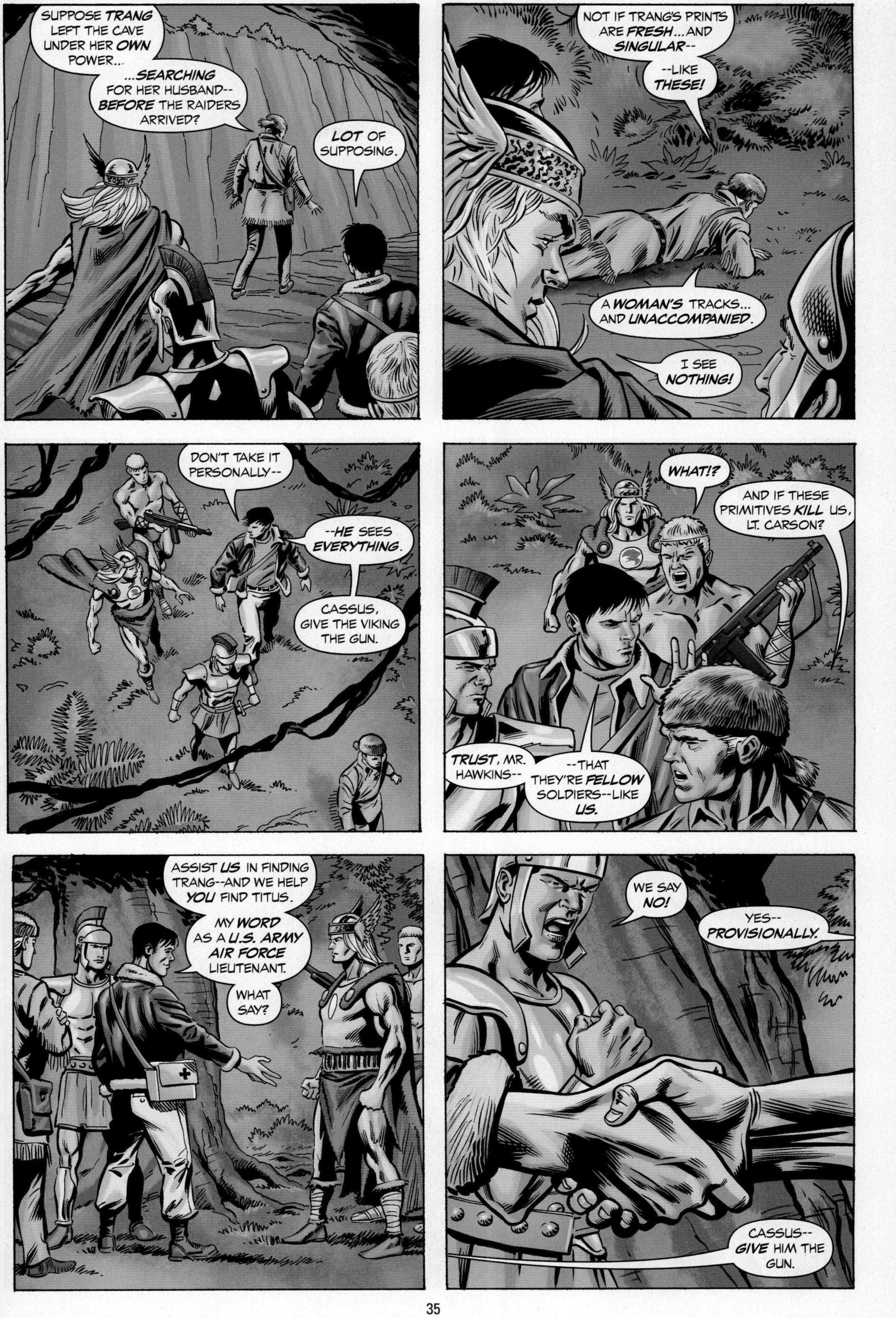
SUPPOSE TRANG LEFT THE CAVE UNDER HER OWN POWER...
...SEARCHING FOR HER HUSBAND-- BEFORE THE RAIDERS ARRIVED?
LOT OF SUPPOSING.
NOT IF TRANG'S PRINTS ARE FRESH...AND SINGULAR--
--LIKE THESE!
A WOMAN'S TRACKS... AND UNACCOMPANIED.
I SEE NOTHING!
DON'T TAKE IT PERSONALLY--
--HE SEES EVERYTHING.
CASSUS, GIVE THE VIKING THE GUN.
WHAT!?
AND IF THESE PRIMITIVES KILL US, LT. CARSON?
TRUST, MR. HAWKINS--
--THAT THEY'RE FELLOW SOLDIERS--LIKE US.
ASSIST US IN FINDING TRANG--AND WE HELP YOU FIND TITUS.
MY WORD AS A U.S. ARMY AIR FORCE LIEUTENANT.
WHAT SAY?
WE SAY NO!
YES-- PROVISIONALLY.
CASSUS-- GIVE HIM THE GUN.

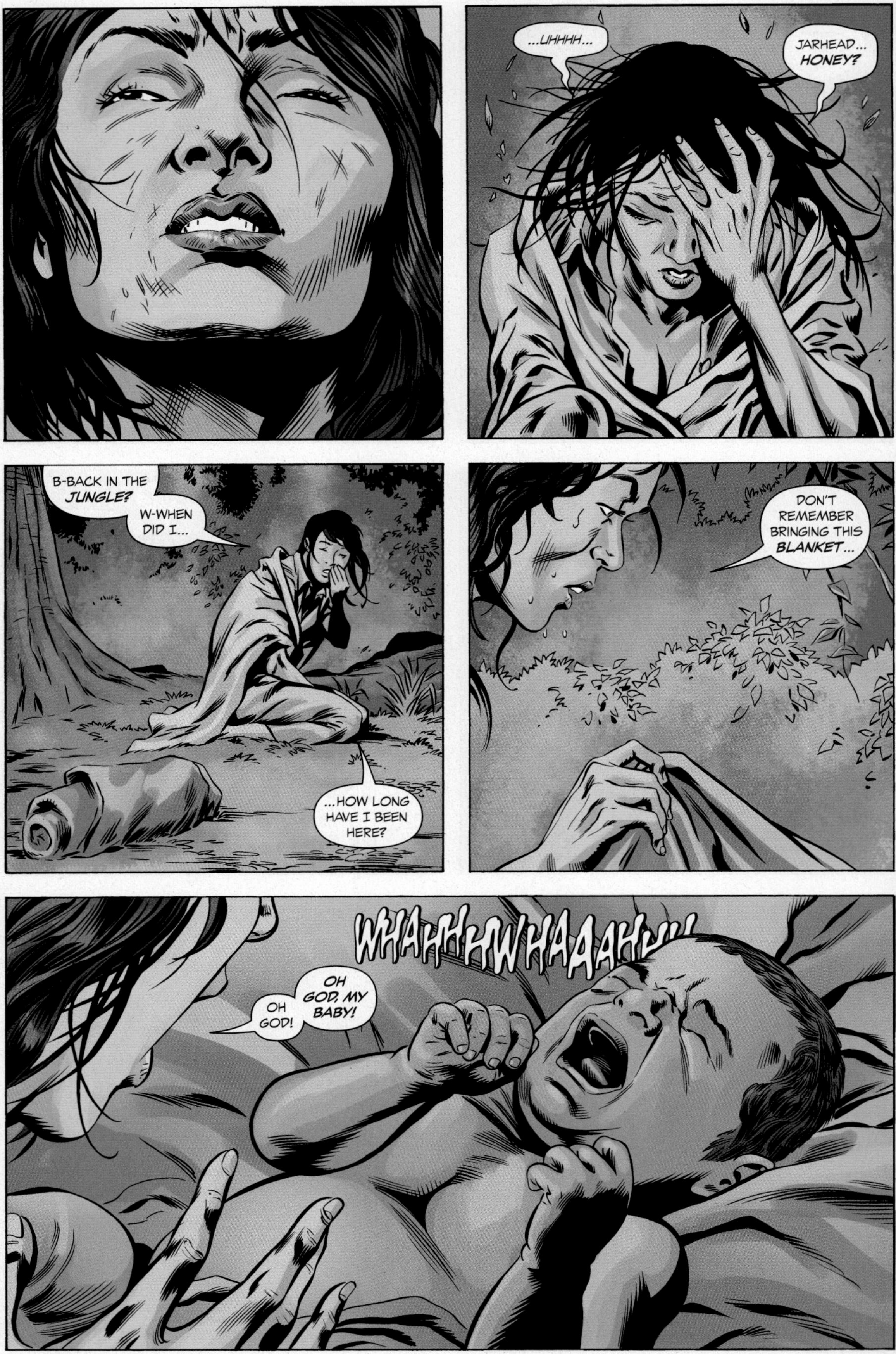
...UHHHH...
JARHEAD... HONEY?
B-BACK IN THE JUNGLE?
W-WHEN DID I...
...HOW LONG HAVE I BEEN HERE?
DON'T REMEMBER BRINGING THIS BLANKET...
WHAHHHWHAAAAH
OH GOD!
OH GOD, MY BABY!

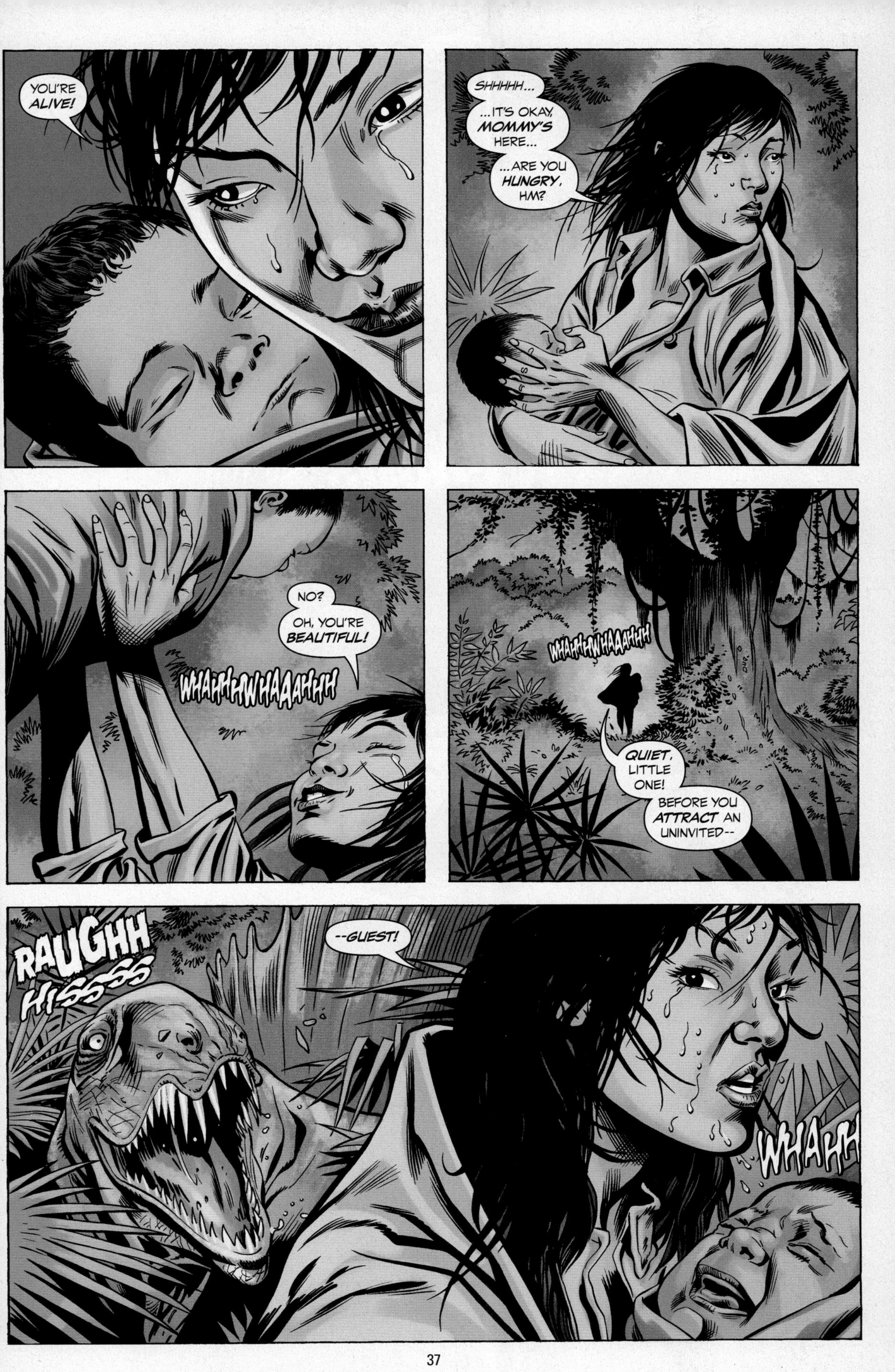

YOU'RE ALIVE!
SHHHHH...
...IT'S OKAY, MOMMY'S HERE...
...ARE YOU HUNGRY, HM?
NO?
OH, YOU'RE BEAUTIFUL!
WHAHHWHAAAHHH
WHAHHWHAAAHHH
QUIET, LITTLE ONE!
BEFORE YOU ATTRACT AN UNINVITED--
RAUGHH
HISSSS
--GUEST!
WHAHH

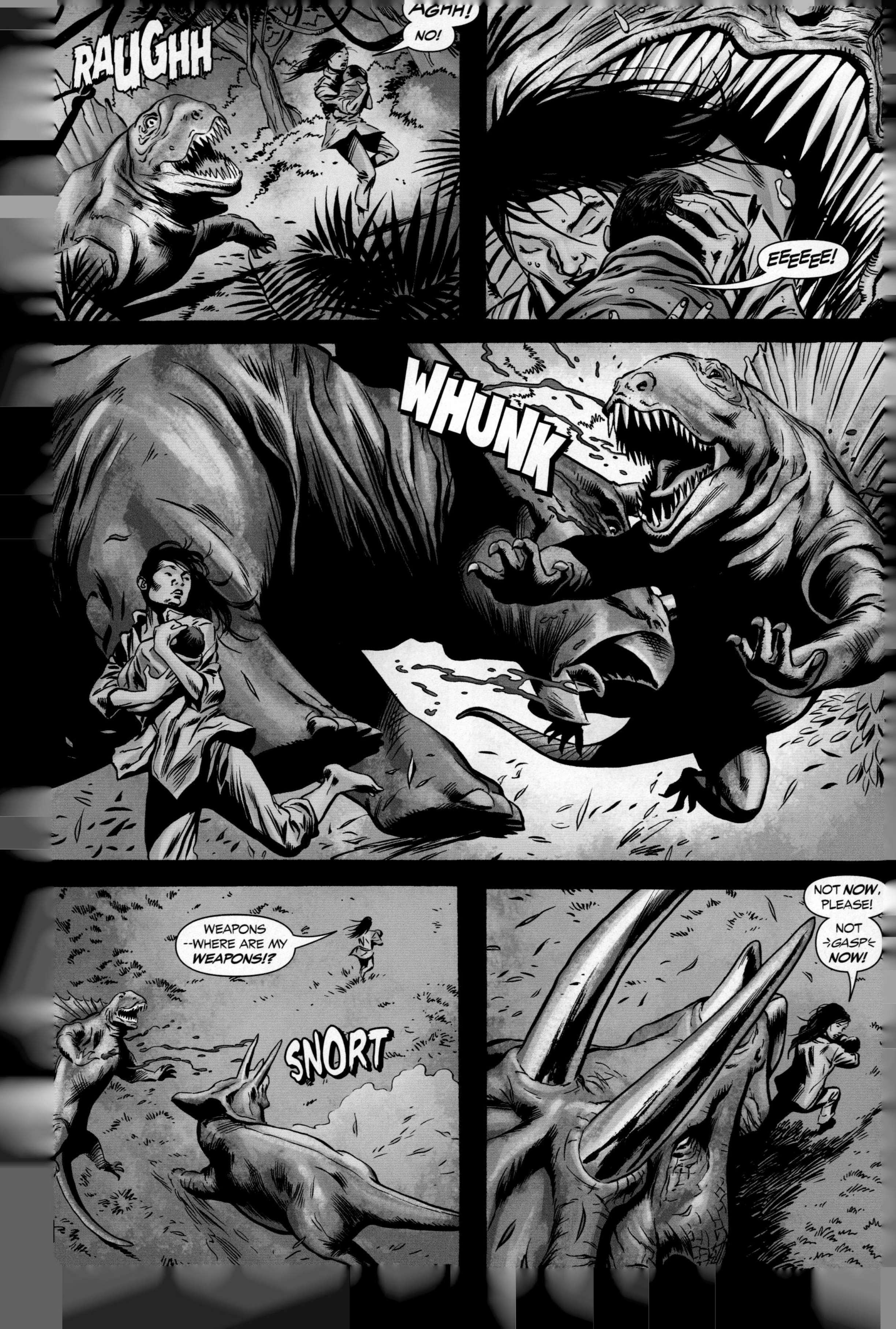

RAUGHH
AGHH! NO!
EEEEEE!
WHUNK
WEAPONS --WHERE ARE MY WEAPONS!?
SNORT
NOT NOW. PLEASE!
NOT ~GASP~ NOW!

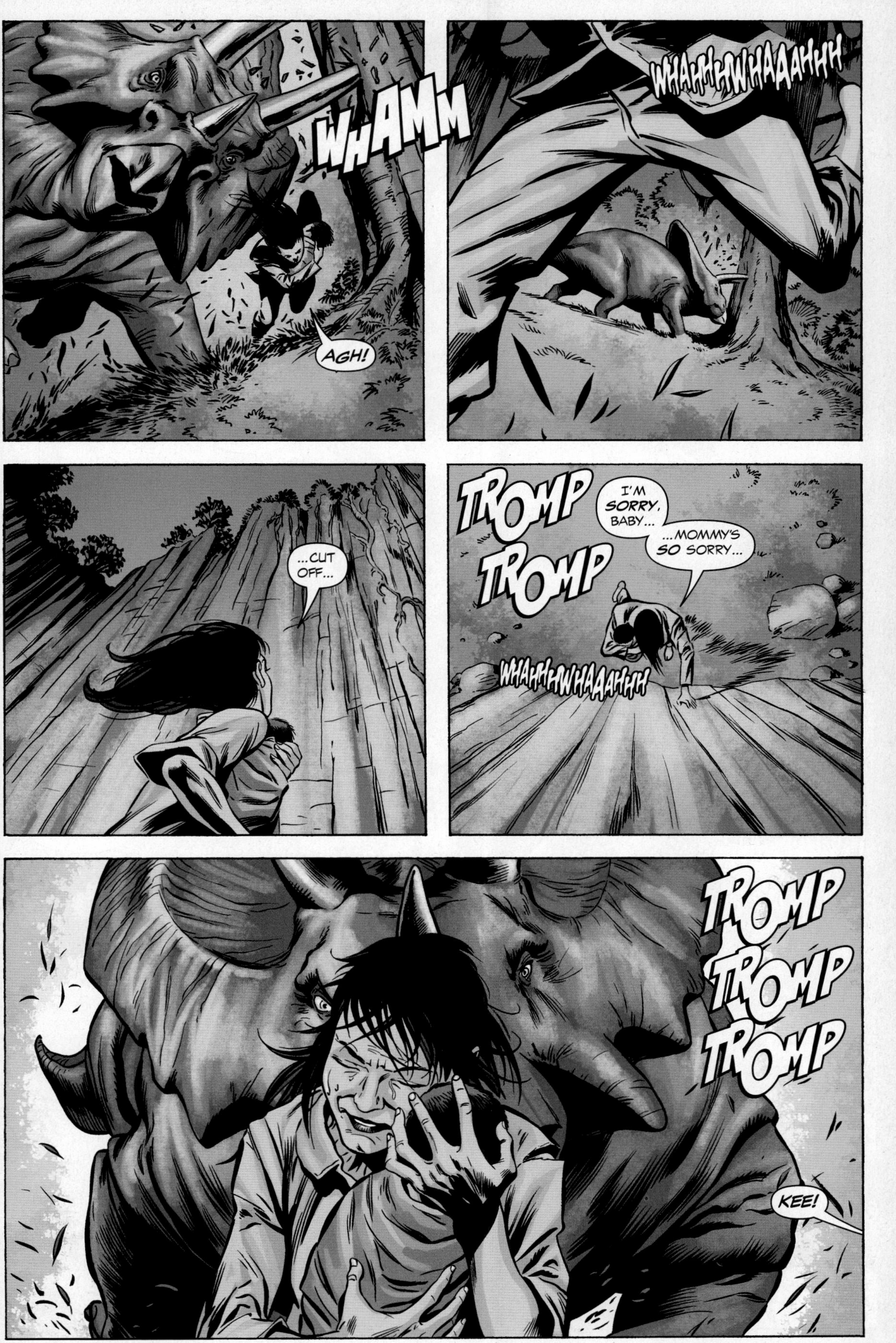
WHAMM
AGH!
WHAHHHWHAAAHHH
...CUT OFF...
TROMP
TROMP
I'M SORRY, BABY...
...MOMMY'S SO SORRY...
WHAHHHWHAAAHHH
TROMP
TROMP
TROMP
KEE!

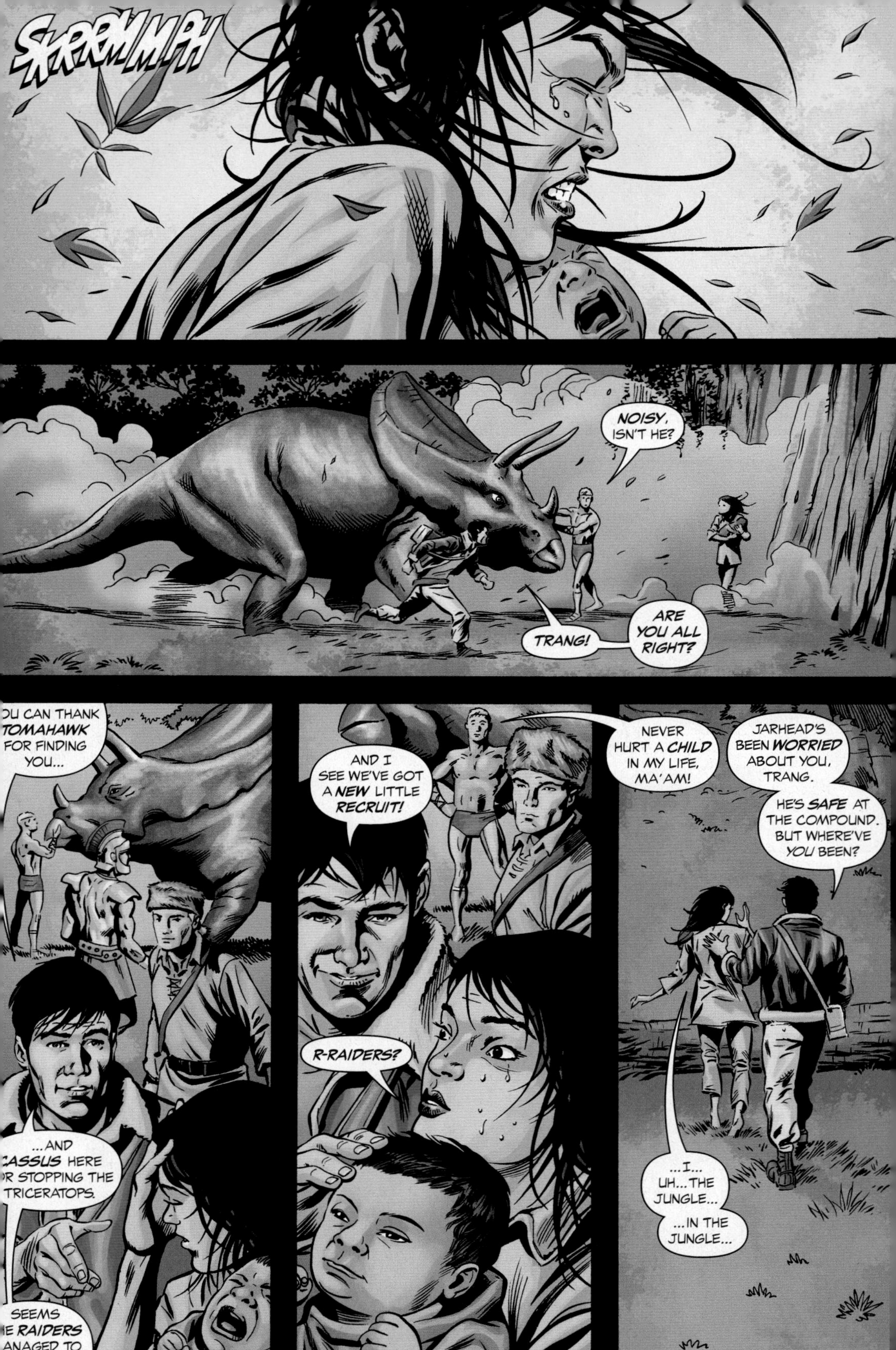
SKRRMMPH
NOISY, ISN'T HE?
TRANG!
ARE YOU ALL RIGHT?
OU CAN THANK TOMAHAWK FOR FINDING YOU...
...AND CASSUS HERE OR STOPPING THE TRICERATOPS.
SEEMS E RAIDERS ANAGED TO RAIN THEM.
AND I SEE WE'VE GOT A NEW LITTLE RECRUIT!
R-RAIDERS?
NEVER HURT A CHILD IN MY LIFE, MA'AM!
JARHEAD'S BEEN WORRIED ABOUT YOU, TRANG.
HE'S SAFE AT THE COMPOUND. BUT WHERE'VE YOU BEEN?
...I... UH...THE JUNGLE...
...IN THE JUNGLE...

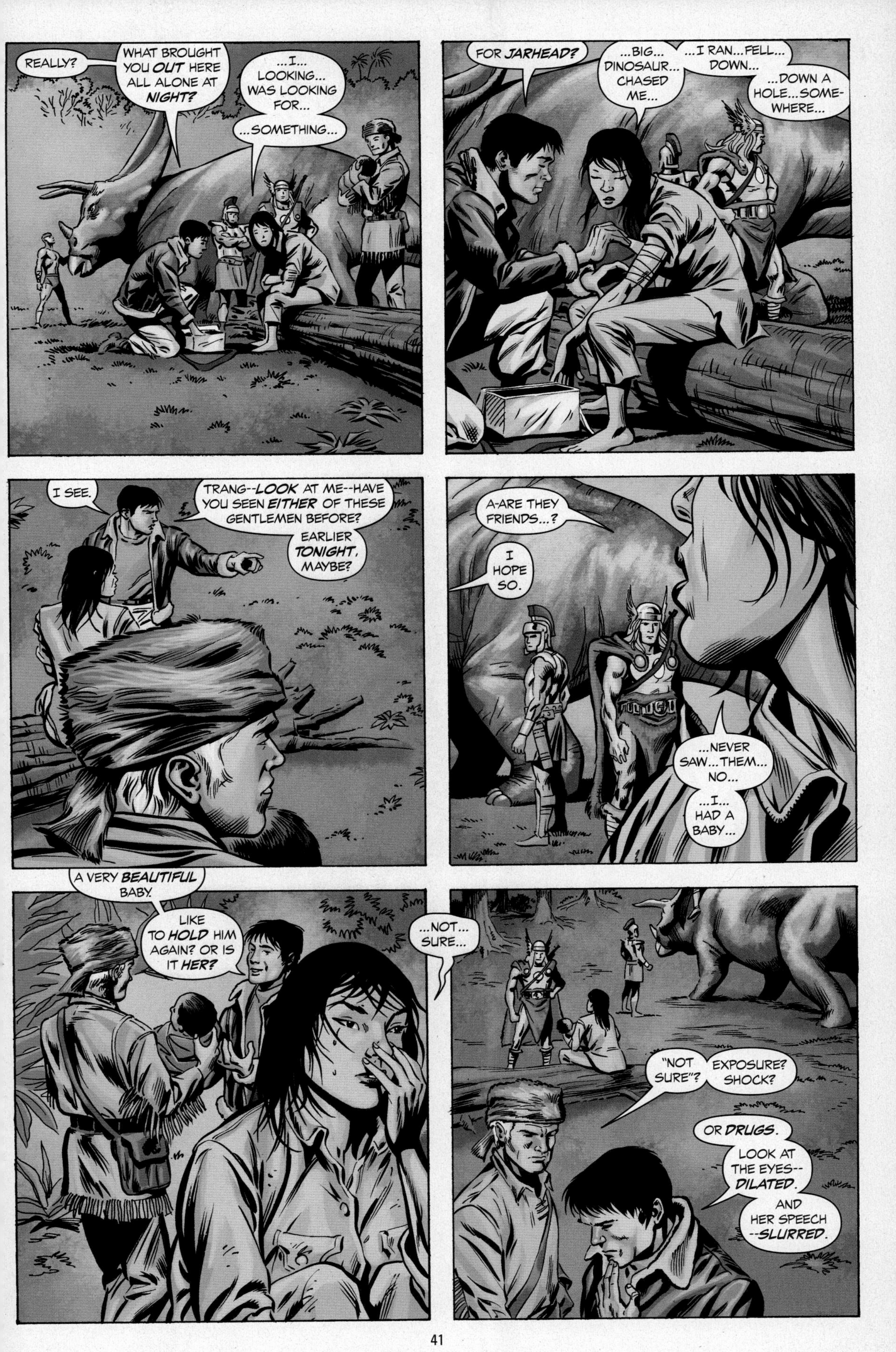
REALLY?
WHAT BROUGHT YOU OUT HERE ALL ALONE AT NIGHT?
...I... LOOKING... WAS LOOKING FOR...
...SOMETHING...
FOR JARHEAD?
...BIG... DINOSAUR... CHASED ME...
...I RAN...FELL... DOWN...
...DOWN A HOLE...SOME-WHERE...
I SEE.
TRANG--LOOK AT ME--HAVE YOU SEEN EITHER OF THESE GENTLEMEN BEFORE?
EARLIER TONIGHT, MAYBE?
A-ARE THEY FRIENDS...?
I HOPE SO.
...NEVER SAW...THEM... NO...
...I... HAD A BABY...
A VERY BEAUTIFUL BABY.
LIKE TO HOLD HIM AGAIN? OR IS IT HER?
...NOT... SURE...
"NOT SURE"?
EXPOSURE? SHOCK?
OR DRUGS.
LOOK AT THE EYES--DILATED.
AND HER SPEECH --SLURRED.

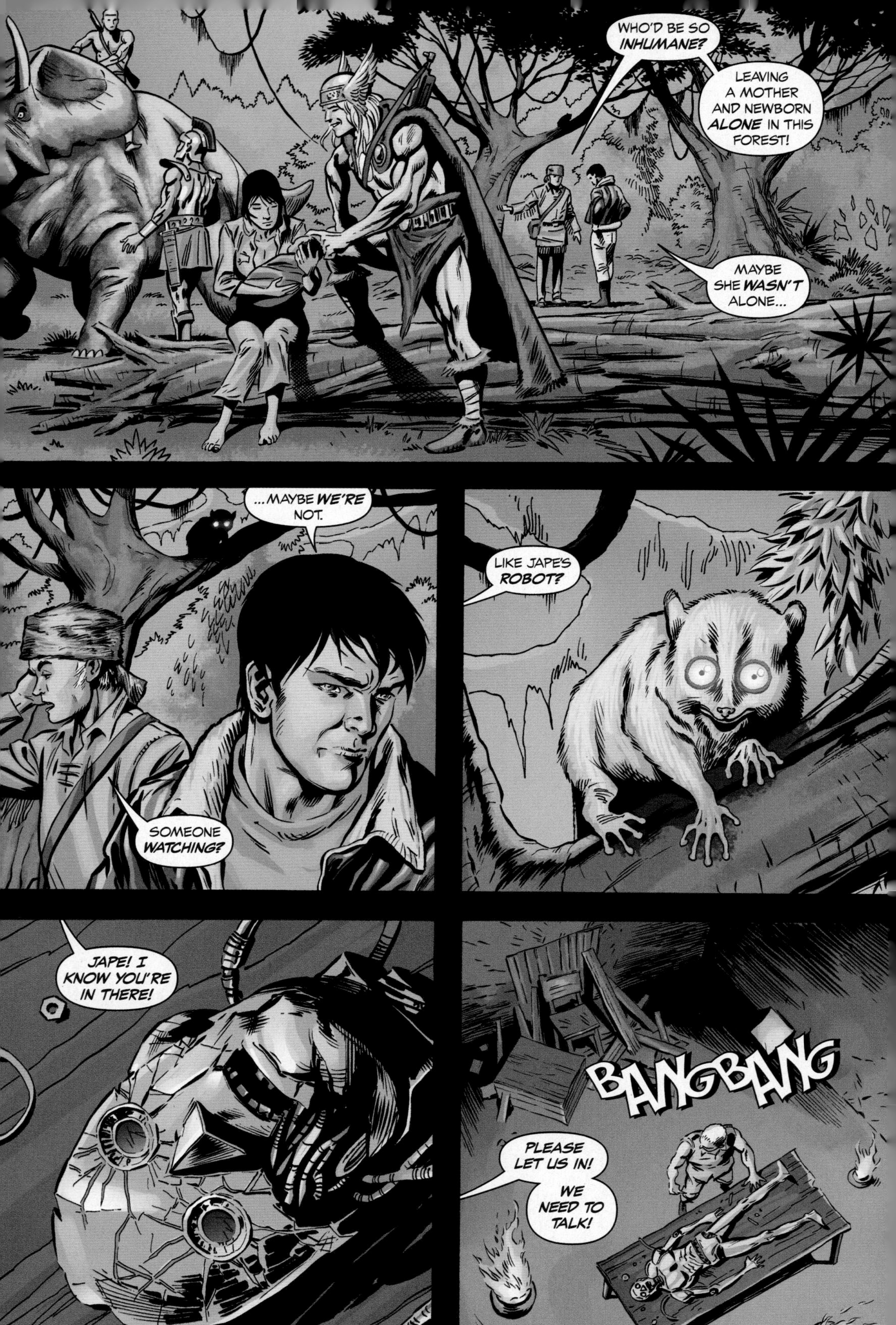
WHO'D BE SO INHUMANE?
LEAVING A MOTHER AND NEWBORN ALONE IN THIS FOREST!
MAYBE SHE WASN'T ALONE...
...MAYBE WE'RE NOT.
SOMEONE WATCHING?
LIKE JAPE'S ROBOT?
JAPE! I KNOW YOU'RE IN THERE!
BANGBANG
PLEASE LET US IN!
WE NEED TO TALK!

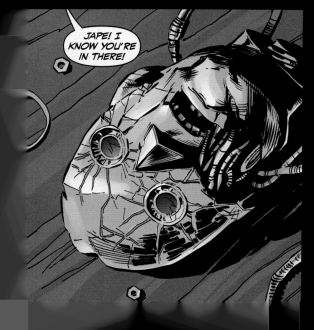

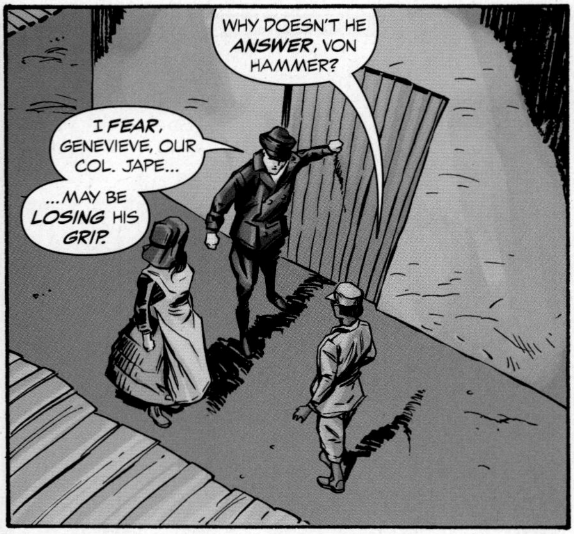
WHY DOESN'T HE ANSWER, VON HAMMER?
I FEAR, GENEVIEVE, OUR COL. JAPE...
...MAY BE LOSING HIS GRIP.

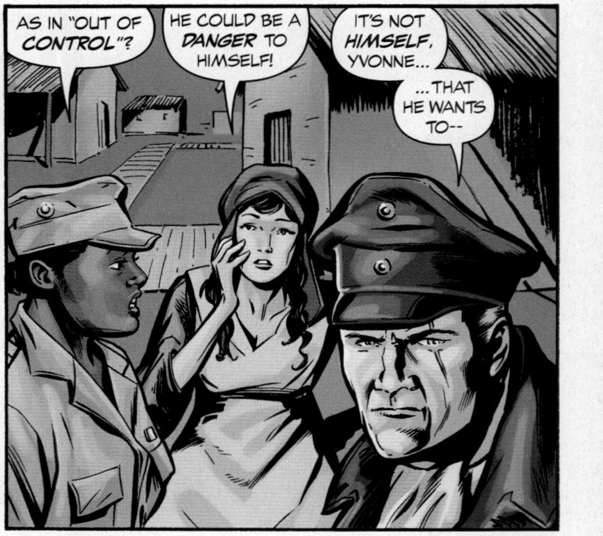
AS IN "OUT OF CONTROL"?
HE COULD BE A DANGER TO HIMSELF!
IT'S NOT HIMSELF, YVONNE...
...THAT HE WANTS TO--

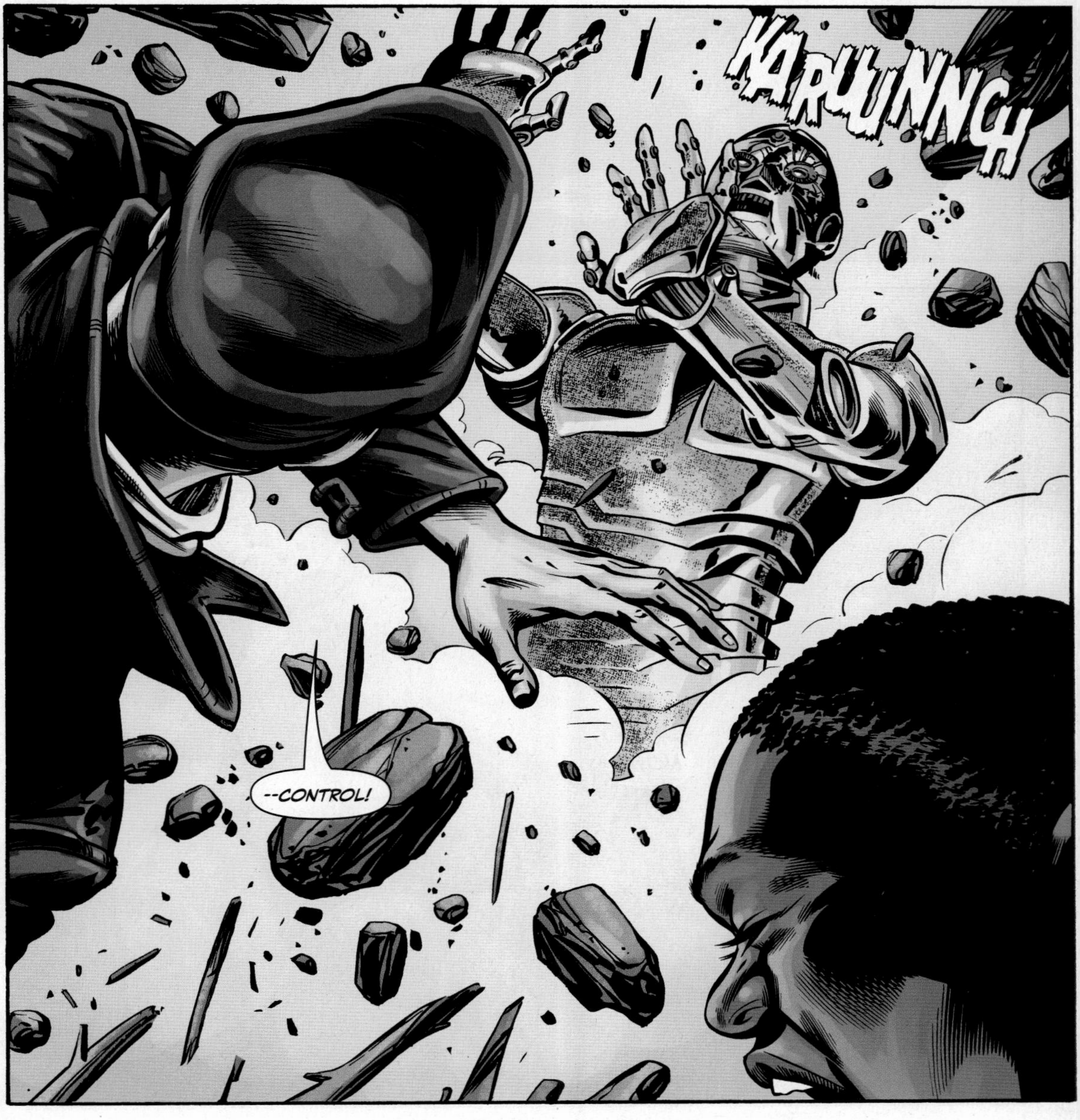
KARUUNNCH
--CONTROL!

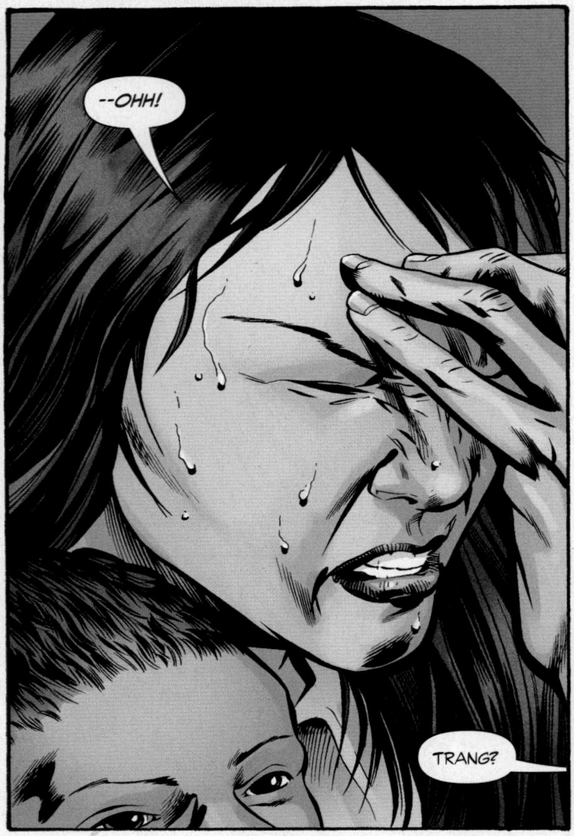
--OHH!
TRANG?

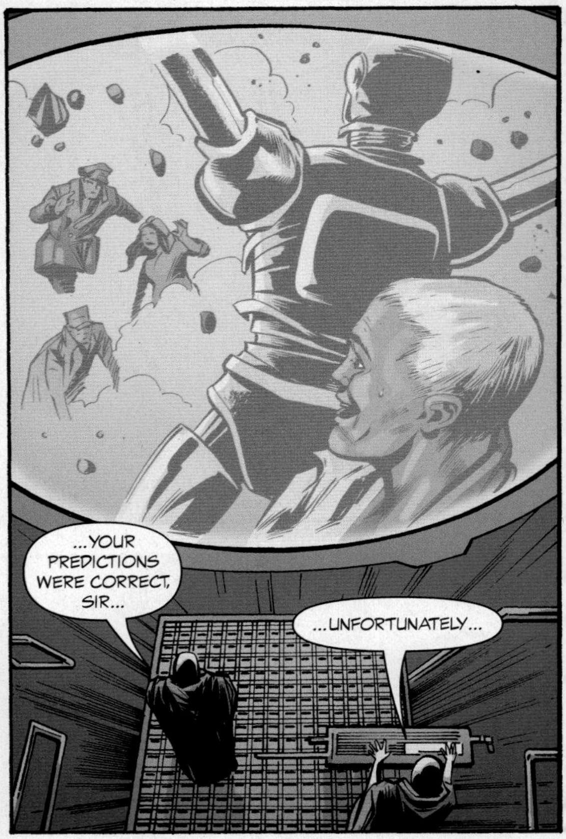
...YOUR PREDICTIONS WERE CORRECT, SIR...
...UNFORTUNATELY...

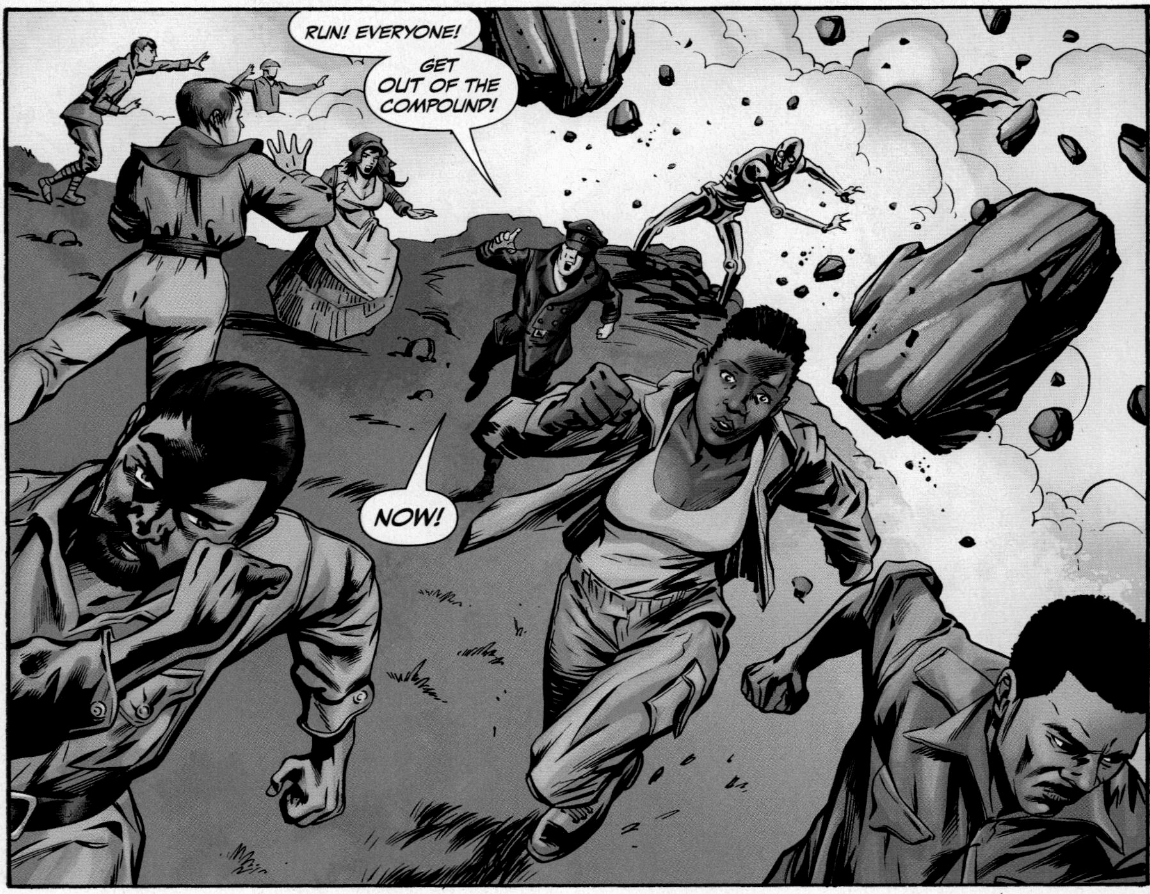
RUN! EVERYONE!
GET OUT OF THE COMPOUND!
NOW!

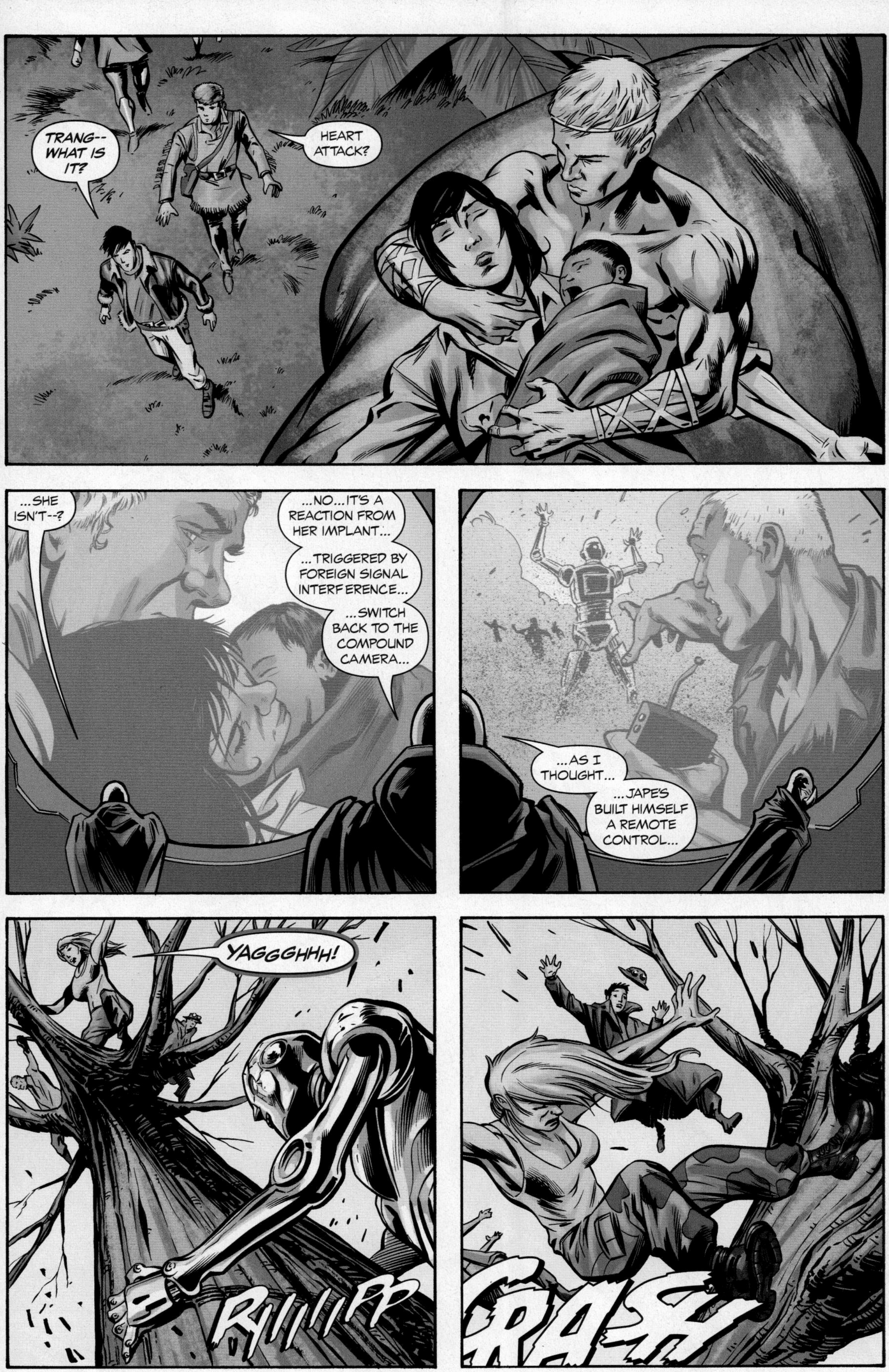
TRANG--
WHAT IS
IT?
HEART
ATTACK?
...SHE
ISN'T--?
...NO...IT'S A
REACTION FROM
HER IMPLANT...
...TRIGGERED BY
FOREIGN SIGNAL
INTERFERENCE...
...SWITCH
BACK TO THE
COMPOUND
CAMERA...
...AS I
THOUGHT...
...JAPE'S
BUILT HIMSELF
A REMOTE
CONTROL...
YAGGGHHH!
RIIIIPP
CRASH

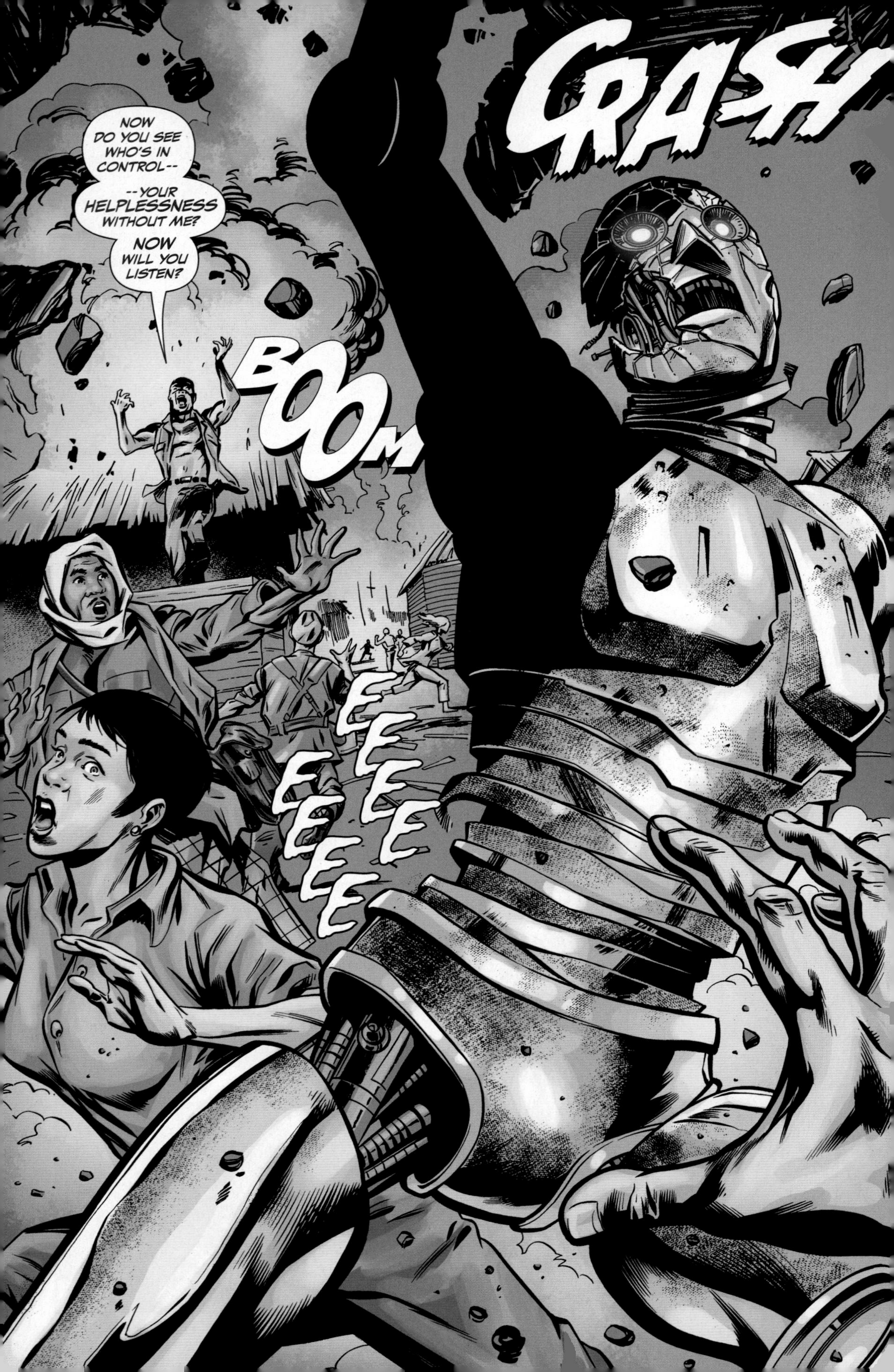
CRASH
NOW DO YOU SEE WHO'S IN CONTROL--
--YOUR HELPLESSNESS WITHOUT ME?
NOW WILL YOU LISTEN?
BOOOM
EEEEEEEE

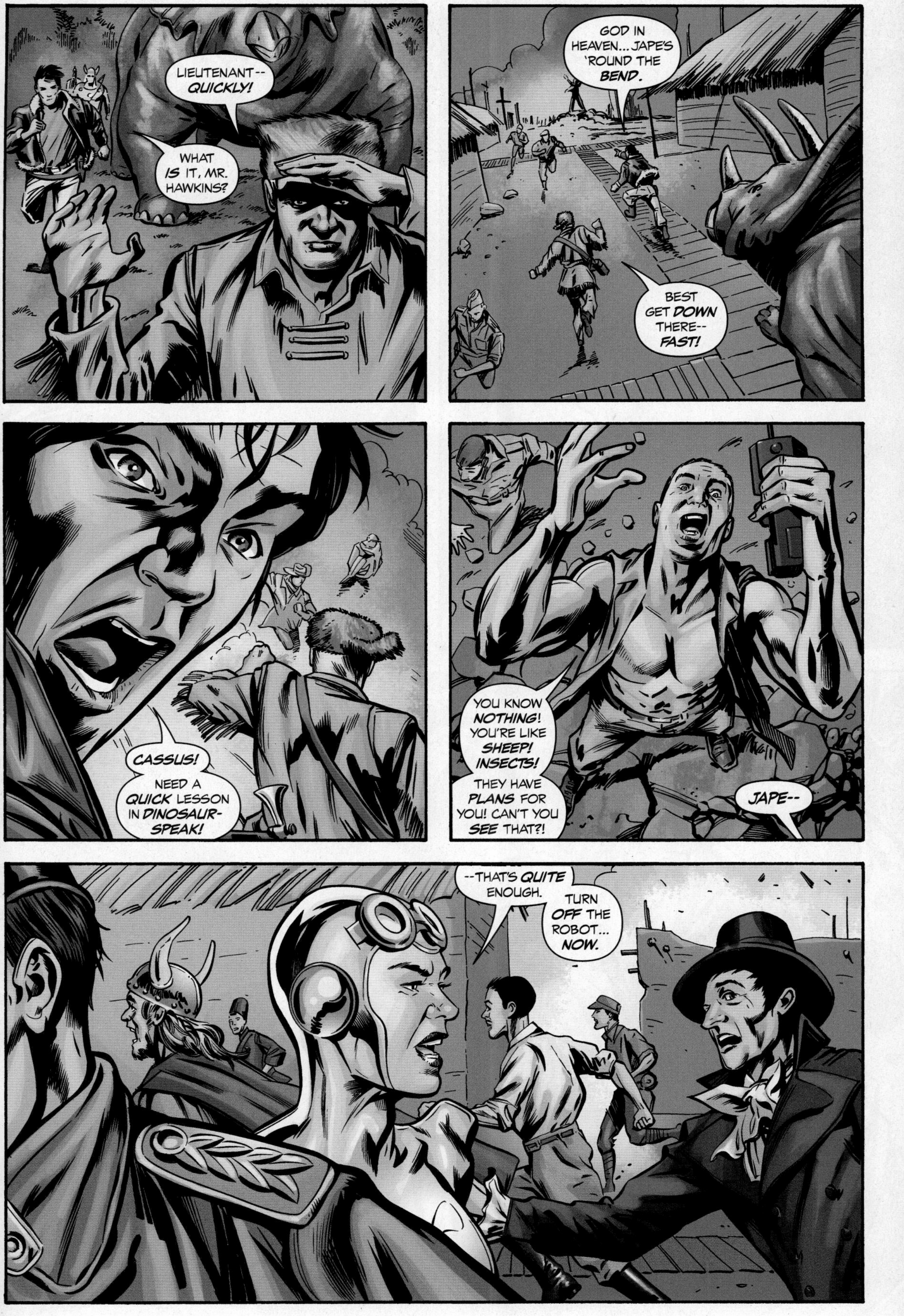
LIEUTENANT--
QUICKLY!
WHAT IS IT, MR. HAWKINS?
GOD IN HEAVEN... JAPE'S 'ROUND THE BEND.
BEST GET DOWN THERE-- FAST!
CASSUS!
NEED A QUICK LESSON IN DINOSAUR-SPEAK!
YOU KNOW NOTHING! YOU'RE LIKE SHEEP! INSECTS!
THEY HAVE PLANS FOR YOU! CAN'T YOU SEE THAT?!
JAPE--
--THAT'S QUITE ENOUGH.
TURN OFF THE ROBOT... NOW.

NO!

CHOKE
PLEASE!

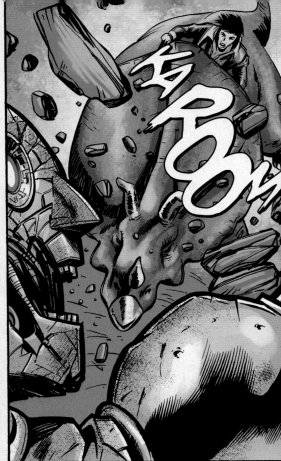

KAROOM!

WHUMP

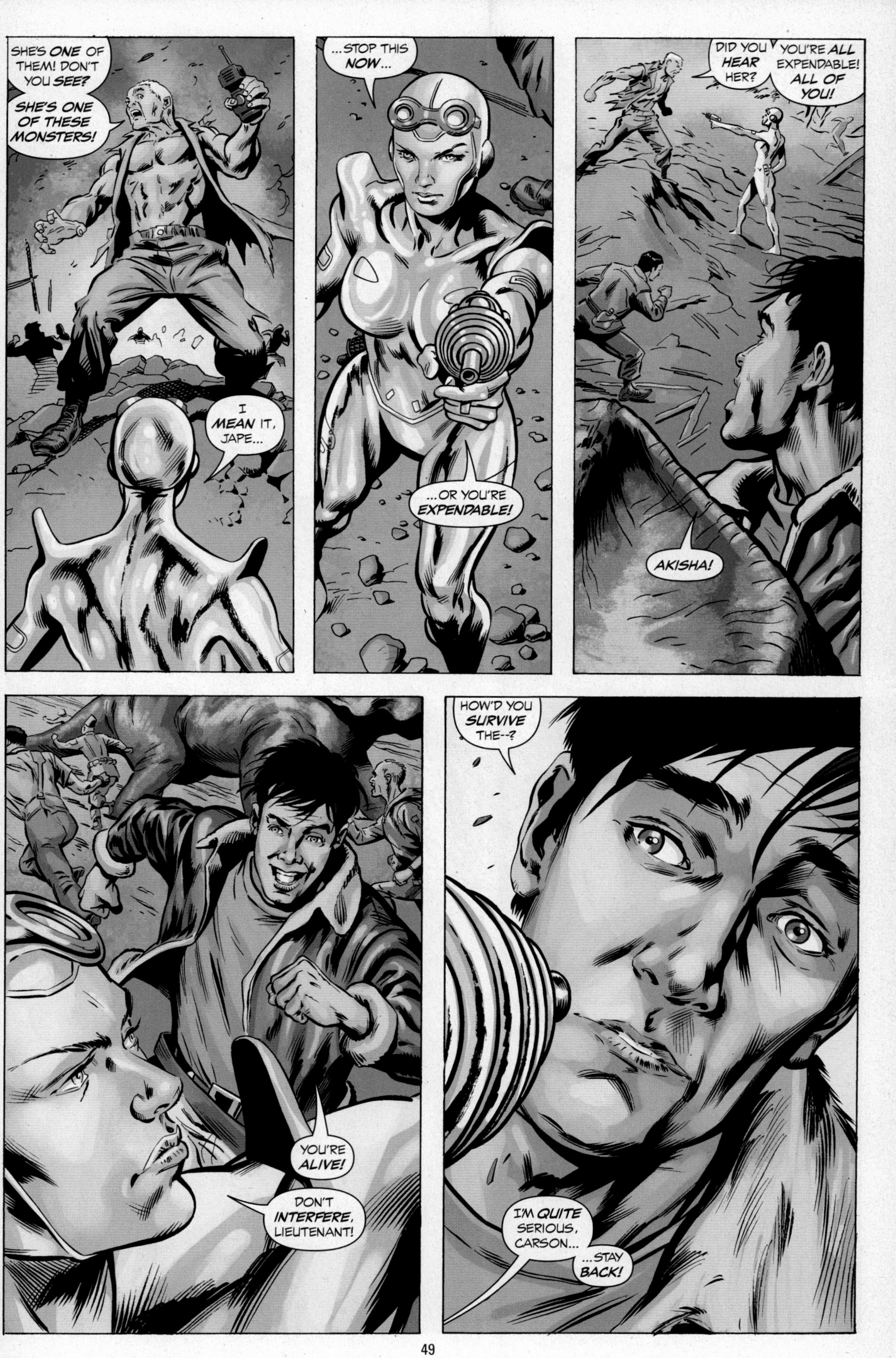

SHE'S ONE OF THEM! DON'T YOU SEE?
SHE'S ONE OF THESE MONSTERS!
I MEAN IT, JAPE...
...STOP THIS NOW...
...OR YOU'RE EXPENDABLE!
DID YOU HEAR HER?
YOU'RE ALL EXPENDABLE! ALL OF YOU!
AKISHA!
YOU'RE ALIVE!
DON'T INTERFERE, LIEUTENANT!
HOW'D YOU SURVIVE THE--?
I'M QUITE SERIOUS, CARSON...
...STAY BACK!

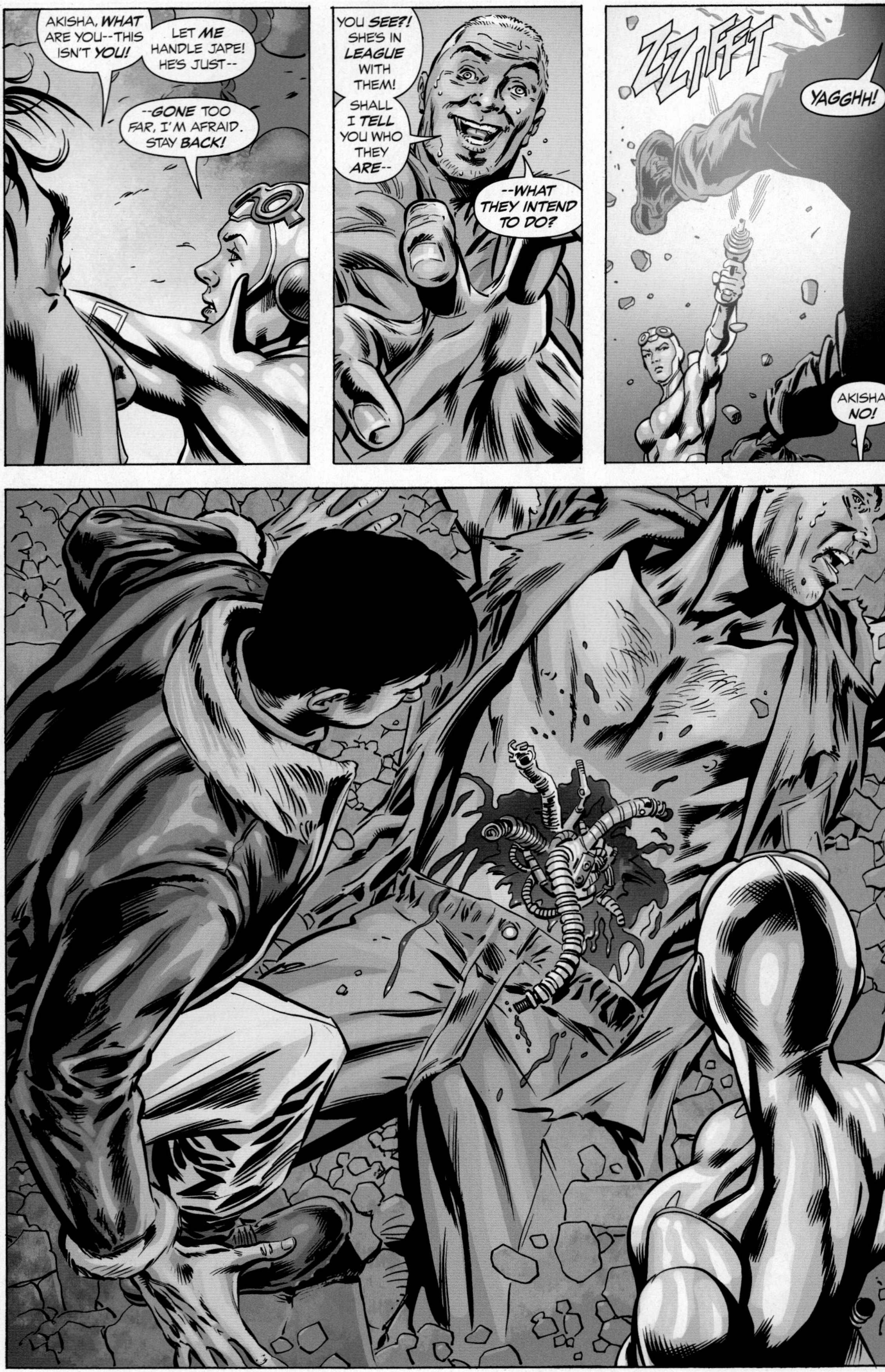

AKISHA, WHAT ARE YOU--THIS ISN'T YOU!
LET ME HANDLE JAPE! HE'S JUST--
--GONE TOO FAR, I'M AFRAID. STAY BACK!
YOU SEE?! SHE'S IN LEAGUE WITH THEM!
SHALL I TELL YOU WHO THEY ARE--
--WHAT THEY INTEND TO DO?
ZZIFFT
YAGGHH!
AKISHA, NO!

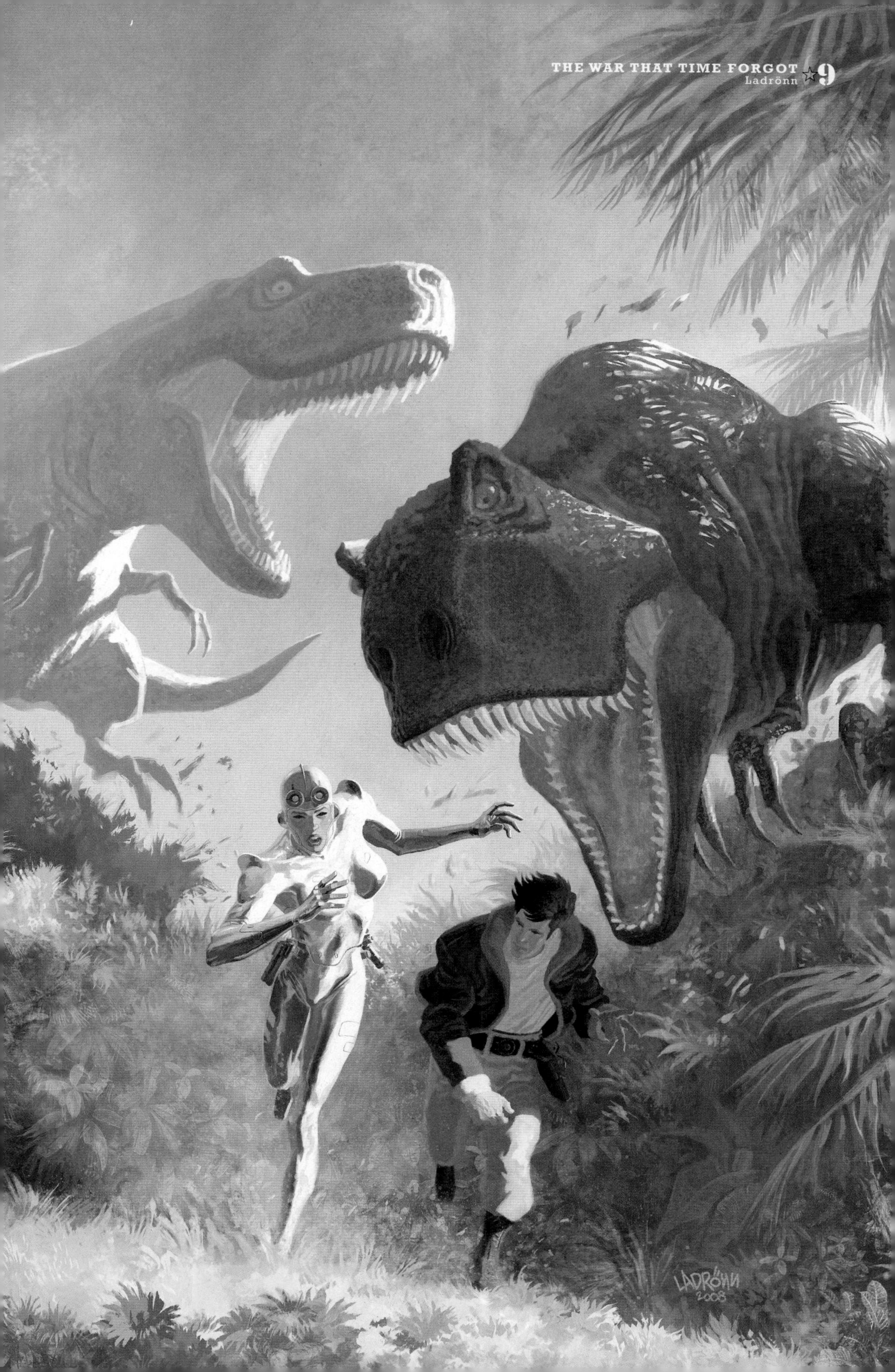
THE WAR THAT TIME FORGOT ☆9
Ladrönn
LADRÖNN
2008

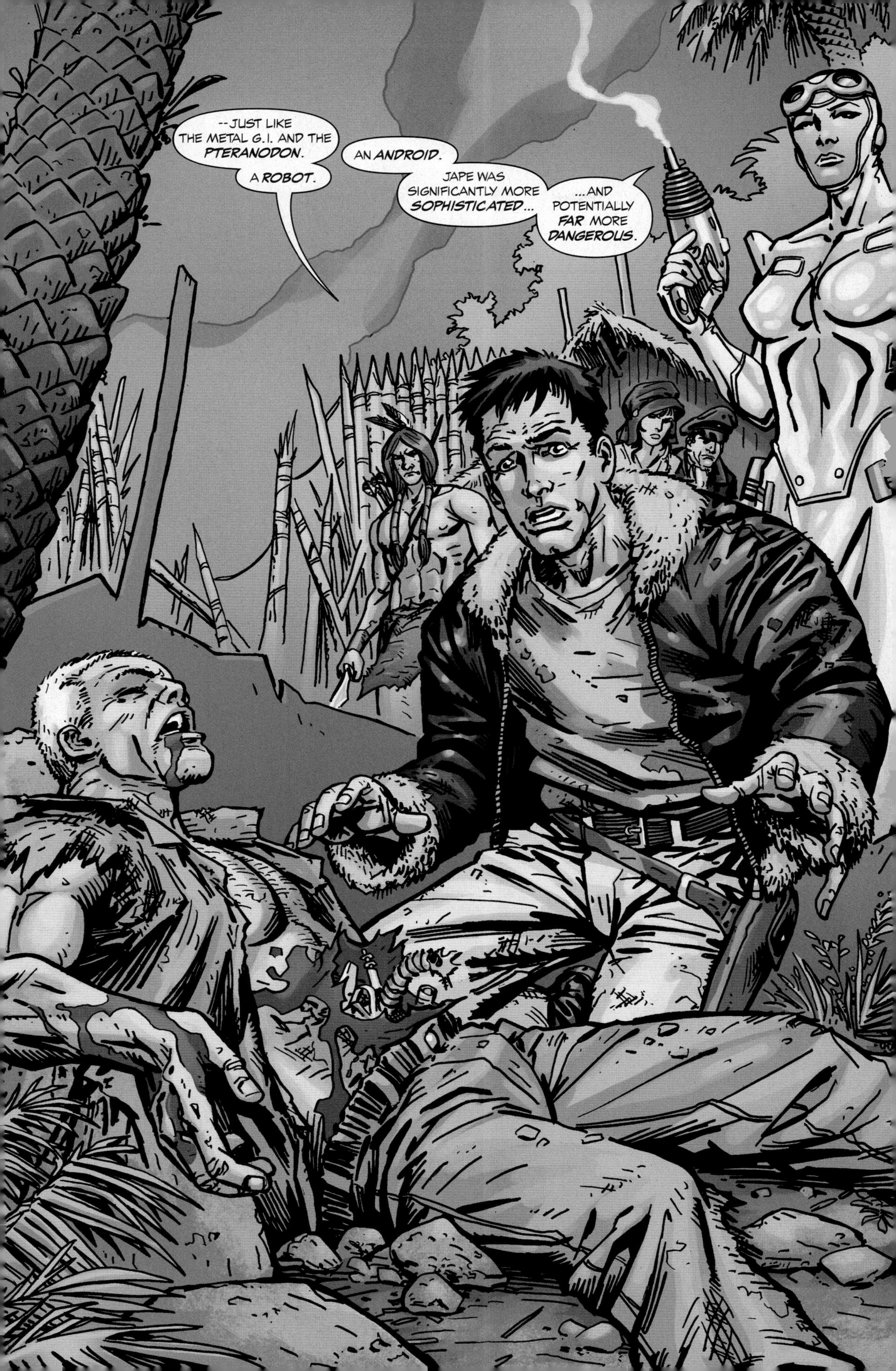
--JUST LIKE THE METAL G.I. AND THE PTERANODON.
A ROBOT.
AN ANDROID.
JAPE WAS SIGNIFICANTLY MORE SOPHISTICATED...
...AND POTENTIALLY FAR MORE DANGEROUS.

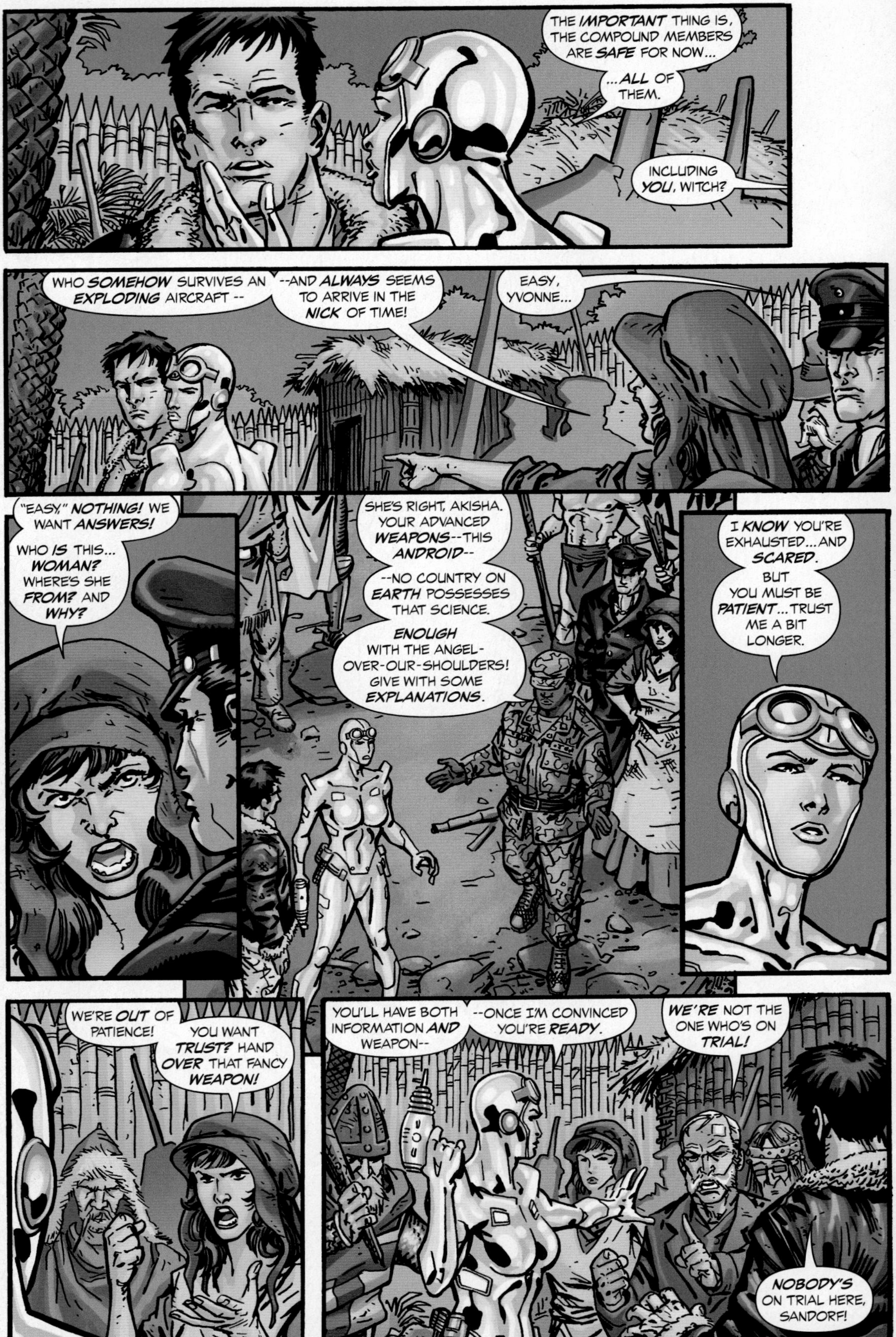
THE IMPORTANT THING IS, THE COMPOUND MEMBERS ARE SAFE FOR NOW...
...ALL OF THEM.
INCLUDING YOU, WITCH?
WHO SOMEHOW SURVIVES AN EXPLODING AIRCRAFT --
--AND ALWAYS SEEMS TO ARRIVE IN THE NICK OF TIME!
EASY, YVONNE...
"EASY," NOTHING! WE WANT ANSWERS!
WHO IS THIS... WOMAN? WHERE'S SHE FROM? AND WHY?
SHE'S RIGHT, AKISHA. YOUR ADVANCED WEAPONS--THIS ANDROID--
--NO COUNTRY ON EARTH POSSESSES THAT SCIENCE.
ENOUGH WITH THE ANGEL-OVER-OUR-SHOULDERS! GIVE WITH SOME EXPLANATIONS.
I KNOW YOU'RE EXHAUSTED...AND SCARED.
BUT YOU MUST BE PATIENT...TRUST ME A BIT LONGER.
WE'RE OUT OF PATIENCE!
YOU WANT TRUST? HAND OVER THAT FANCY WEAPON!
YOU'LL HAVE BOTH INFORMATION AND WEAPON--
--ONCE I'M CONVINCED YOU'RE READY.
WE'RE NOT THE ONE WHO'S ON TRIAL!
NOBODY'S ON TRIAL HERE, SANDORF!

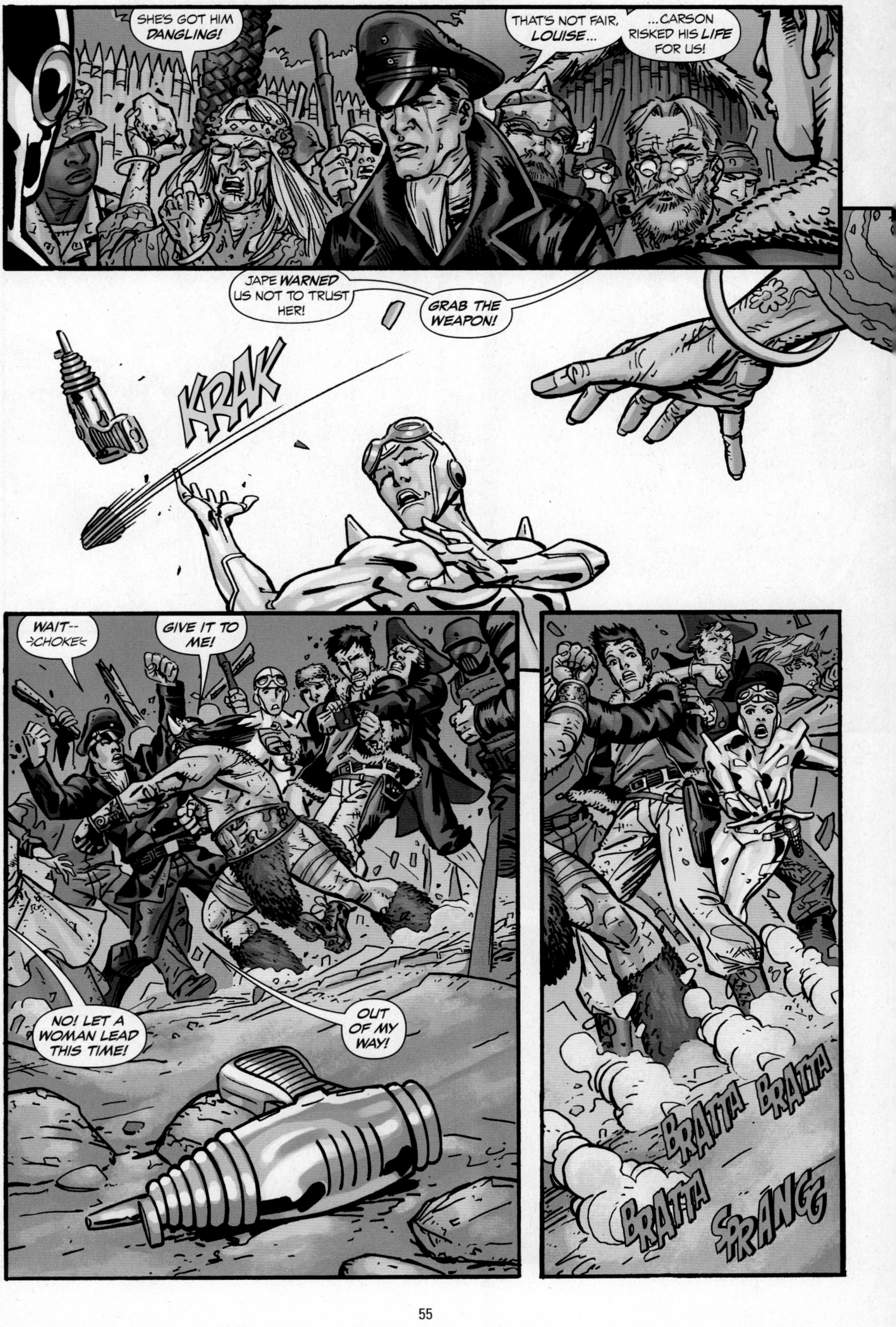
SHE'S GOT HIM DANGLING!
THAT'S NOT FAIR, LOUISE...
...CARSON RISKED HIS LIFE FOR US!
JAPE WARNED US NOT TO TRUST HER!
GRAB THE WEAPON!
KRAK
WAIT-- CHOKE
GIVE IT TO ME!
NO! LET A WOMAN LEAD THIS TIME!
OUT OF MY WAY!
BRATTA BRATTA
BRATTA
SPRANGG

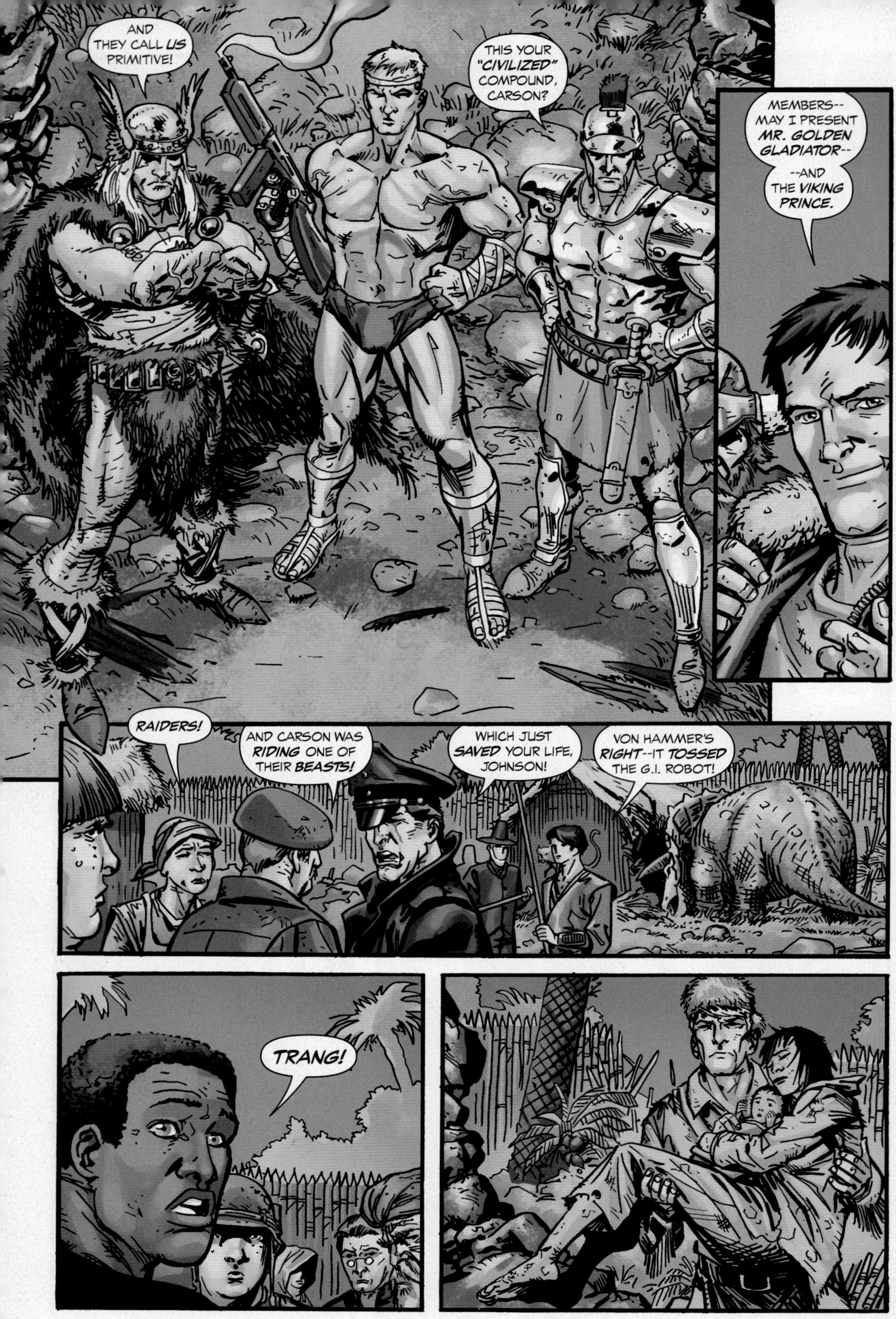
AND THEY CALL US PRIMITIVE!
THIS YOUR "CIVILIZED" COMPOUND, CARSON?
MEMBERS-- MAY I PRESENT MR. GOLDEN GLADIATOR--
--AND THE VIKING PRINCE.
RAIDERS!
AND CARSON WAS RIDING ONE OF THEIR BEASTS!
WHICH JUST SAVED YOUR LIFE, JOHNSON!
VON HAMMER'S RIGHT--IT TOSSED THE G.I. ROBOT!
TRANG!

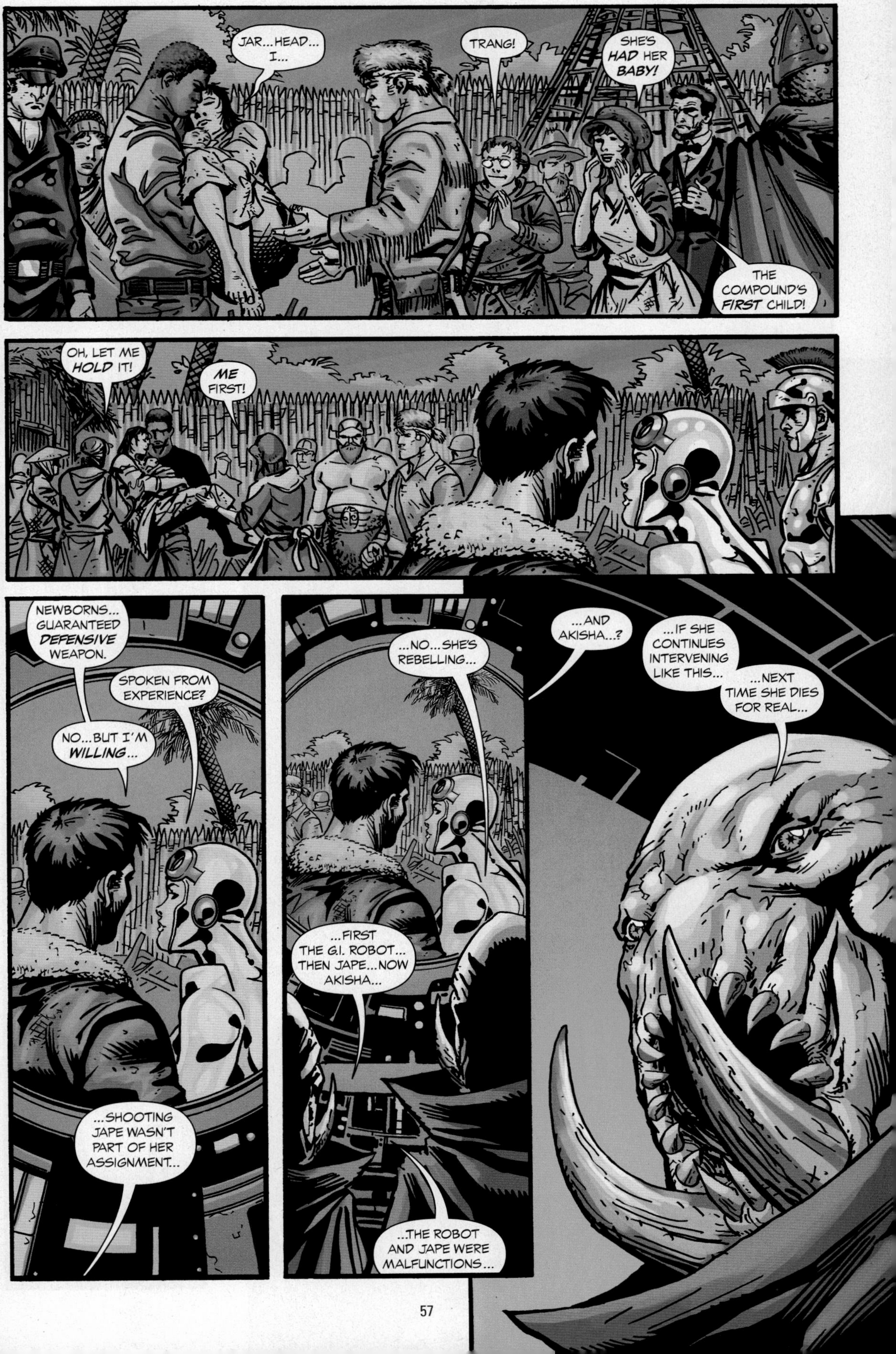

JAR...HEAD... I...
TRANG!
SHE'S HAD HER BABY!
THE COMPOUND'S FIRST CHILD!
OH, LET ME HOLD IT!
ME FIRST!
NEWBORNS... GUARANTEED DEFENSIVE WEAPON.
SPOKEN FROM EXPERIENCE?
NO...BUT I'M WILLING...
...SHOOTING JAPE WASN'T PART OF HER ASSIGNMENT...
...NO...SHE'S REBELLING...
...FIRST THE G.I. ROBOT... THEN JAPE...NOW AKISHA...
...THE ROBOT AND JAPE WERE MALFUNCTIONS...
...AND AKISHA...?
...IF SHE CONTINUES INTERVENING LIKE THIS...
...NEXT TIME SHE DIES FOR REAL...

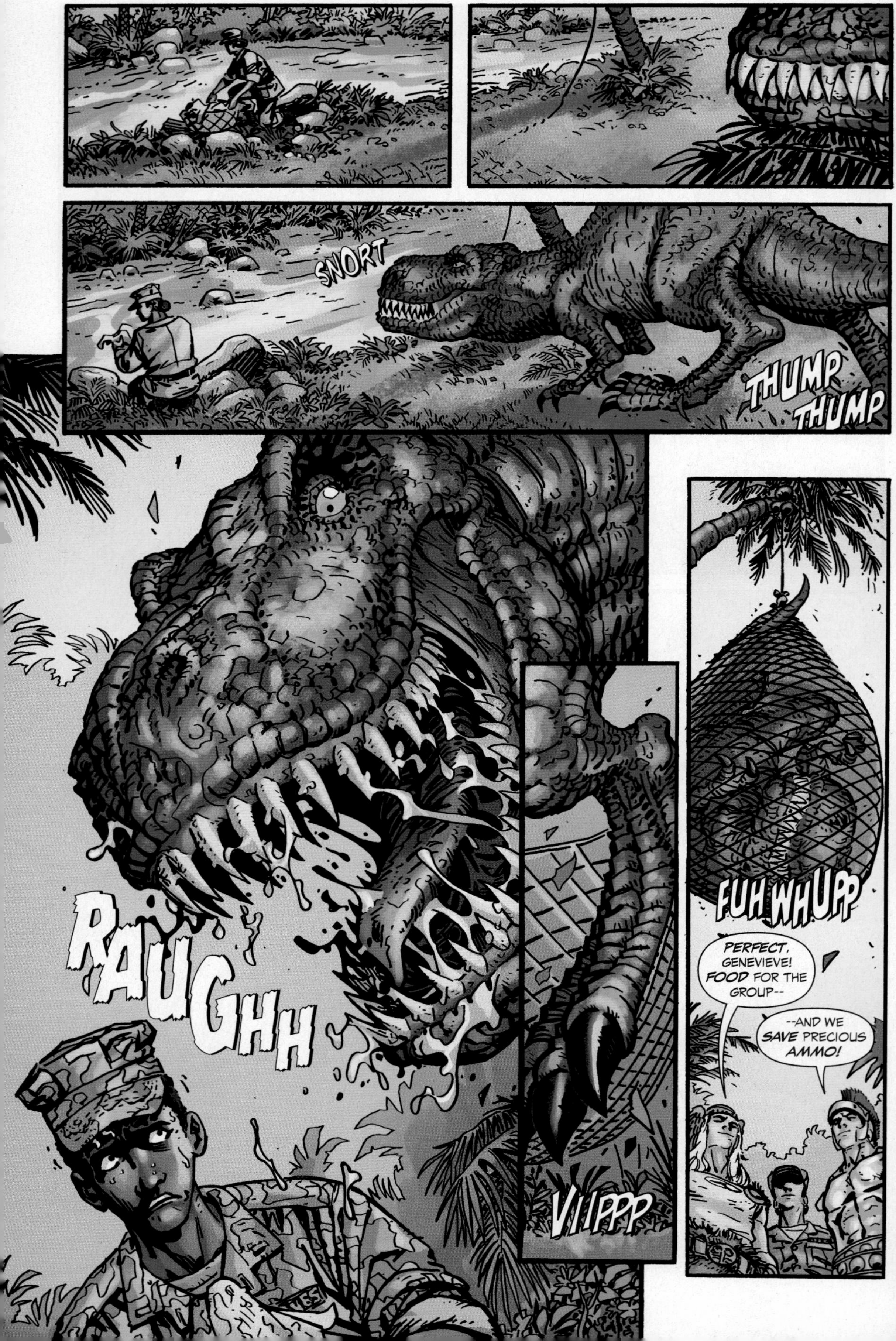
SNORT
THUMP
THUMP
RAUGHH
VIIPPP
FUH WHUPP
PERFECT, GENEVIEVE! FOOD FOR THE GROUP--
--AND WE SAVE PRECIOUS AMMO!

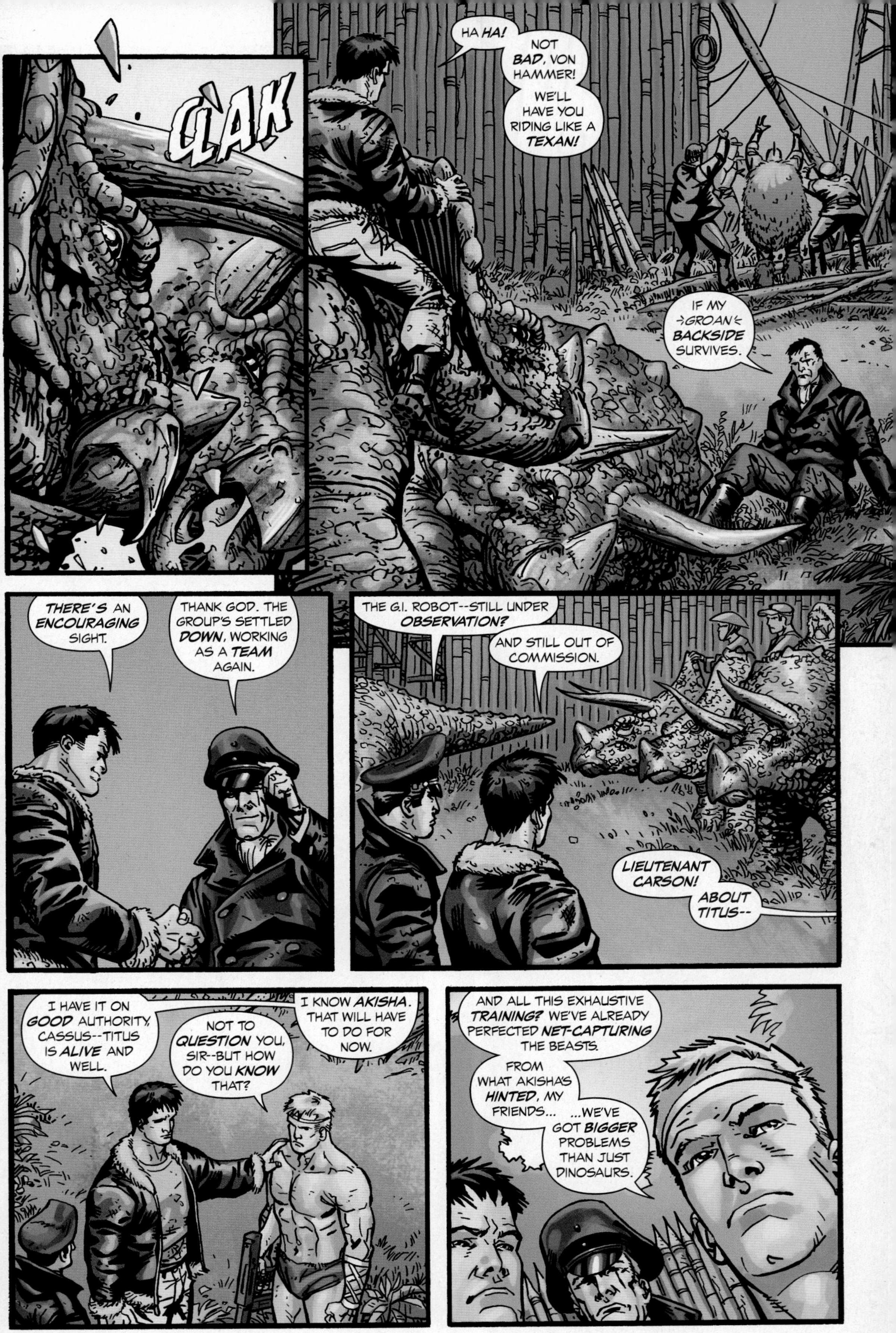
CLAK
HA HA!
NOT BAD, VON HAMMER!
WE'LL HAVE YOU RIDING LIKE A TEXAN!
IF MY -GROAN- BACKSIDE SURVIVES.
THERE'S AN ENCOURAGING SIGHT.
THANK GOD. THE GROUP'S SETTLED DOWN, WORKING AS A TEAM AGAIN.
THE G.I. ROBOT--STILL UNDER OBSERVATION?
AND STILL OUT OF COMMISSION.
LIEUTENANT CARSON!
ABOUT TITUS--
I HAVE IT ON GOOD AUTHORITY, CASSUS--TITUS IS ALIVE AND WELL.
NOT TO QUESTION YOU, SIR--BUT HOW DO YOU KNOW THAT?
I KNOW AKISHA. THAT WILL HAVE TO DO FOR NOW.
AND ALL THIS EXHAUSTIVE TRAINING? WE'VE ALREADY PERFECTED NET-CAPTURING THE BEASTS.
FROM WHAT AKISHA'S HINTED, MY FRIENDS...
...WE'VE GOT BIGGER PROBLEMS THAN JUST DINOSAURS.

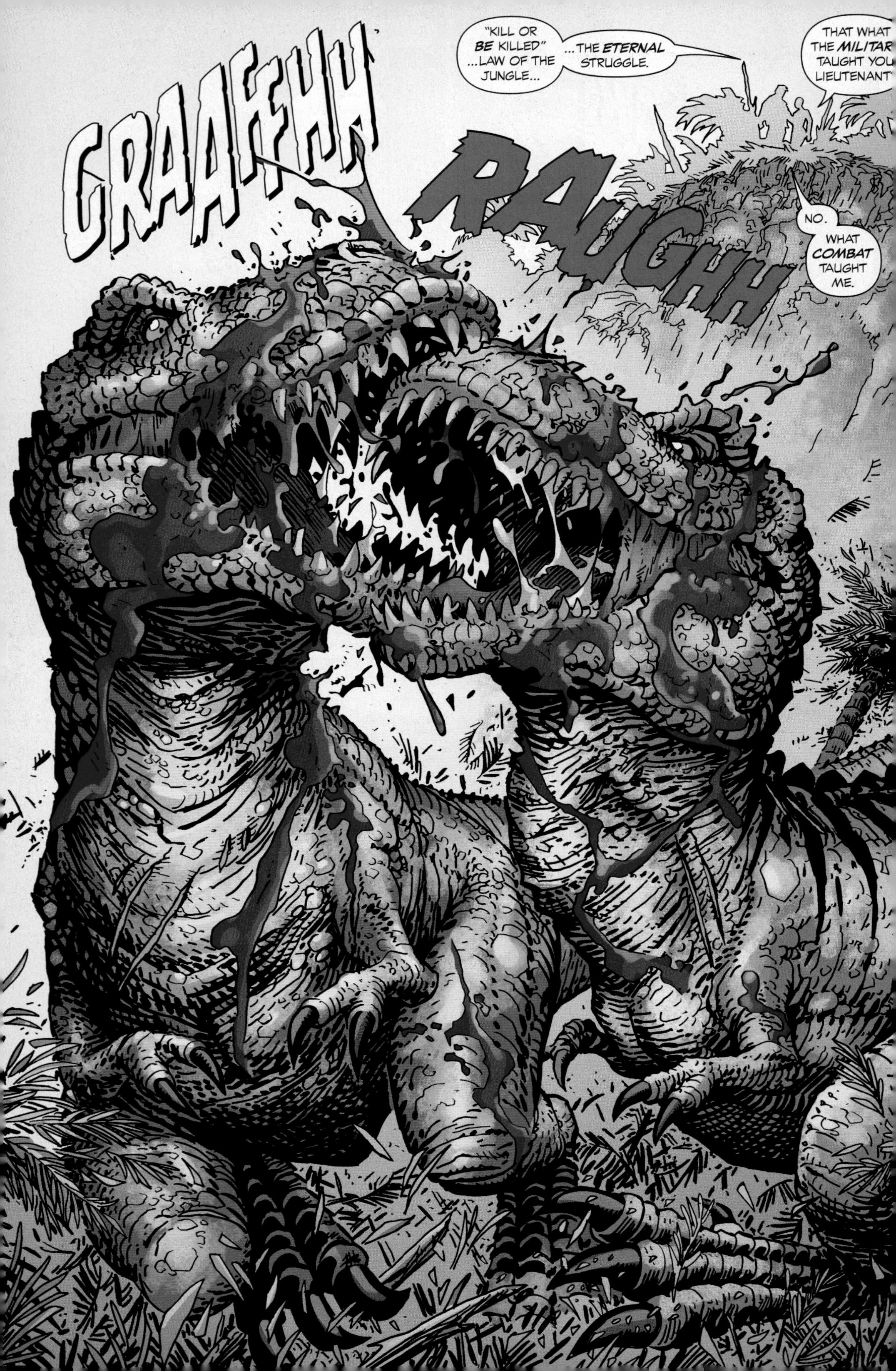
GRAAFHH
"KILL OR BE KILLED" ...LAW OF THE JUNGLE...
...THE ETERNAL STRUGGLE.
THAT WHAT THE MILITAR TAUGHT YOU LIEUTENANT
RAUGHH
NO. WHAT COMBAT TAUGHT ME.

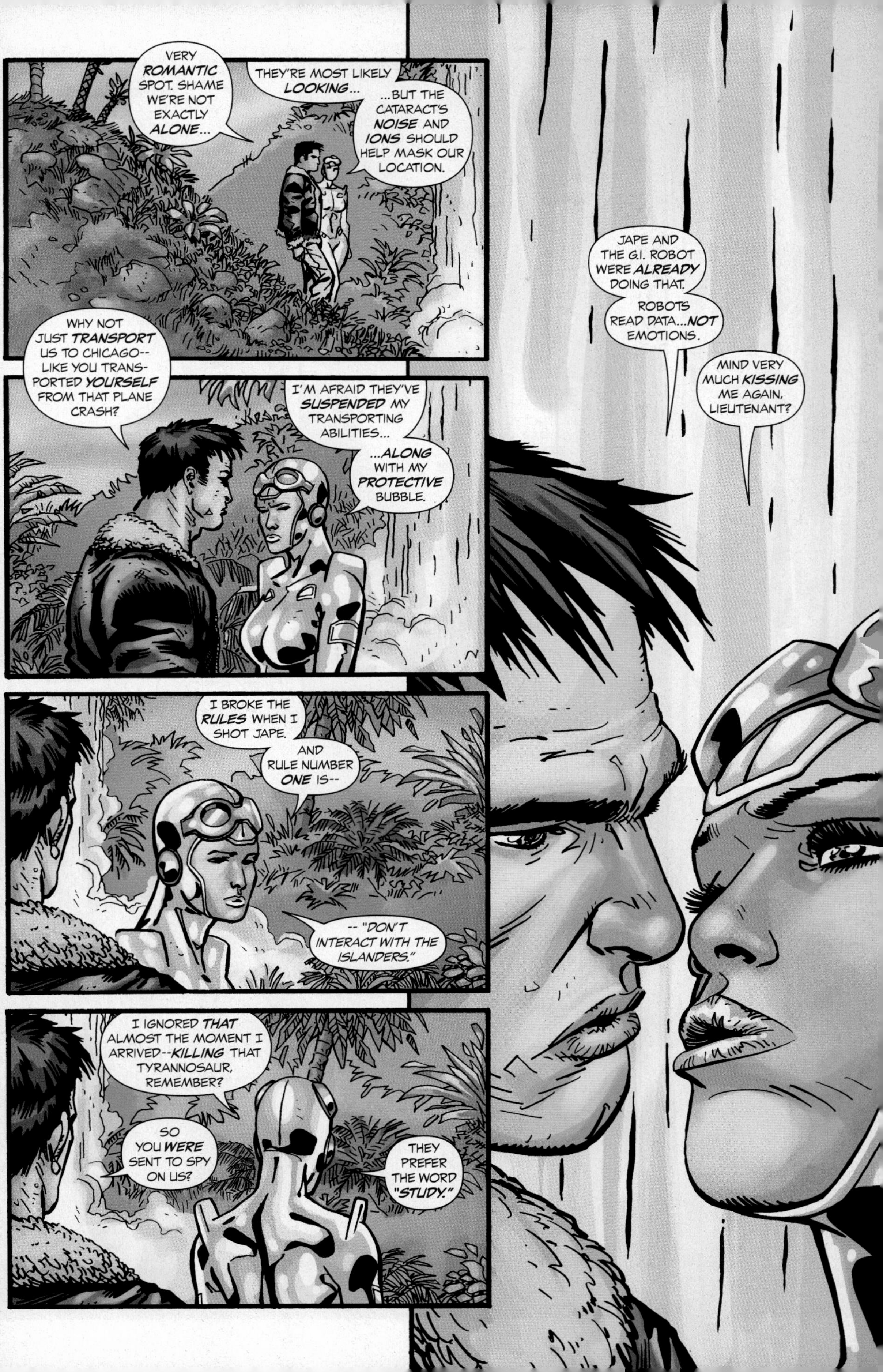

VERY ROMANTIC SPOT. SHAME WE'RE NOT EXACTLY ALONE...
THEY'RE MOST LIKELY LOOKING...
...BUT THE CATARACT'S NOISE AND IONS SHOULD HELP MASK OUR LOCATION.
WHY NOT JUST TRANSPORT US TO CHICAGO--LIKE YOU TRANSPORTED YOURSELF FROM THAT PLANE CRASH?
I'M AFRAID THEY'VE SUSPENDED MY TRANSPORTING ABILITIES...
...ALONG WITH MY PROTECTIVE BUBBLE.
I BROKE THE RULES WHEN I SHOT JAPE.
AND RULE NUMBER ONE IS--
-- "DON'T INTERACT WITH THE ISLANDERS."
I IGNORED THAT ALMOST THE MOMENT I ARRIVED--KILLING THAT TYRANNOSAUR, REMEMBER?
SO YOU WERE SENT TO SPY ON US?
THEY PREFER THE WORD "STUDY."
JAPE AND THE G.I. ROBOT WERE ALREADY DOING THAT.
ROBOTS READ DATA...NOT EMOTIONS.
MIND VERY MUCH KISSING ME AGAIN, LIEUTENANT?

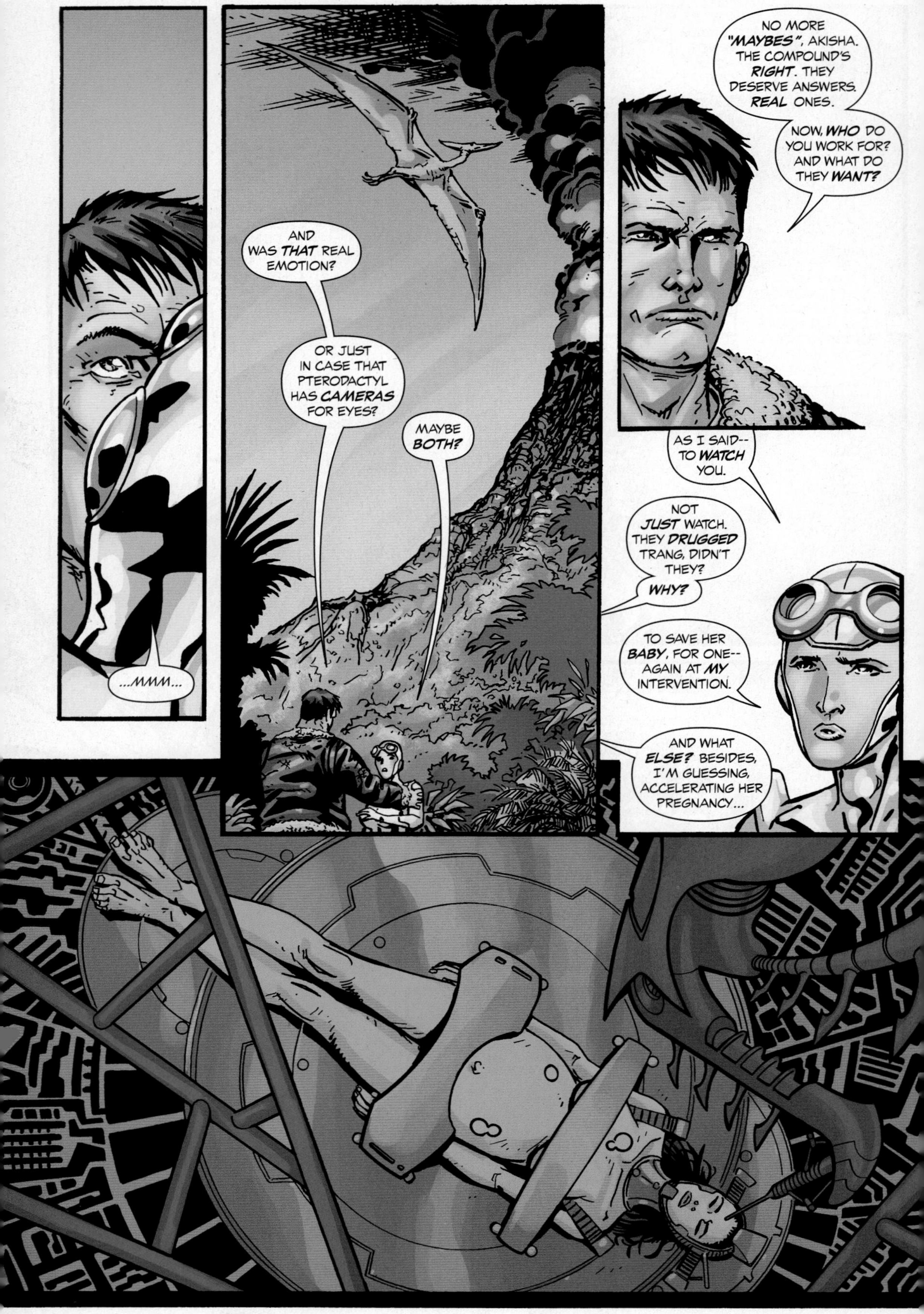
...MMM...
AND WAS THAT REAL EMOTION?
OR JUST IN CASE THAT PTERODACTYL HAS CAMERAS FOR EYES?
MAYBE BOTH?
NO MORE "MAYBES", AKISHA. THE COMPOUND'S RIGHT. THEY DESERVE ANSWERS. REAL ONES.
NOW, WHO DO YOU WORK FOR? AND WHAT DO THEY WANT?
AS I SAID-- TO WATCH YOU.
NOT JUST WATCH. THEY DRUGGED TRANG, DIDN'T THEY?
WHY?
TO SAVE HER BABY, FOR ONE-- AGAIN AT MY INTERVENTION.
AND WHAT ELSE? BESIDES, I'M GUESSING, ACCELERATING HER PREGNANCY...

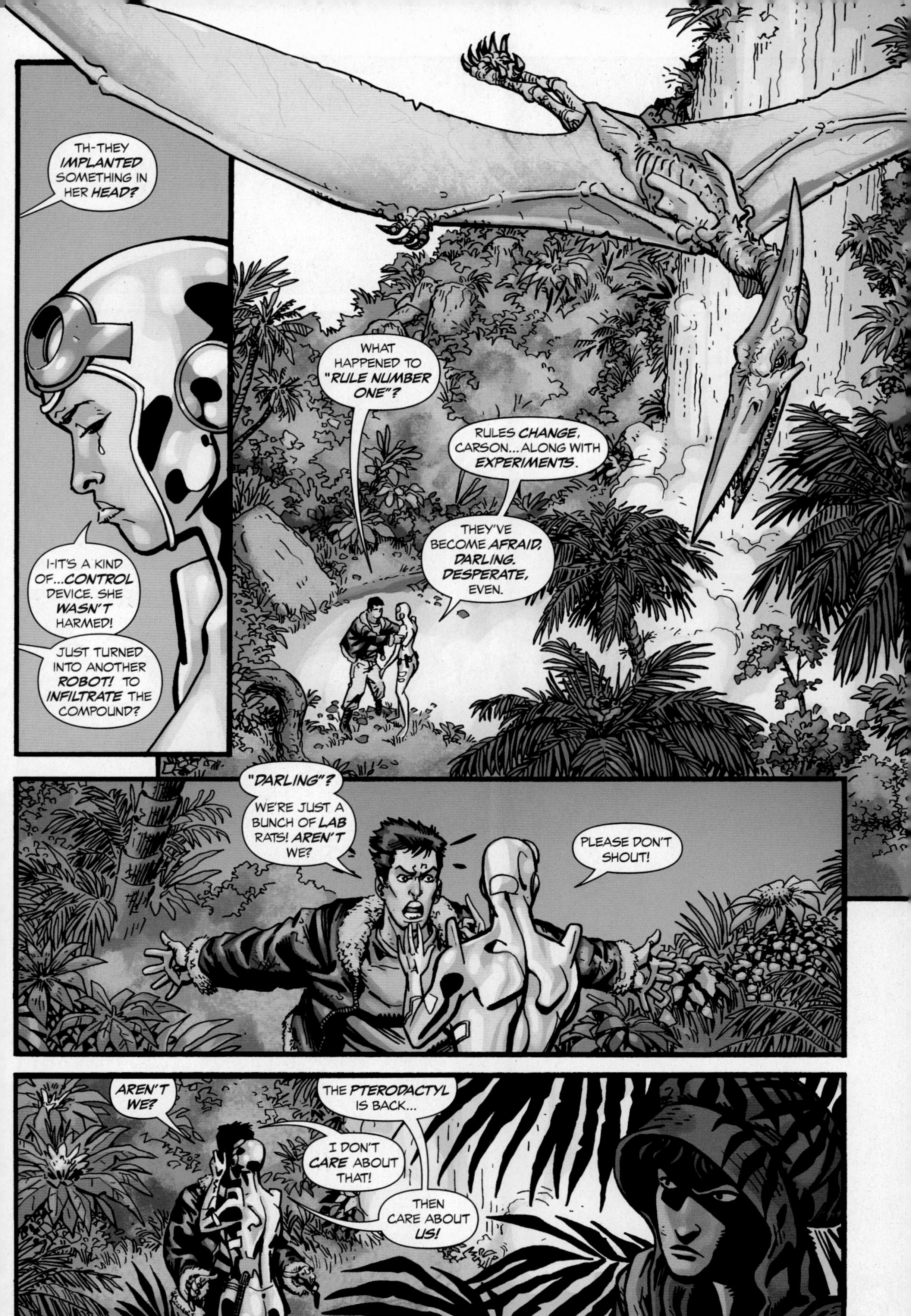
TH-THEY IMPLANTED SOMETHING IN HER HEAD?
WHAT HAPPENED TO "RULE NUMBER ONE"?
RULES CHANGE, CARSON...ALONG WITH EXPERIMENTS.
THEY'VE BECOME AFRAID, DARLING. DESPERATE, EVEN.
I-IT'S A KIND OF...CONTROL DEVICE. SHE WASN'T HARMED!
JUST TURNED INTO ANOTHER ROBOT! TO INFILTRATE THE COMPOUND?
"DARLING"?
WE'RE JUST A BUNCH OF LAB RATS! AREN'T WE?
PLEASE DON'T SHOUT!
AREN'T WE?
THE PTERODACTYL IS BACK...
I DON'T CARE ABOUT THAT!
THEN CARE ABOUT US!

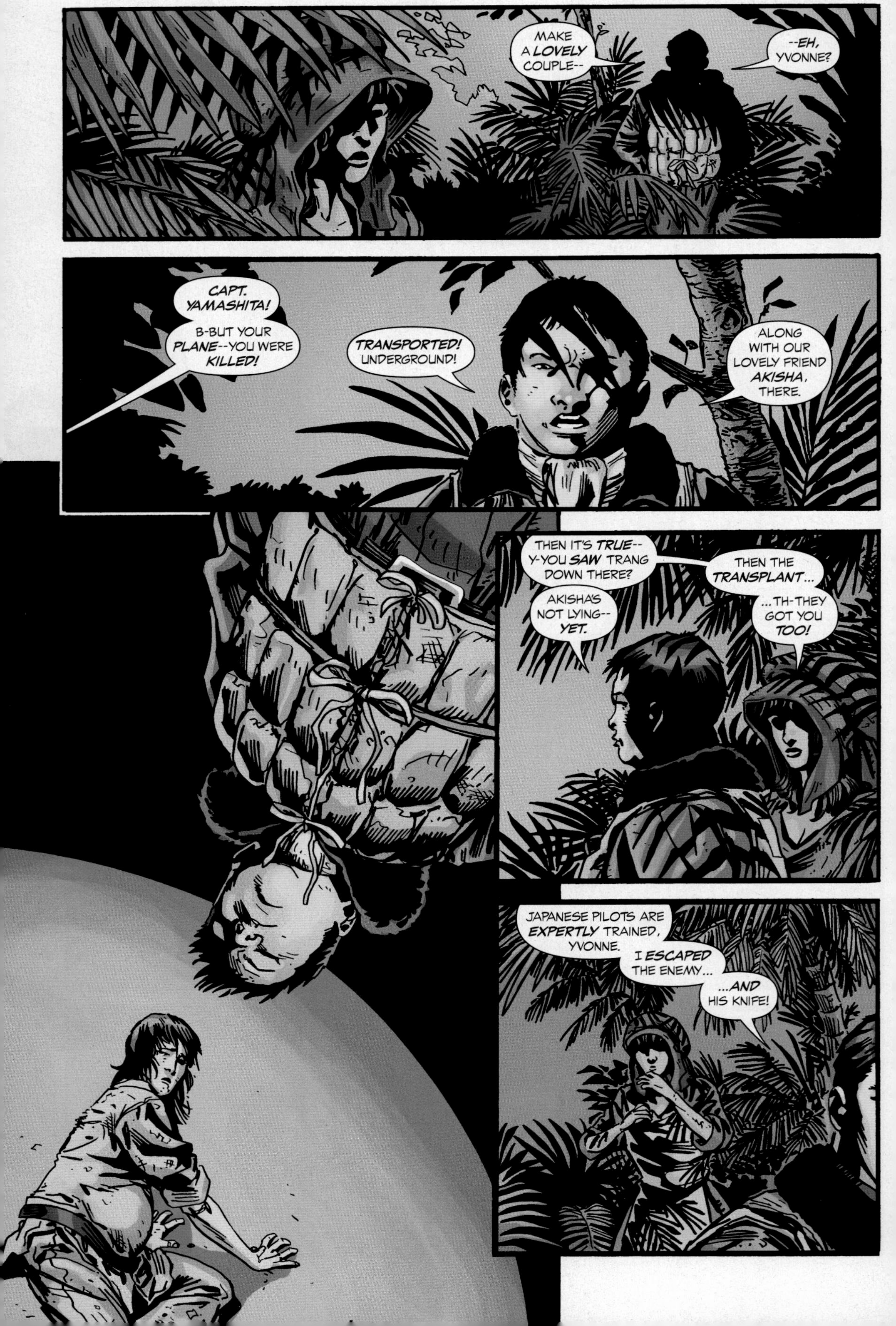
MAKE A LOVELY COUPLE--
--EH, YVONNE?
CAPT. YAMASHITA!
B-BUT YOUR PLANE--YOU WERE KILLED!
TRANSPORTED! UNDERGROUND!
ALONG WITH OUR LOVELY FRIEND AKISHA, THERE.
THEN IT'S TRUE-- Y-YOU SAW TRANG DOWN THERE?
AKISHA'S NOT LYING-- YET.
THEN THE TRANSPLANT...
...TH-THEY GOT YOU TOO!
JAPANESE PILOTS ARE EXPERTLY TRAINED, YVONNE.
I ESCAPED THE ENEMY...
...AND HIS KNIFE!

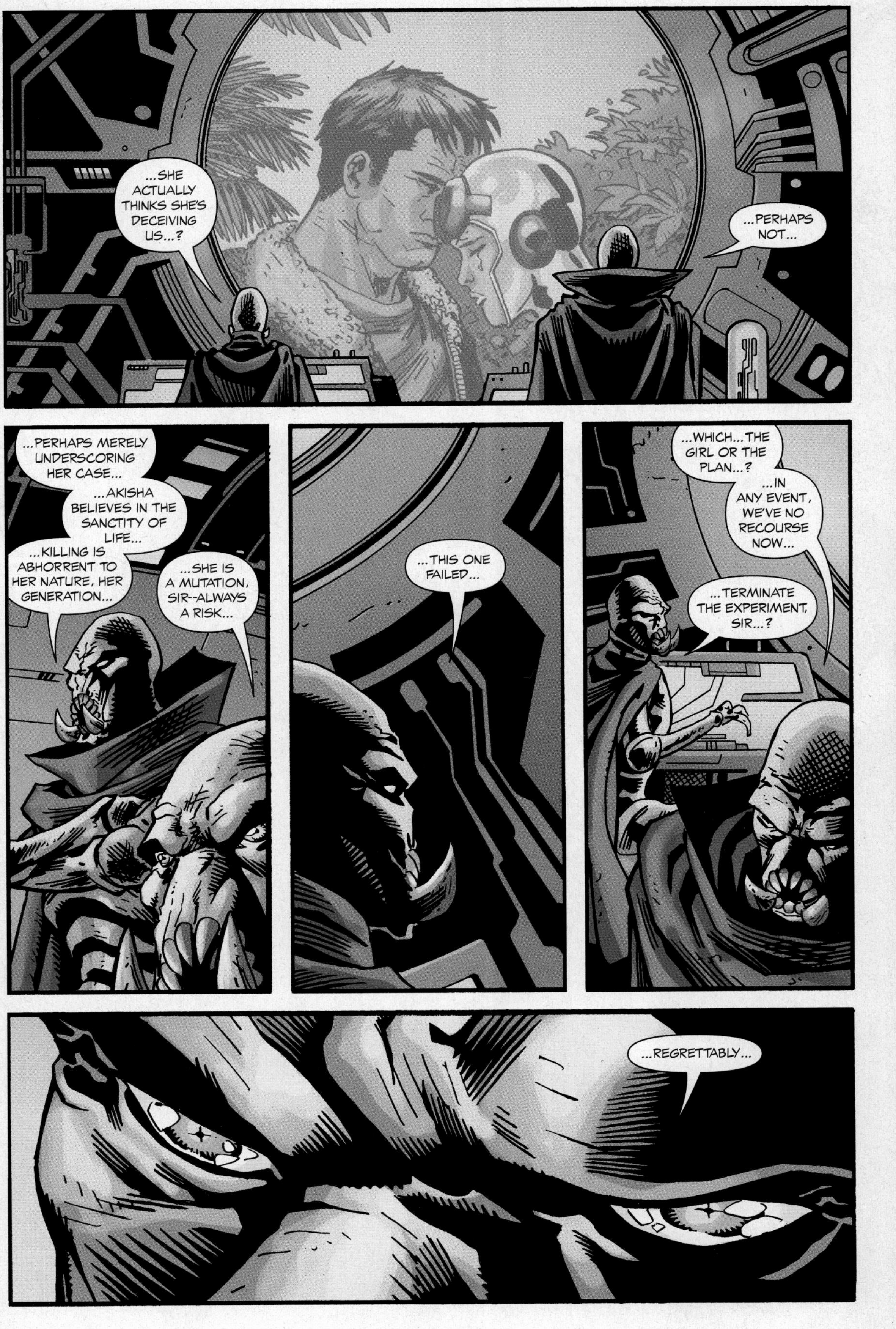
...SHE ACTUALLY THINKS SHE'S DECEIVING US...?
...PERHAPS NOT...
...PERHAPS MERELY UNDERSCORING HER CASE...
...AKISHA BELIEVES IN THE SANCTITY OF LIFE...
...KILLING IS ABHORRENT TO HER NATURE, HER GENERATION...
...SHE IS A MUTATION, SIR--ALWAYS A RISK...
...THIS ONE FAILED...
...WHICH...THE GIRL OR THE PLAN...?
...IN ANY EVENT, WE'VE NO RECOURSE NOW...
...TERMINATE THE EXPERIMENT, SIR...?
...REGRETTABLY...

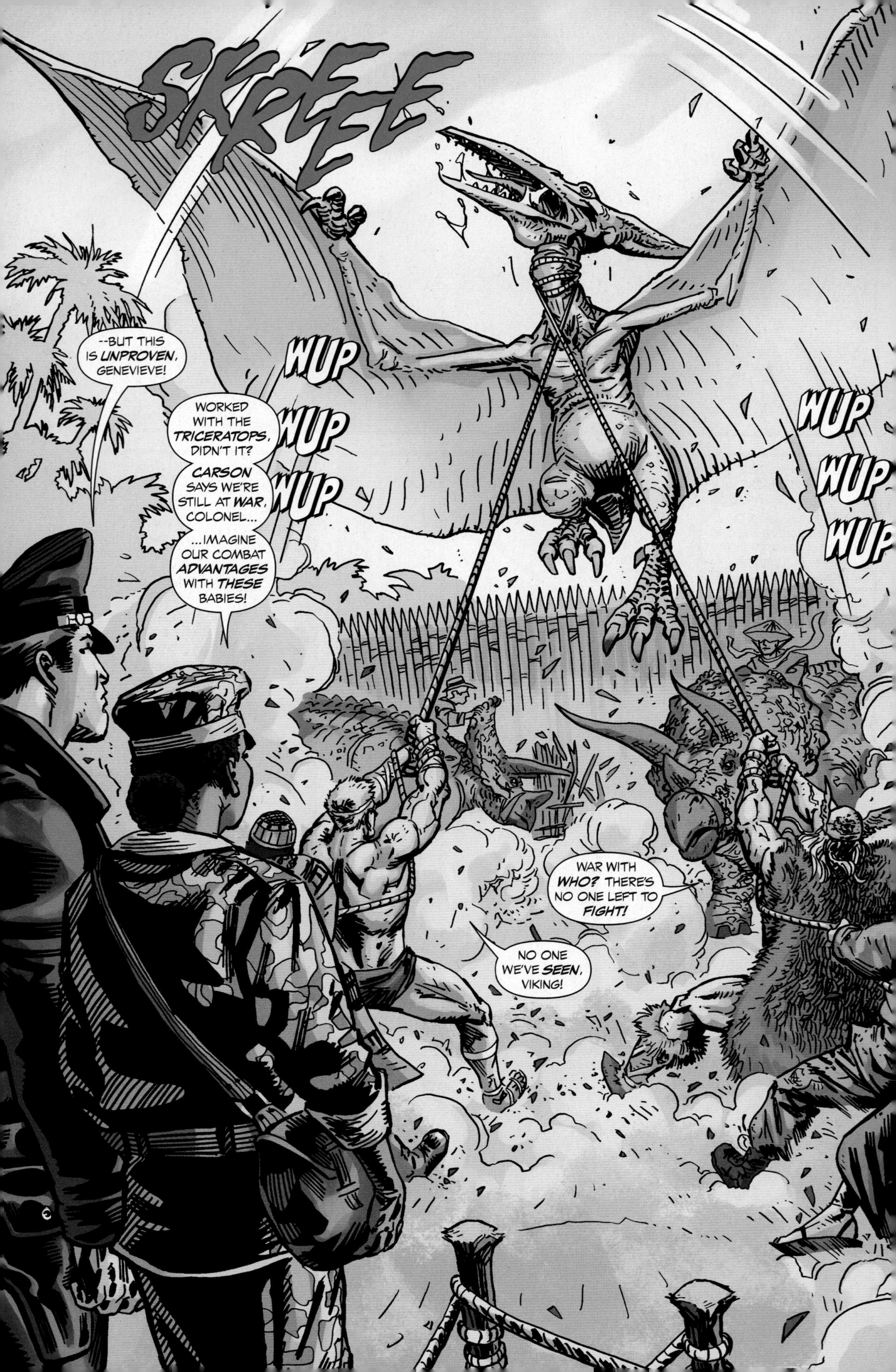
SKREEE
--BUT THIS IS UNPROVEN, GENEVIEVE!
WORKED WITH THE TRICERATOPS, DIDN'T IT?
CARSON SAYS WE'RE STILL AT WAR, COLONEL...
...IMAGINE OUR COMBAT ADVANTAGES WITH THESE BABIES!
WUP WUP WUP
WUP WUP WUP
WAR WITH WHO? THERE'S NO ONE LEFT TO FIGHT!
NO ONE WE'VE SEEN, VIKING!

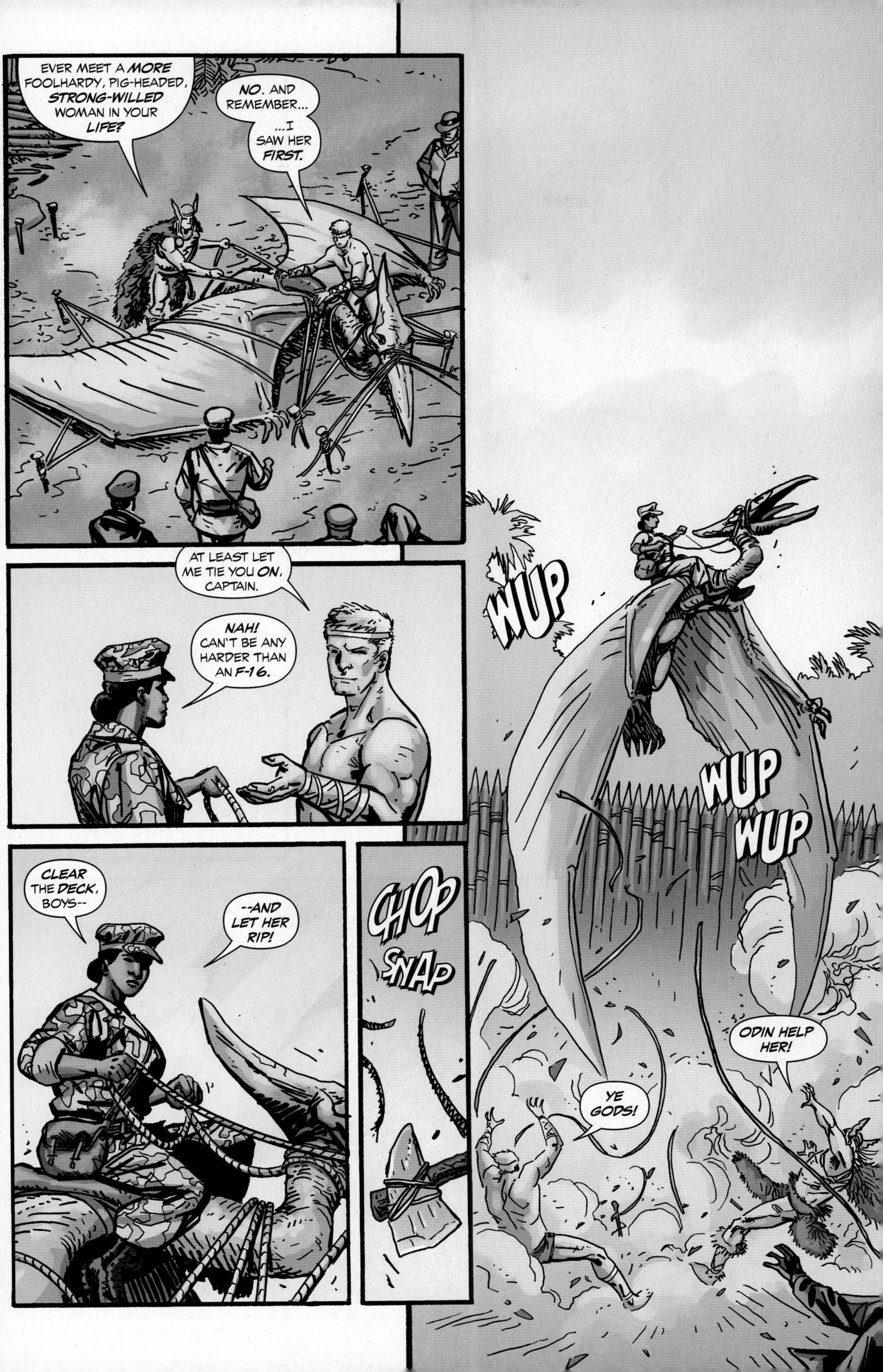

EVER MEET A MORE FOOLHARDY, PIG-HEADED, STRONG-WILLED WOMAN IN YOUR LIFE?
NO. AND REMEMBER...
...I SAW HER FIRST.
AT LEAST LET ME TIE YOU ON, CAPTAIN.
NAH! CAN'T BE ANY HARDER THAN AN F-16.
CLEAR THE DECK, BOYS--
--AND LET HER RIP!
CHOP
SNAP
WUP
WUP WUP
YE GODS!
ODIN HELP HER!

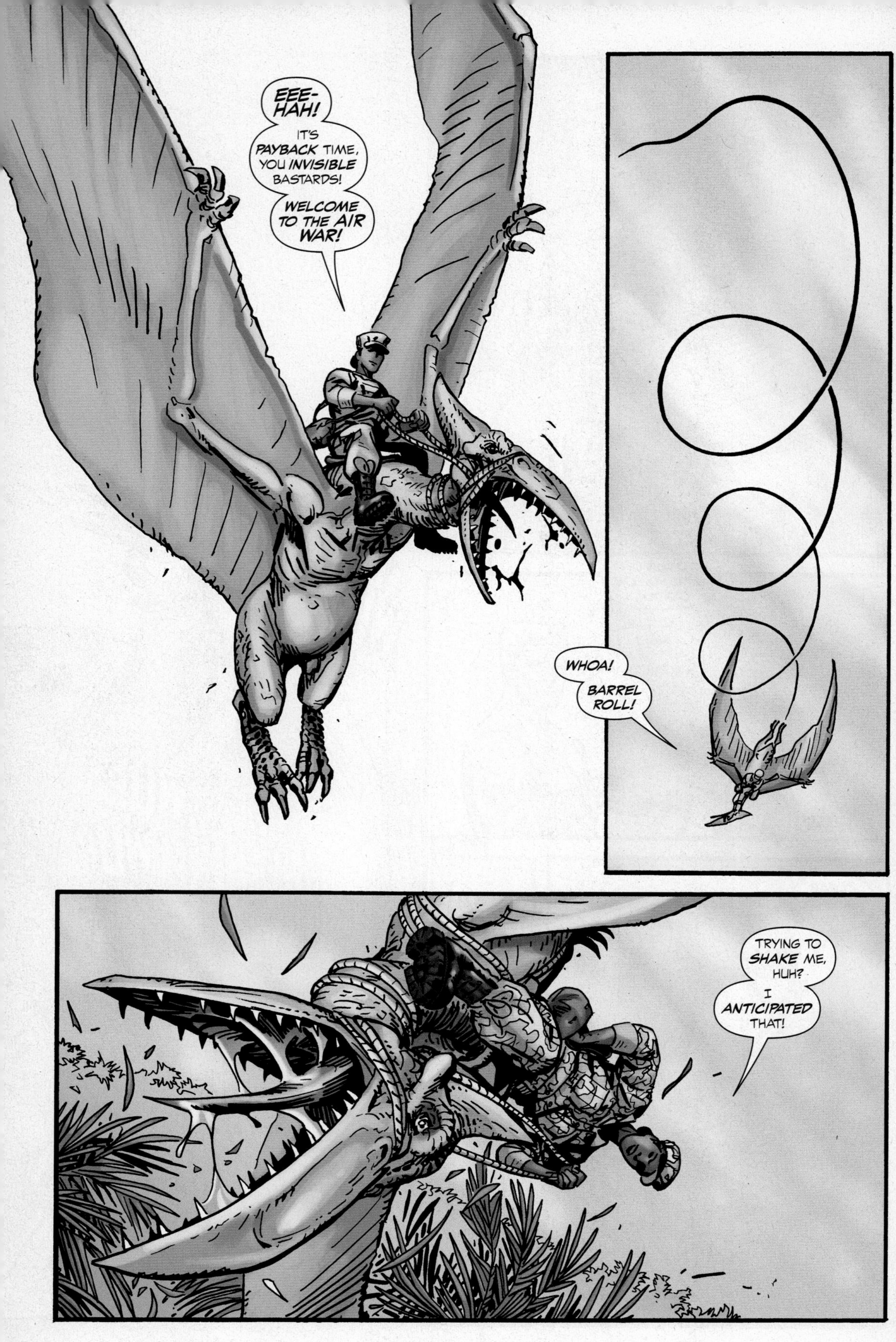
EEE-HAH!
IT'S PAYBACK TIME, YOU INVISIBLE BASTARDS!
WELCOME TO THE AIR WAR!
WHOA! BARREL ROLL!
TRYING TO SHAKE ME, HUH?
I ANTICIPATED THAT!

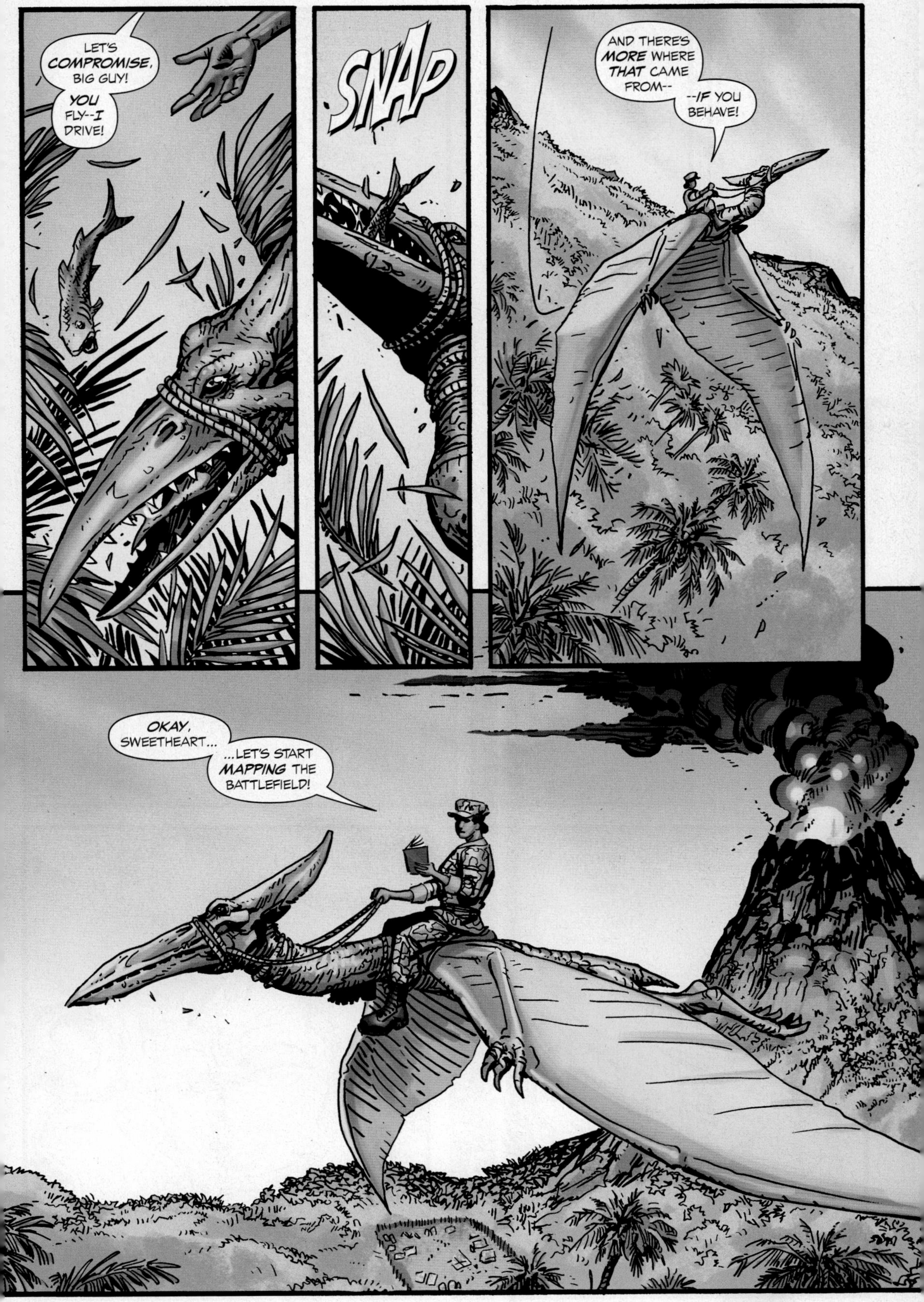
LET'S COMPROMISE, BIG GUY!
YOU FLY--I DRIVE!
SNAP
AND THERE'S MORE WHERE THAT CAME FROM--
--IF YOU BEHAVE!
OKAY, SWEETHEART...
...LET'S START MAPPING THE BATTLEFIELD!

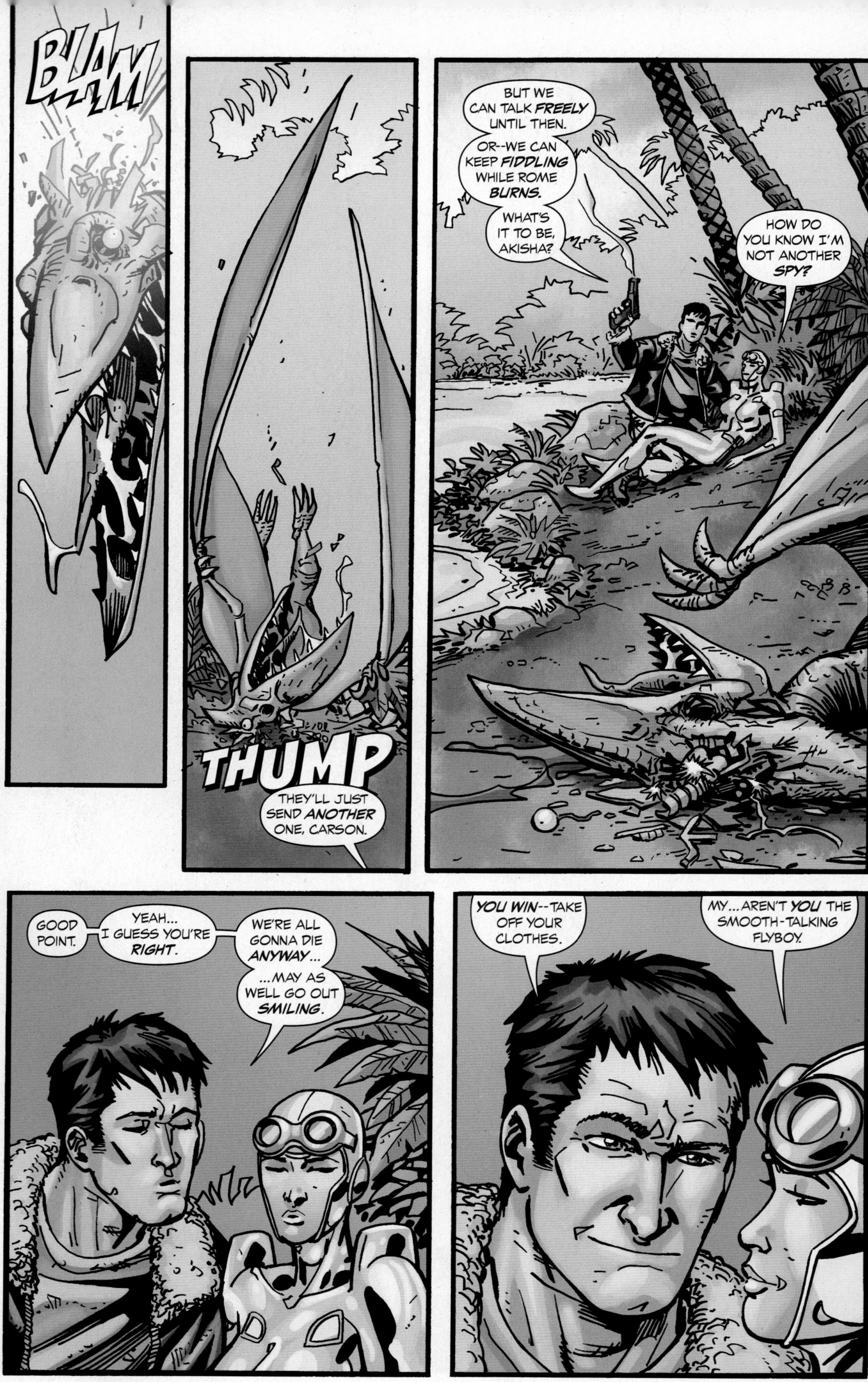
BLAM
THUMP
THEY'LL JUST SEND ANOTHER ONE, CARSON.
BUT WE CAN TALK FREELY UNTIL THEN.
OR--WE CAN KEEP FIDDLING WHILE ROME BURNS.
WHAT'S IT TO BE, AKISHA?
HOW DO YOU KNOW I'M NOT ANOTHER SPY?
GOOD POINT.
YEAH... I GUESS YOU'RE RIGHT.
WE'RE ALL GONNA DIE ANYWAY...
...MAY AS WELL GO OUT SMILING.
YOU WIN--TAKE OFF YOUR CLOTHES.
MY... AREN'T YOU THE SMOOTH-TALKING FLYBOY.

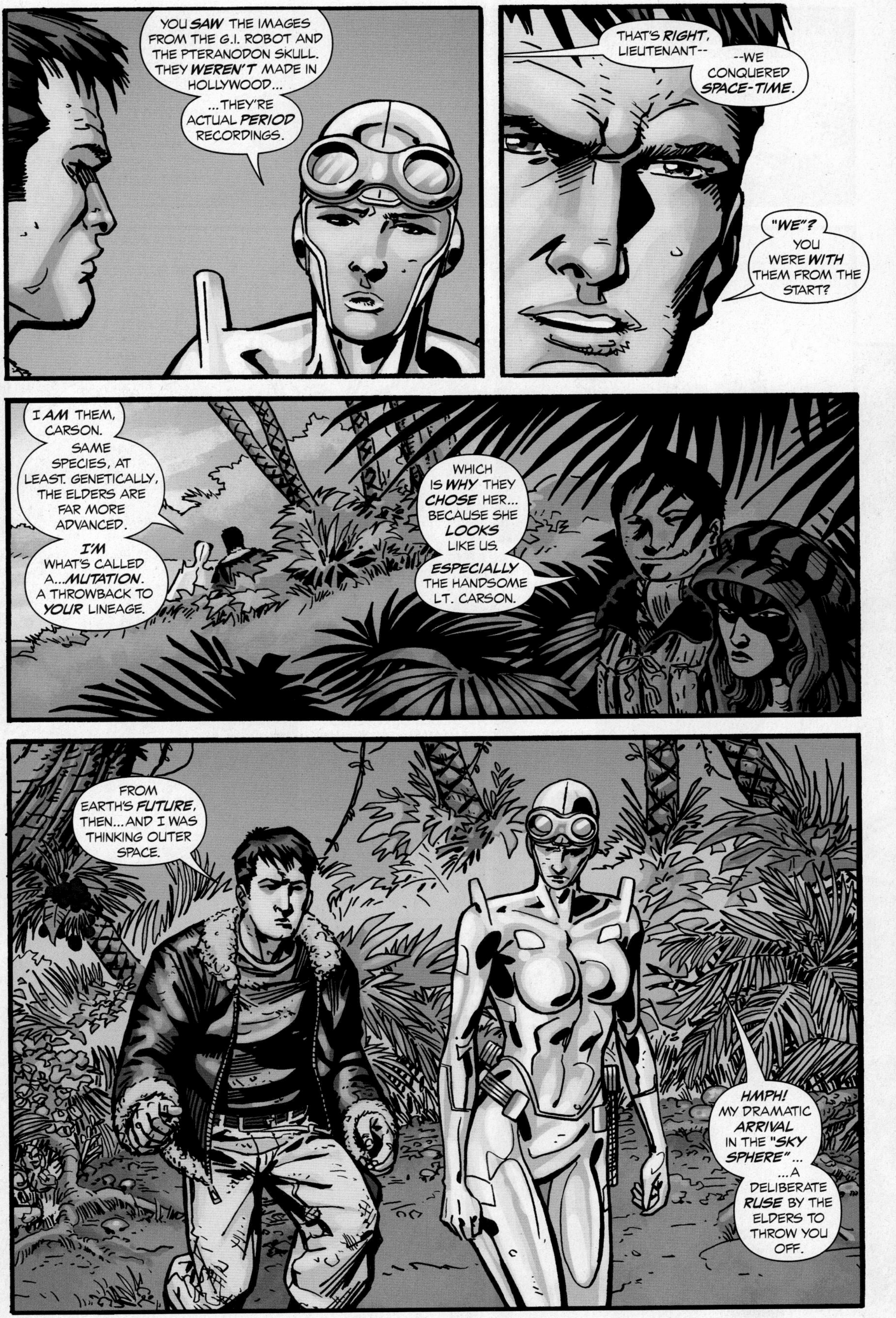
YOU SAW THE IMAGES FROM THE G.I. ROBOT AND THE PTERANODON SKULL. THEY WEREN'T MADE IN HOLLYWOOD...
...THEY'RE ACTUAL PERIOD RECORDINGS.
THAT'S RIGHT, LIEUTENANT--
--WE CONQUERED SPACE-TIME.
"WE"? YOU WERE WITH THEM FROM THE START?
I AM THEM, CARSON. SAME SPECIES, AT LEAST. GENETICALLY, THE ELDERS ARE FAR MORE ADVANCED.
I'M WHAT'S CALLED A...MUTATION. A THROWBACK TO YOUR LINEAGE.
WHICH IS WHY THEY CHOSE HER... BECAUSE SHE LOOKS LIKE US.
ESPECIALLY THE HANDSOME LT. CARSON.
FROM EARTH'S FUTURE, THEN...AND I WAS THINKING OUTER SPACE.
HMPH! MY DRAMATIC ARRIVAL IN THE "SKY SPHERE"...
...A DELIBERATE RUSE BY THE ELDERS TO THROW YOU OFF.

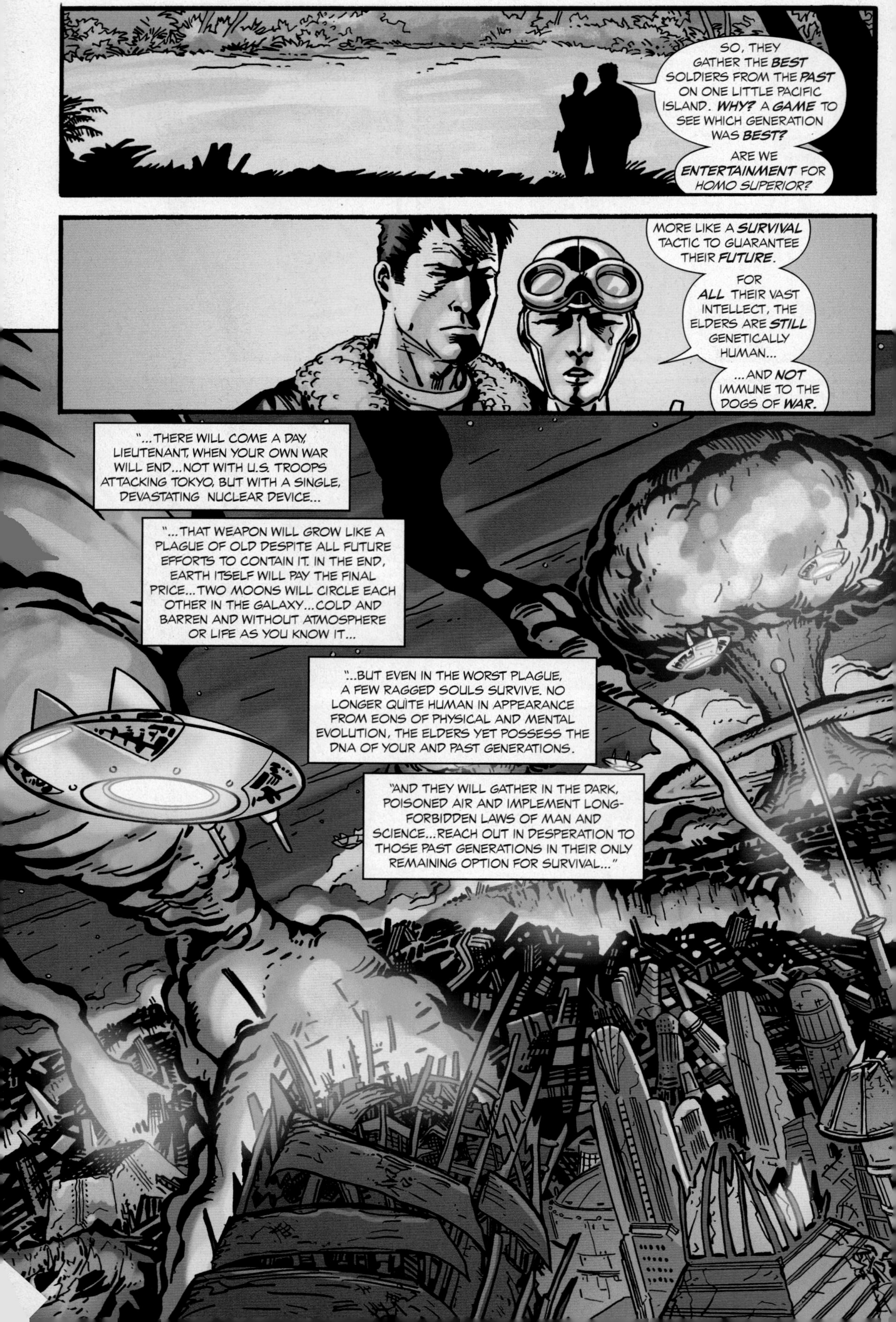
SO, THEY GATHER THE BEST SOLDIERS FROM THE PAST ON ONE LITTLE PACIFIC ISLAND. WHY? A GAME TO SEE WHICH GENERATION WAS BEST?
ARE WE ENTERTAINMENT FOR HOMO SUPERIOR?
MORE LIKE A SURVIVAL TACTIC TO GUARANTEE THEIR FUTURE.
FOR ALL THEIR VAST INTELLECT, THE ELDERS ARE STILL GENETICALLY HUMAN...
...AND NOT IMMUNE TO THE DOGS OF WAR.
"...THERE WILL COME A DAY, LIEUTENANT, WHEN YOUR OWN WAR WILL END...NOT WITH U.S. TROOPS ATTACKING TOKYO, BUT WITH A SINGLE, DEVASTATING NUCLEAR DEVICE...
"...THAT WEAPON WILL GROW LIKE A PLAGUE OF OLD DESPITE ALL FUTURE EFFORTS TO CONTAIN IT. IN THE END, EARTH ITSELF WILL PAY THE FINAL PRICE...TWO MOONS WILL CIRCLE EACH OTHER IN THE GALAXY...COLD AND BARREN AND WITHOUT ATMOSPHERE OR LIFE AS YOU KNOW IT...
"...BUT EVEN IN THE WORST PLAGUE, A FEW RAGGED SOULS SURVIVE. NO LONGER QUITE HUMAN IN APPEARANCE FROM EONS OF PHYSICAL AND MENTAL EVOLUTION, THE ELDERS YET POSSESS THE DNA OF YOUR AND PAST GENERATIONS.
"AND THEY WILL GATHER IN THE DARK, POISONED AIR AND IMPLEMENT LONG-FORBIDDEN LAWS OF MAN AND SCIENCE...REACH OUT IN DESPERATION TO THOSE PAST GENERATIONS IN THEIR ONLY REMAINING OPTION FOR SURVIVAL..."

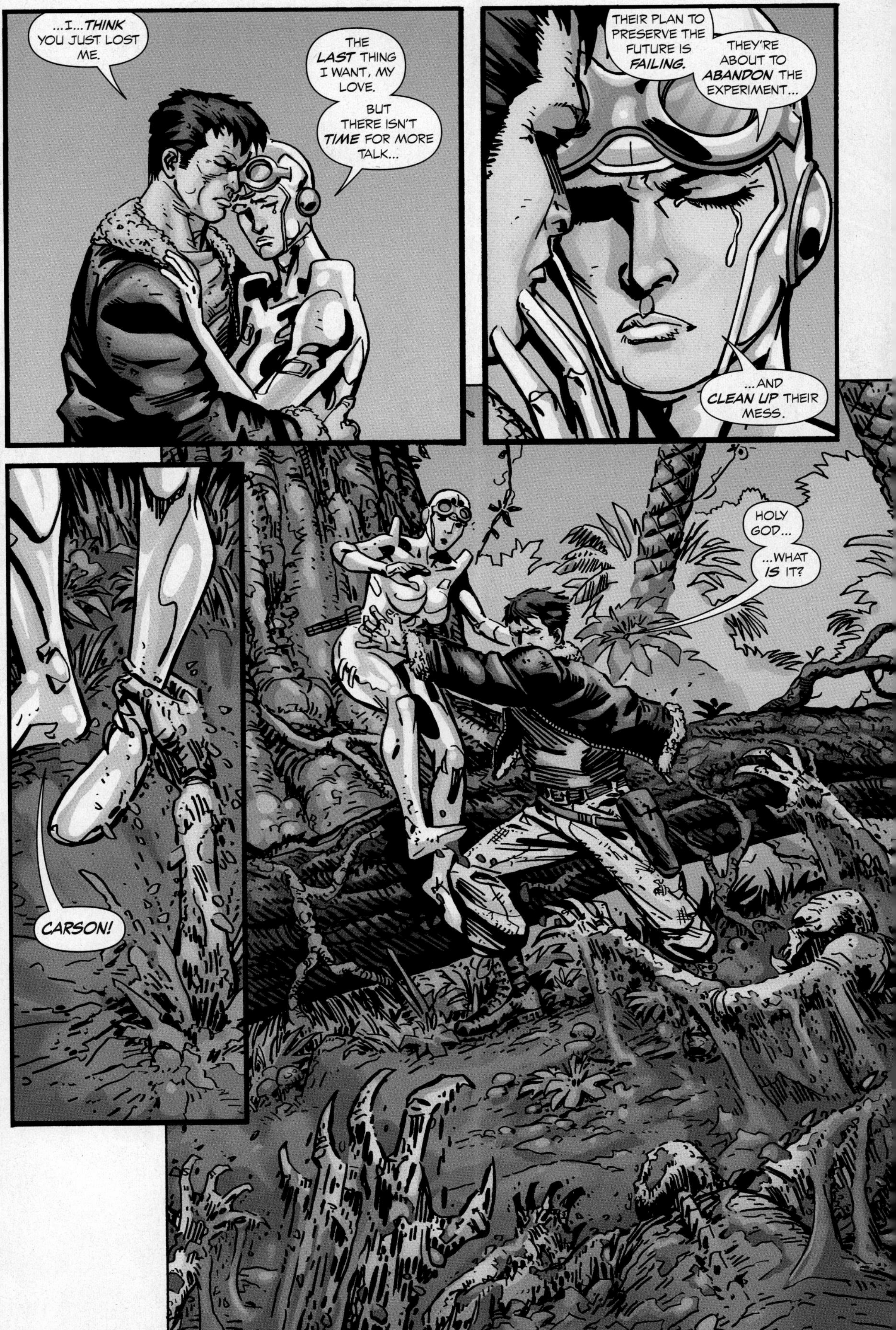
...I...THINK YOU JUST LOST ME.
THE LAST THING I WANT, MY LOVE.
BUT THERE ISN'T TIME FOR MORE TALK...
THEIR PLAN TO PRESERVE THE FUTURE IS FAILING.
THEY'RE ABOUT TO ABANDON THE EXPERIMENT...
...AND CLEAN UP THEIR MESS.
CARSON!
HOLY GOD...
...WHAT IS IT?

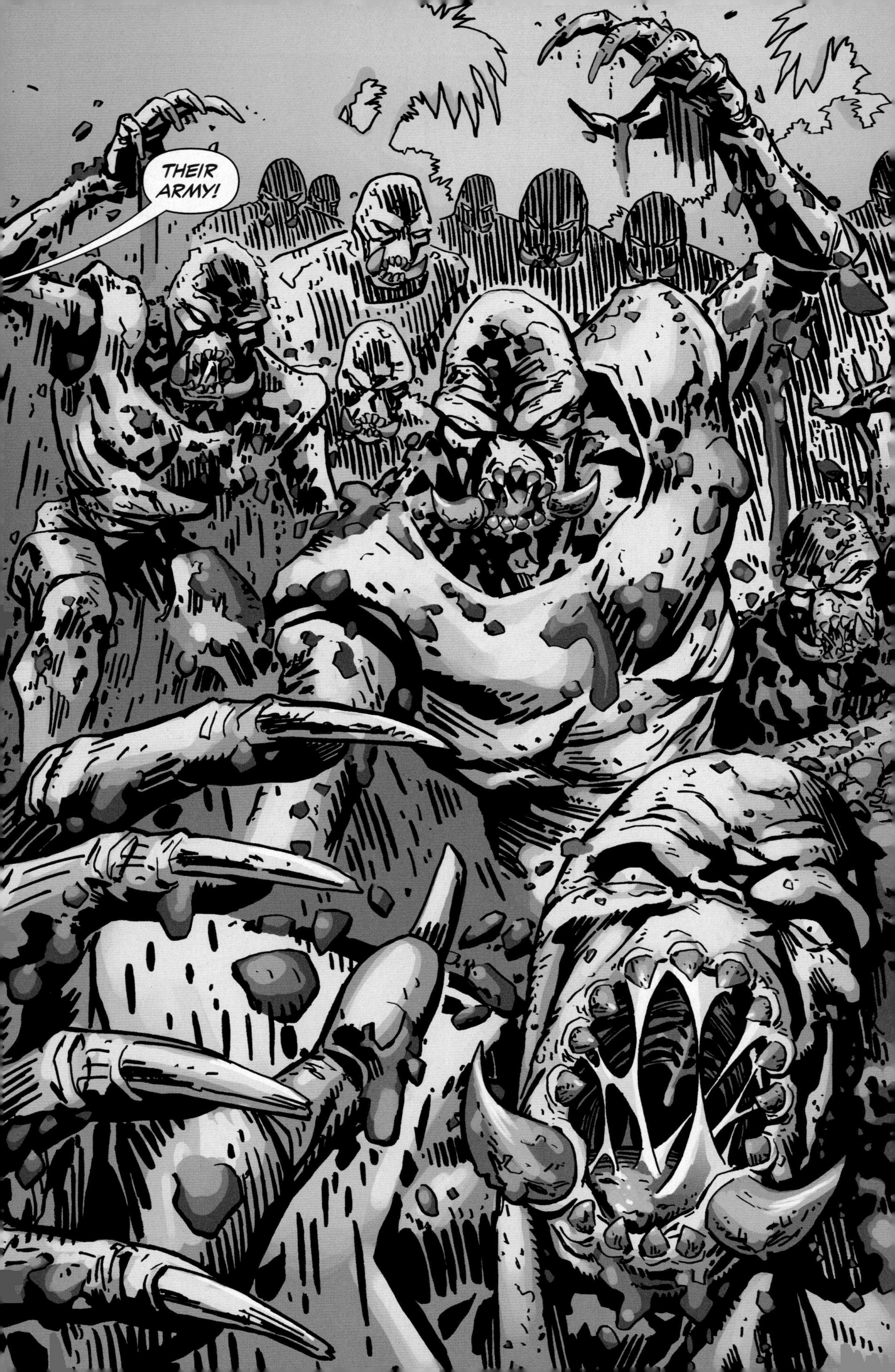
THEIR ARMY!

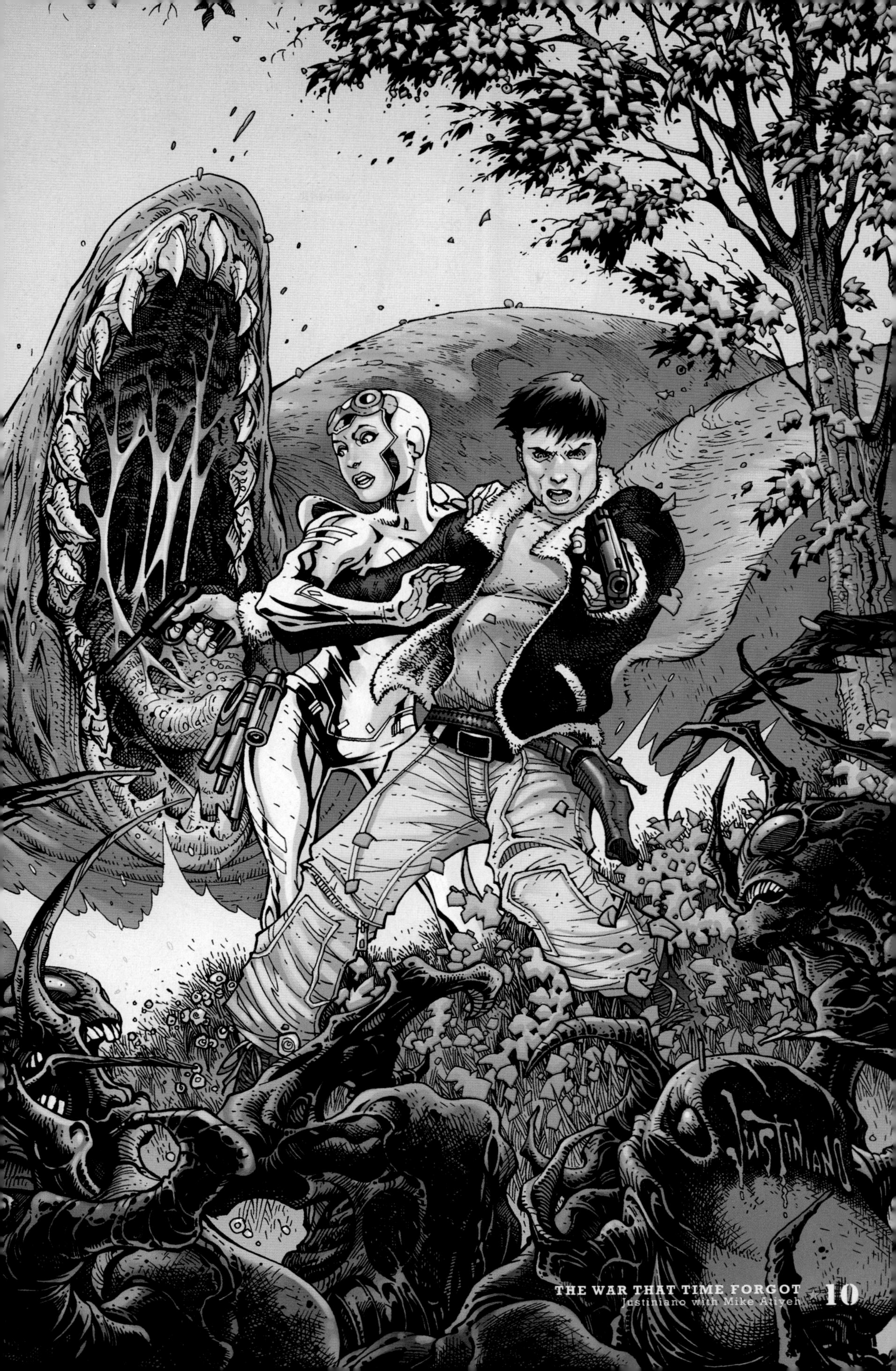
JUSTINIANO

THE WAR THAT TIME FORGOT ★ 10
Justiniano with Mike Atiyeh

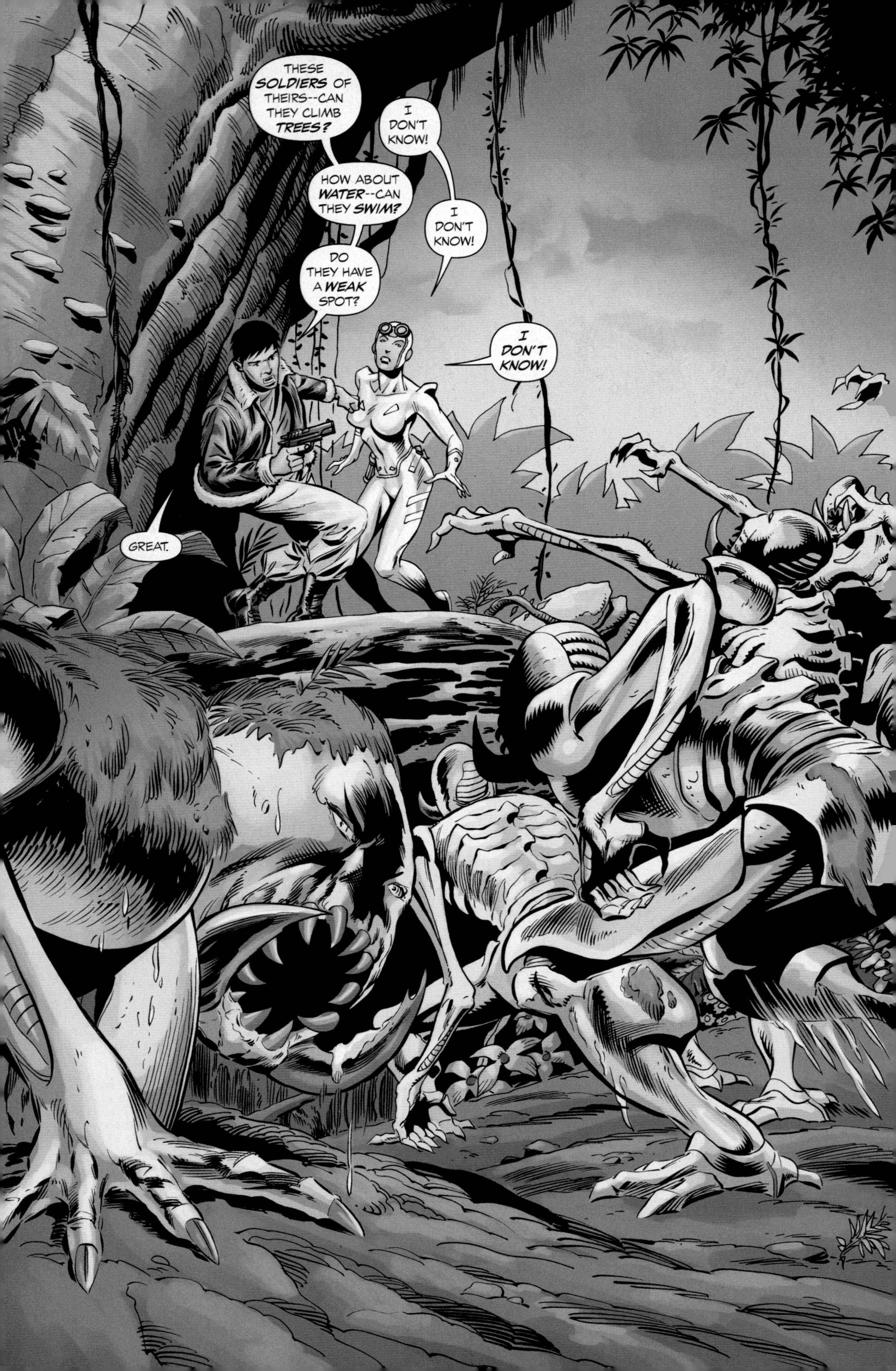
THESE SOLDIERS OF THEIRS--CAN THEY CLIMB TREES?
I DON'T KNOW!
HOW ABOUT WATER--CAN THEY SWIM?
I DON'T KNOW!
DO THEY HAVE A WEAK SPOT?
I DON'T KNOW!
GREAT.

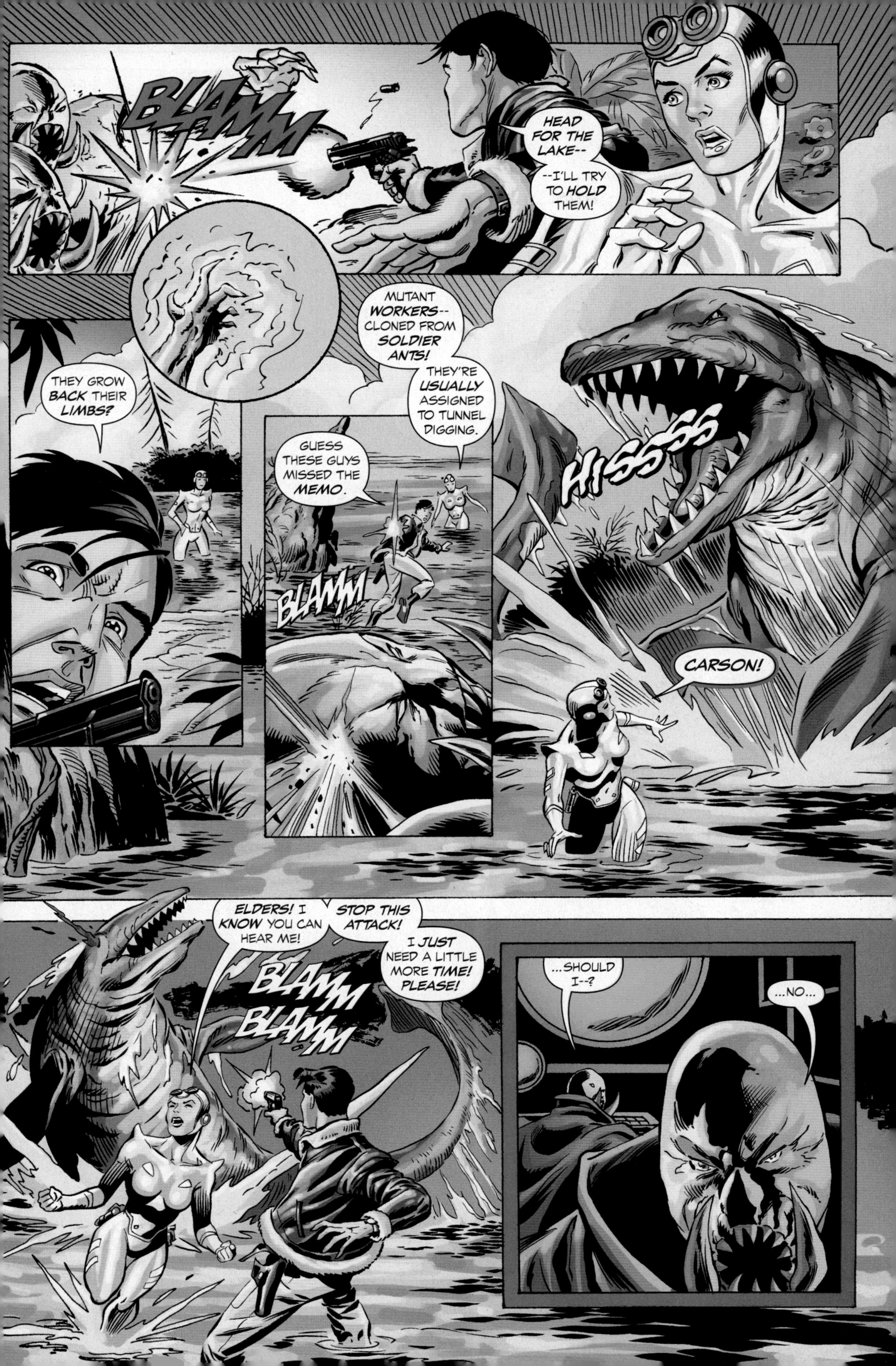
BLAMM
HEAD FOR THE LAKE--
--I'LL TRY TO HOLD THEM!
THEY GROW BACK THEIR LIMBS?
MUTANT WORKERS-- CLONED FROM SOLDIER ANTS!
THEY'RE USUALLY ASSIGNED TO TUNNEL DIGGING.
GUESS THESE GUYS MISSED THE MEMO.
BLAMM
HISSSS
CARSON!
ELDERS! I KNOW YOU CAN HEAR ME!
STOP THIS ATTACK!
I JUST NEED A LITTLE MORE TIME! PLEASE!
BLAMM BLAMM
...SHOULD I--?
...NO...

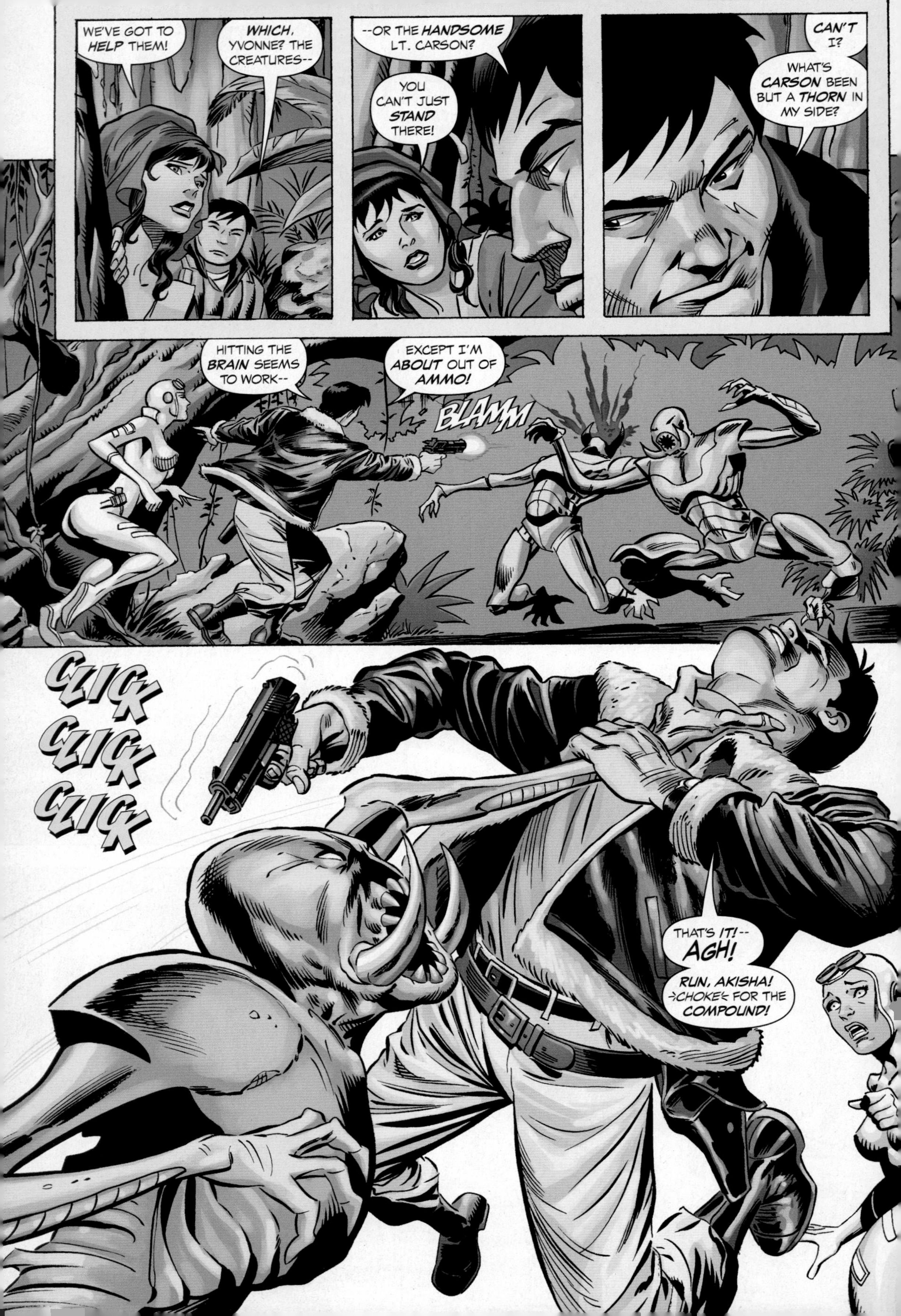

WE'VE GOT TO HELP THEM!
WHICH, YVONNE? THE CREATURES--
--OR THE HANDSOME LT. CARSON?
YOU CAN'T JUST STAND THERE!
CAN'T I?
WHAT'S CARSON BEEN BUT A THORN IN MY SIDE?
HITTING THE BRAIN SEEMS TO WORK--
EXCEPT I'M ABOUT OUT OF AMMO!
BLAMM
CLICK CLICK CLICK
THAT'S IT!-- AGH!
RUN, AKISHA! >CHOKE< FOR THE COMPOUND!

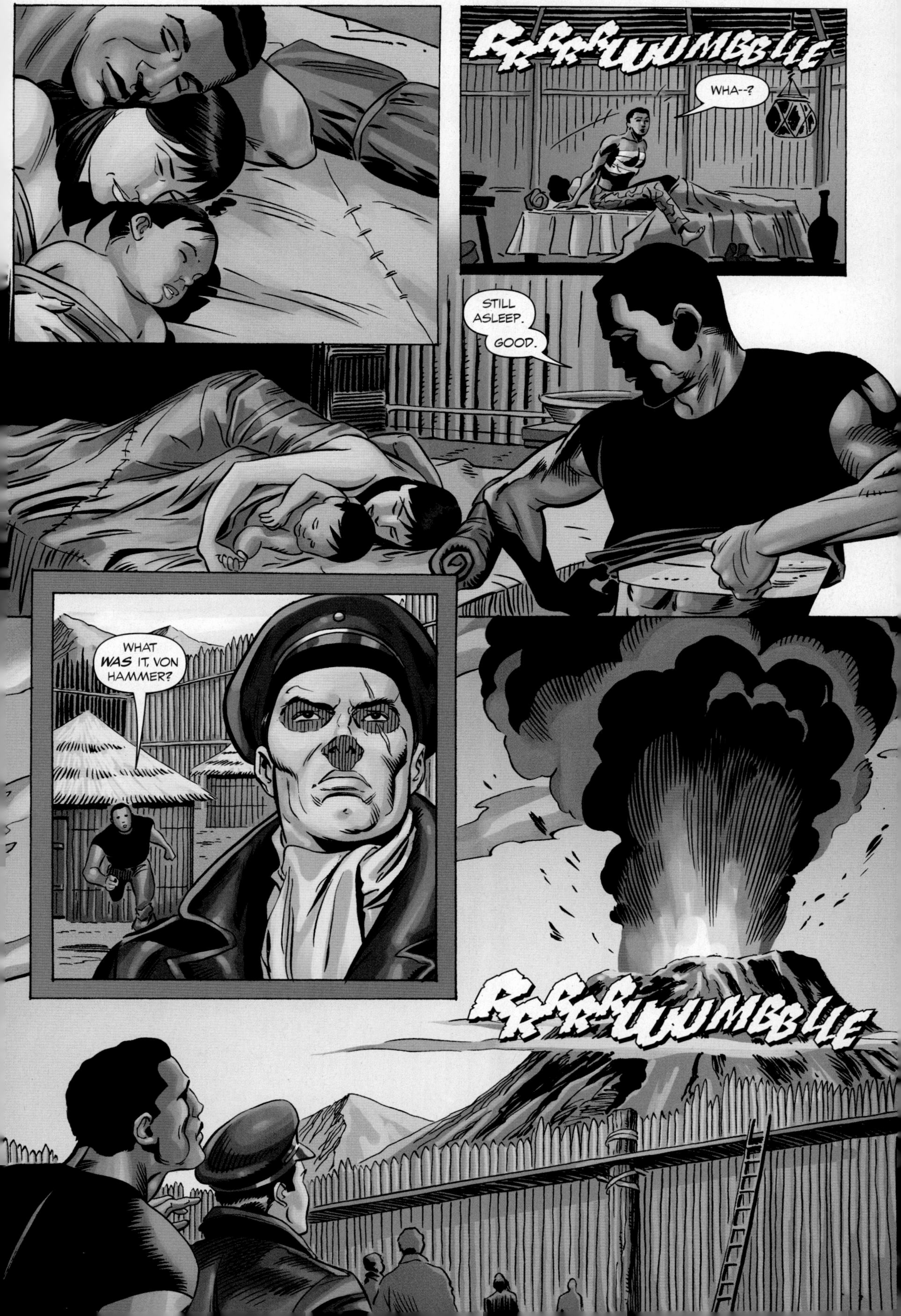
RRRRRUUUMBBLLE
WHA--?
STILL ASLEEP.
GOOD.
WHAT WAS IT, VON HAMMER?
RRRRRUUUMBBLLE

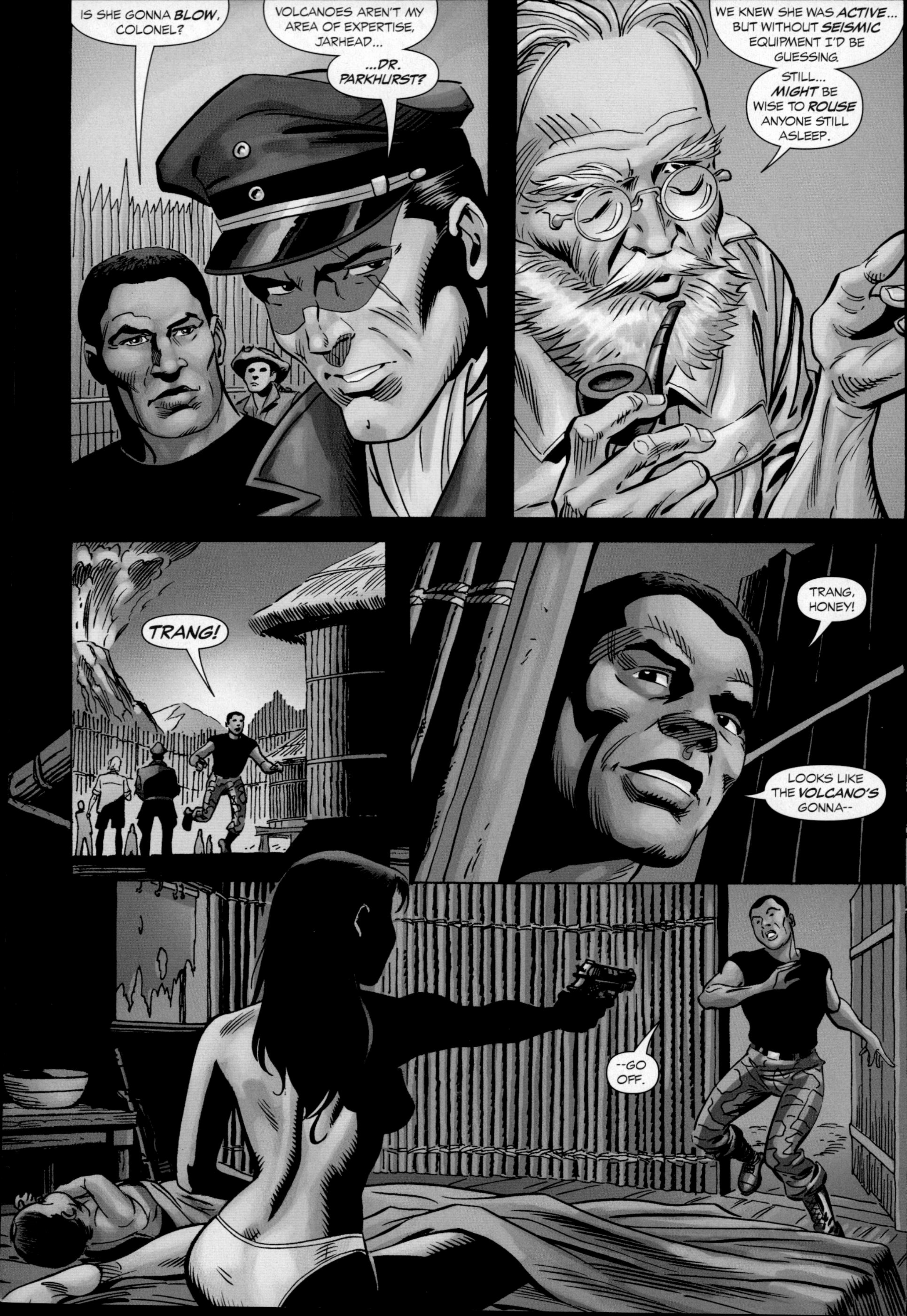

IS SHE GONNA BLOW, COLONEL?
VOLCANOES AREN'T MY AREA OF EXPERTISE, JARHEAD...
...DR. PARKHURST?
WE KNEW SHE WAS ACTIVE... BUT WITHOUT SEISMIC EQUIPMENT I'D BE GUESSING.
STILL... MIGHT BE WISE TO ROUSE ANYONE STILL ASLEEP.
TRANG!
TRANG, HONEY!
LOOKS LIKE THE VOLCANO'S GONNA--
--GO OFF.

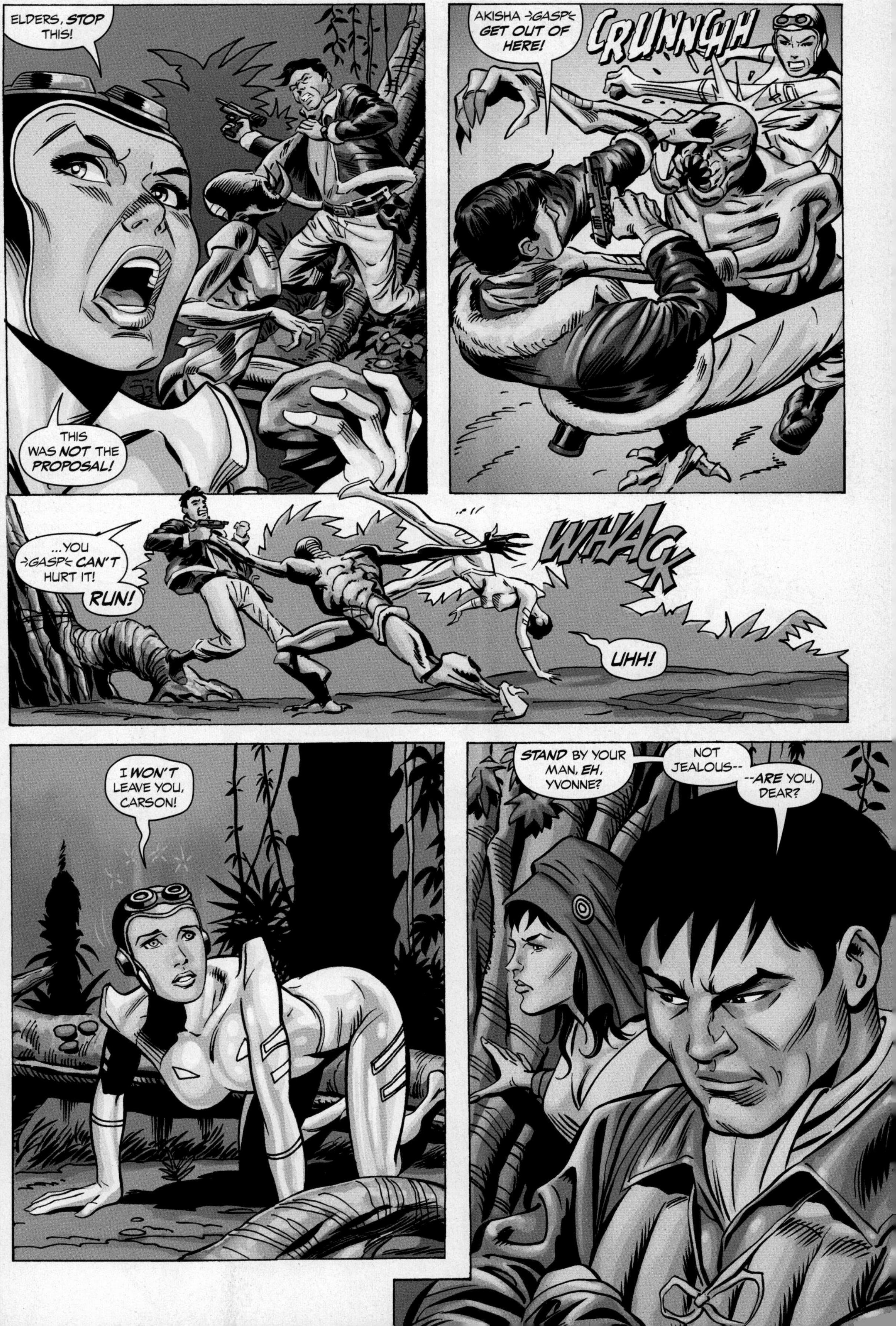
ELDERS, STOP THIS!
THIS WAS NOT THE PROPOSAL!
AKISHA -GASP- GET OUT OF HERE!
CRUNNGHH
...YOU -GASP- CAN'T HURT IT!
RUN!
WHACK
UHH!
I WON'T LEAVE YOU, CARSON!
STAND BY YOUR MAN, EH, YVONNE?
NOT JEALOUS--
--ARE YOU, DEAR?

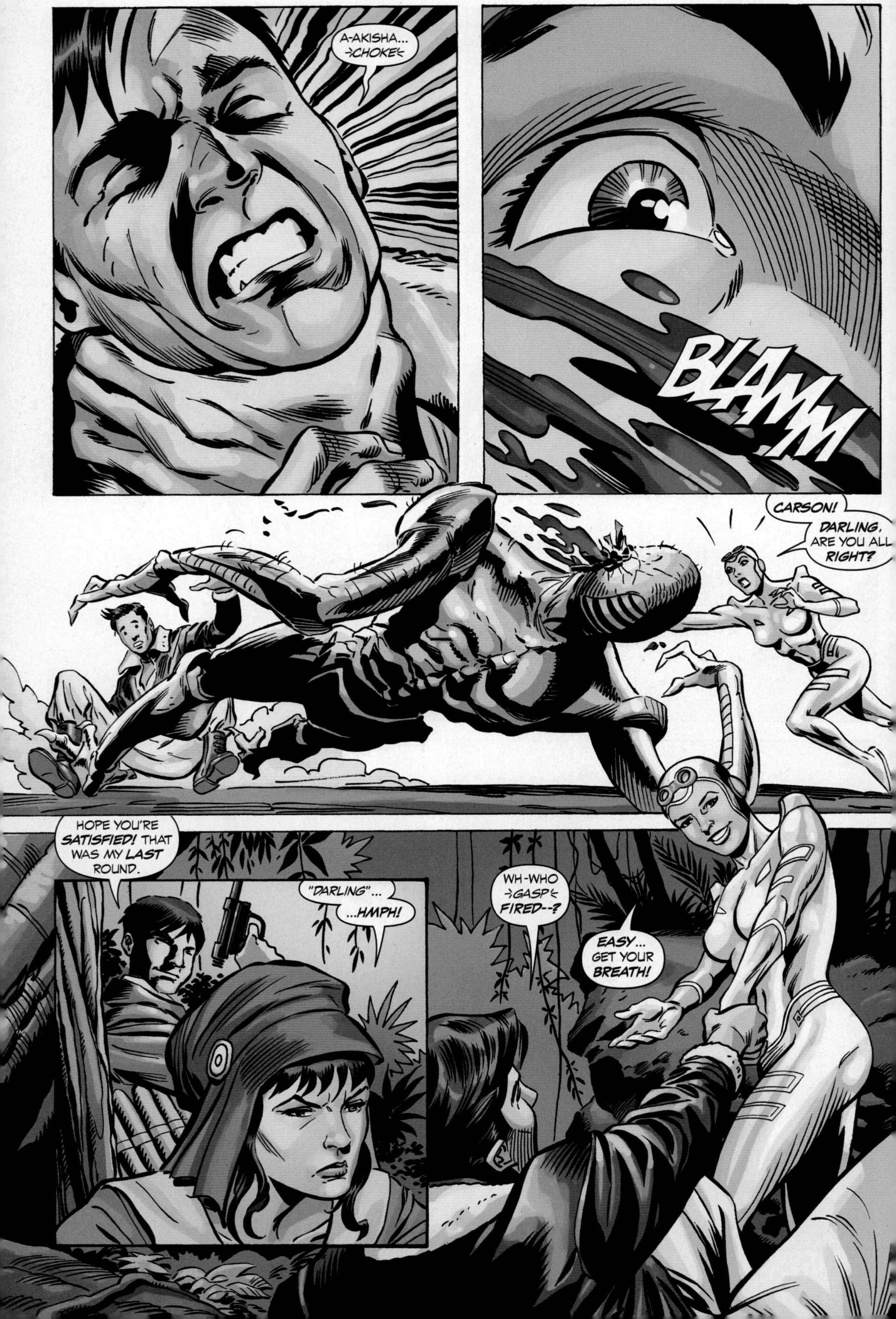
A-AKISHA...
-CHOKE-
BLAMM
CARSON!
DARLING, ARE YOU ALL RIGHT?
HOPE YOU'RE SATISFIED! THAT WAS MY LAST ROUND.
"DARLING"...
...HMPH!
WH-WHO -GASP- FIRED--?
EASY... GET YOUR BREATH!

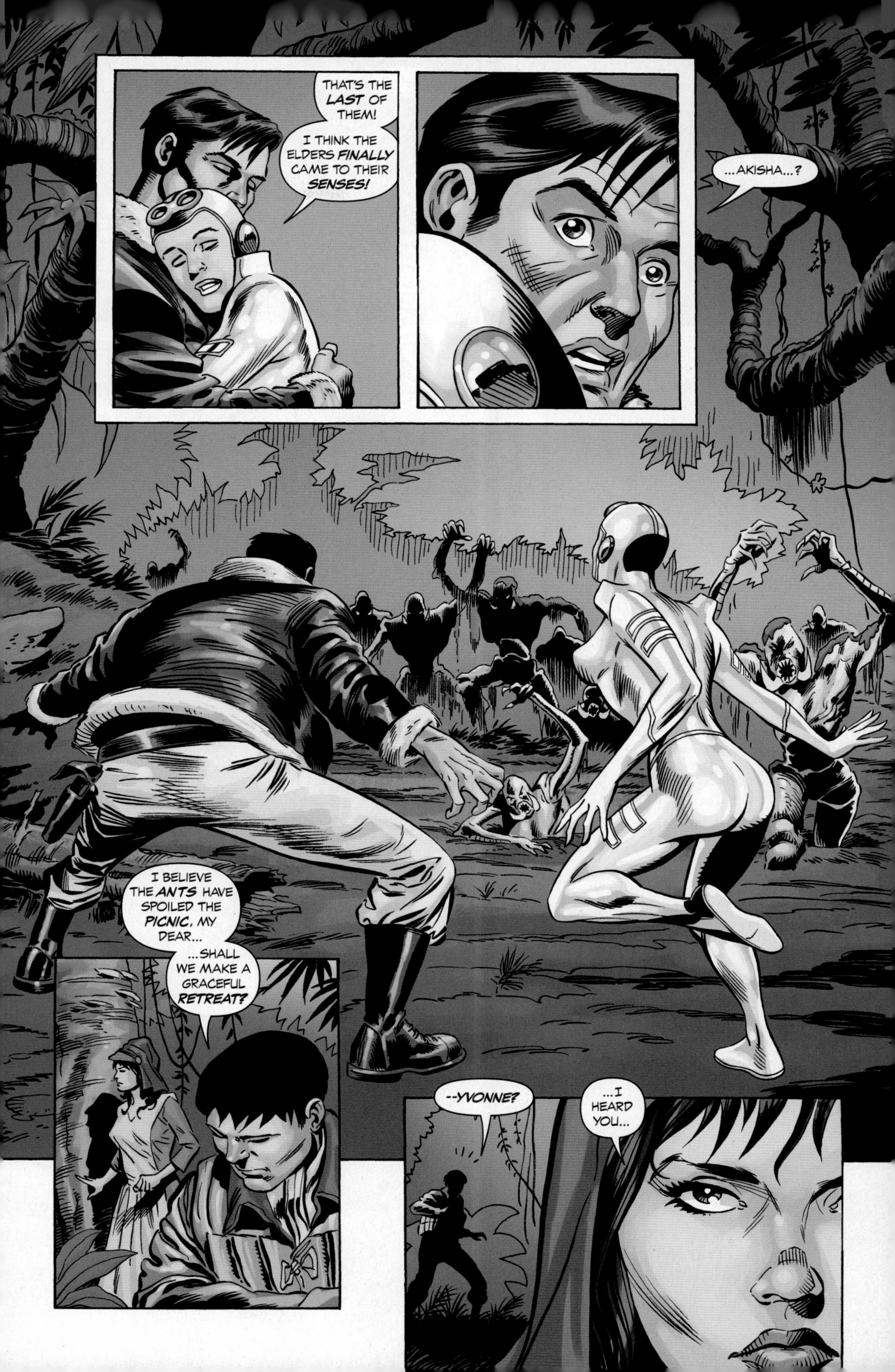
THAT'S THE LAST OF THEM!
I THINK THE ELDERS FINALLY CAME TO THEIR SENSES!
...AKISHA...?
I BELIEVE THE ANTS HAVE SPOILED THE PICNIC, MY DEAR...
...SHALL WE MAKE A GRACEFUL RETREAT?
--YVONNE?
...I HEARD YOU...

T-TRANG?

HONEY?

I-IT'S *ME*, BABY! IT'S *JARHEAD!*

SWEETIE?

IT'S *OKAY* NOW...PUT *DOWN* THE GUN...

THAT'S IT... THAT'S MY GIRL...

...DON'T WANNA *SHOOT* YER OLE *MAN*, DO WE--?

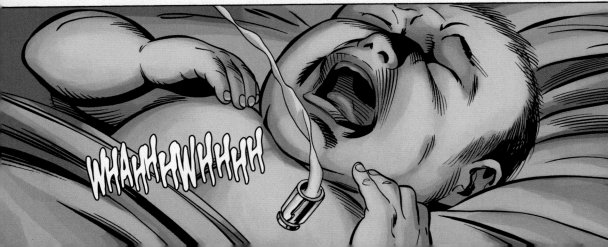

WHAHHHWHHHH

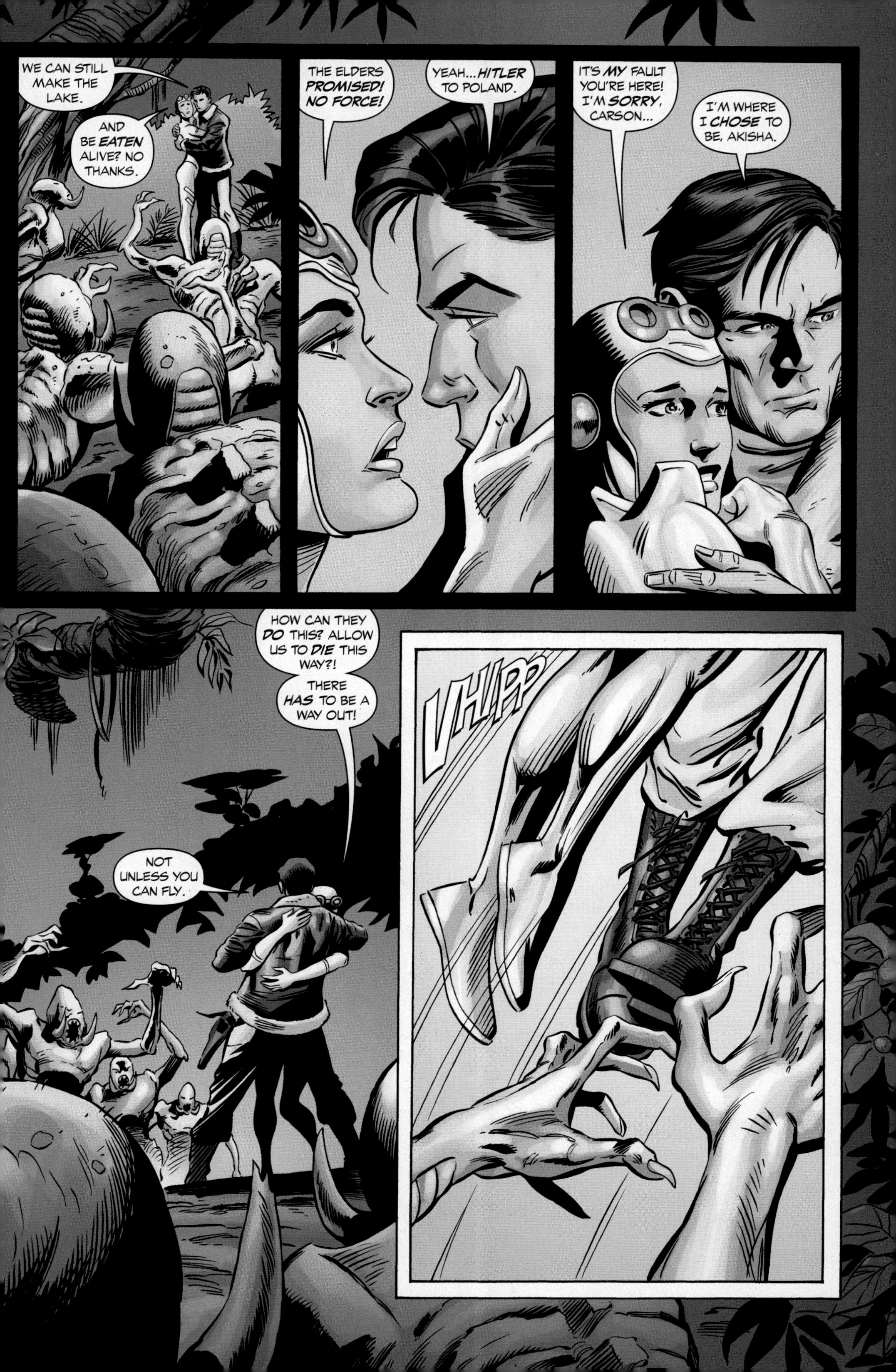
WE CAN STILL MAKE THE LAKE.
AND BE EATEN ALIVE? NO THANKS.
THE ELDERS PROMISED! NO FORCE!
YEAH...HITLER TO POLAND.
IT'S MY FAULT YOU'RE HERE! I'M SORRY, CARSON...
I'M WHERE I CHOSE TO BE, AKISHA.
HOW CAN THEY DO THIS? ALLOW US TO DIE THIS WAY?!
THERE HAS TO BE A WAY OUT!
NOT UNLESS YOU CAN FLY.
VHIPP

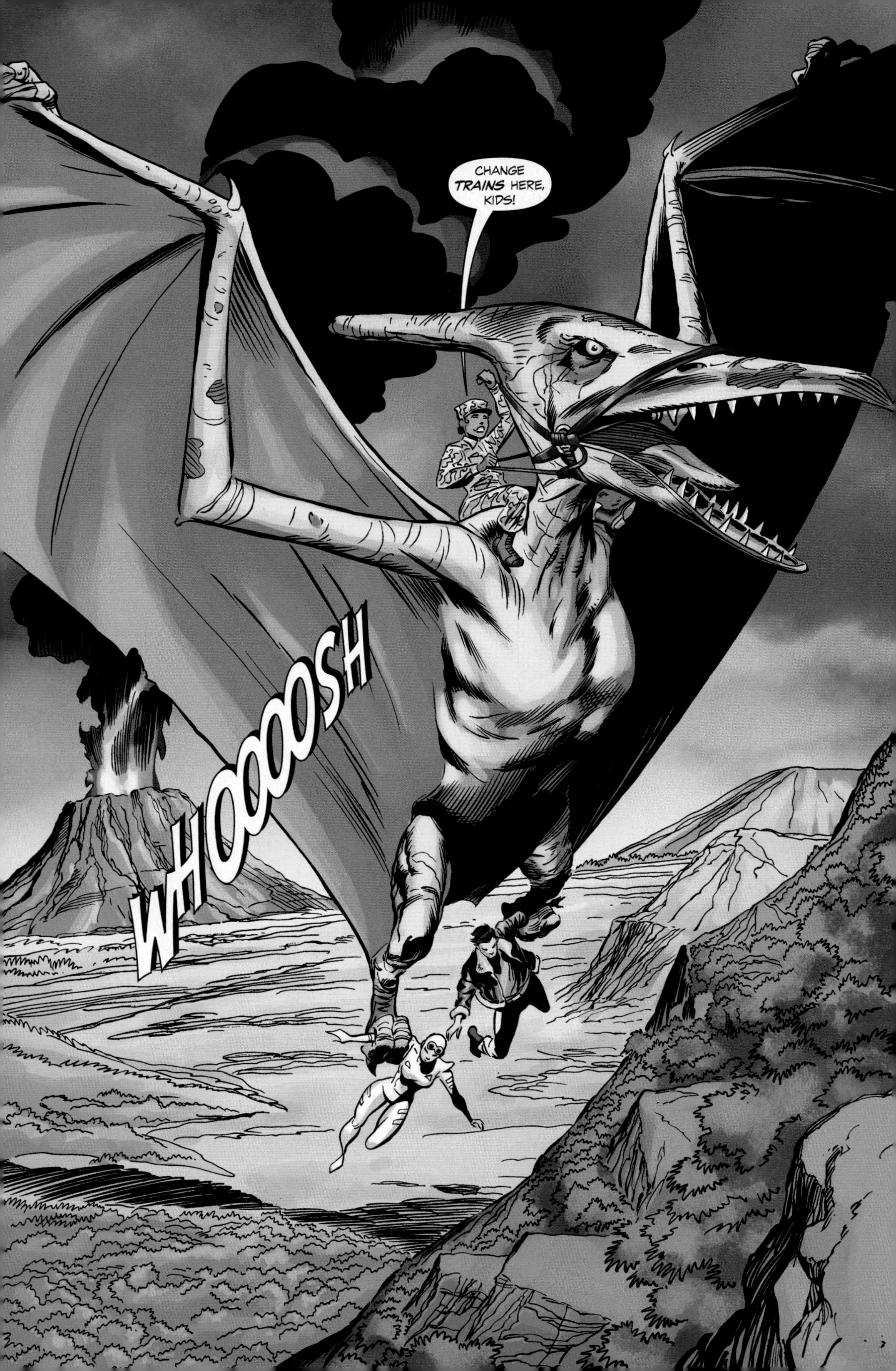
CHANGE TRAINS HERE, KIDS!
WHOOOOSH

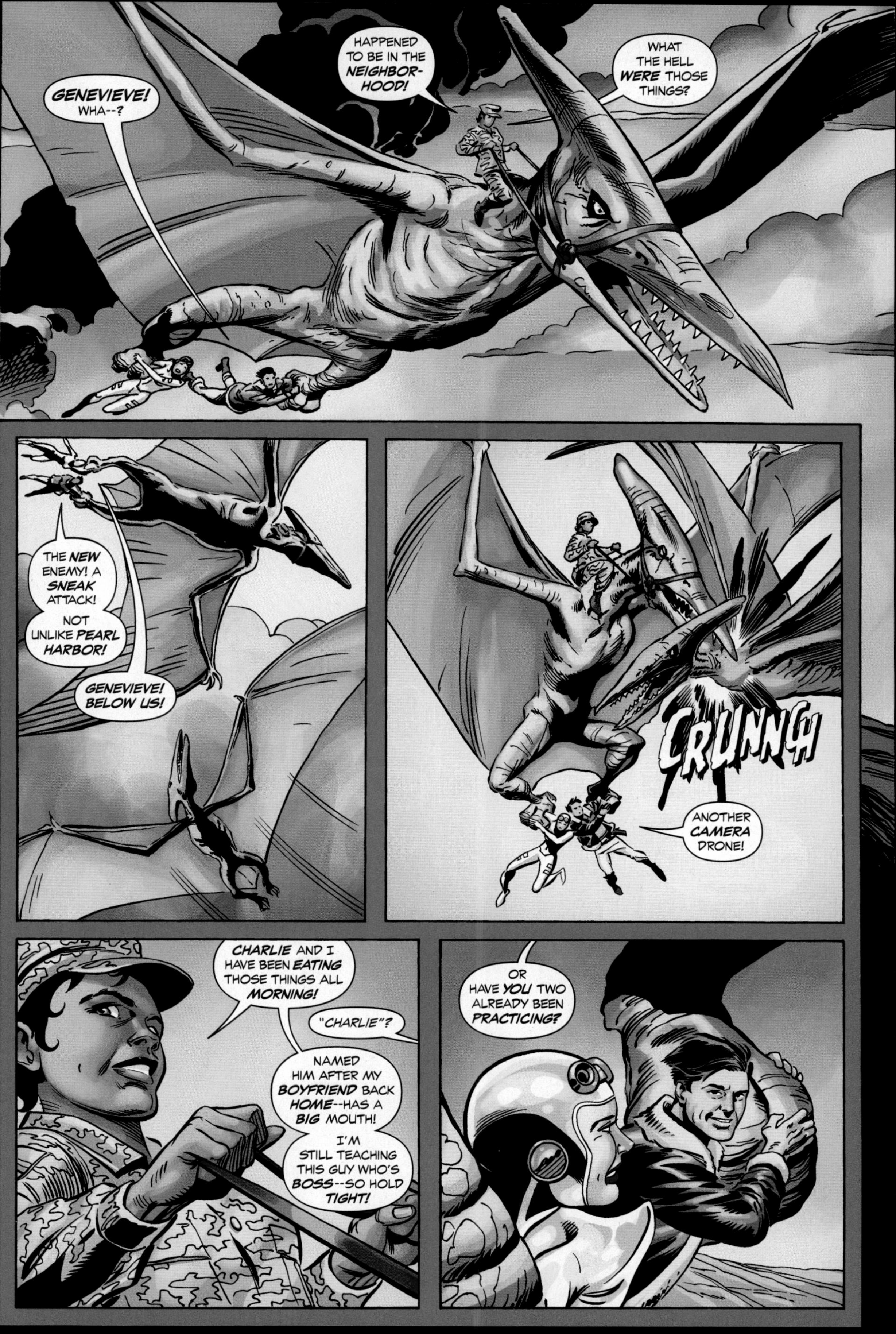
GENEVIEVE! WHA--?
HAPPENED TO BE IN THE NEIGHBOR-HOOD!
WHAT THE HELL WERE THOSE THINGS?
THE NEW ENEMY! A SNEAK ATTACK!
NOT UNLIKE PEARL HARBOR!
GENEVIEVE! BELOW US!
CRUNNCH
ANOTHER CAMERA DRONE!
CHARLIE AND I HAVE BEEN EATING THOSE THINGS ALL MORNING!
"CHARLIE"?
NAMED HIM AFTER MY BOYFRIEND BACK HOME--HAS A BIG MOUTH!
I'M STILL TEACHING THIS GUY WHO'S BOSS--SO HOLD TIGHT!
OR HAVE YOU TWO ALREADY BEEN PRACTICING?

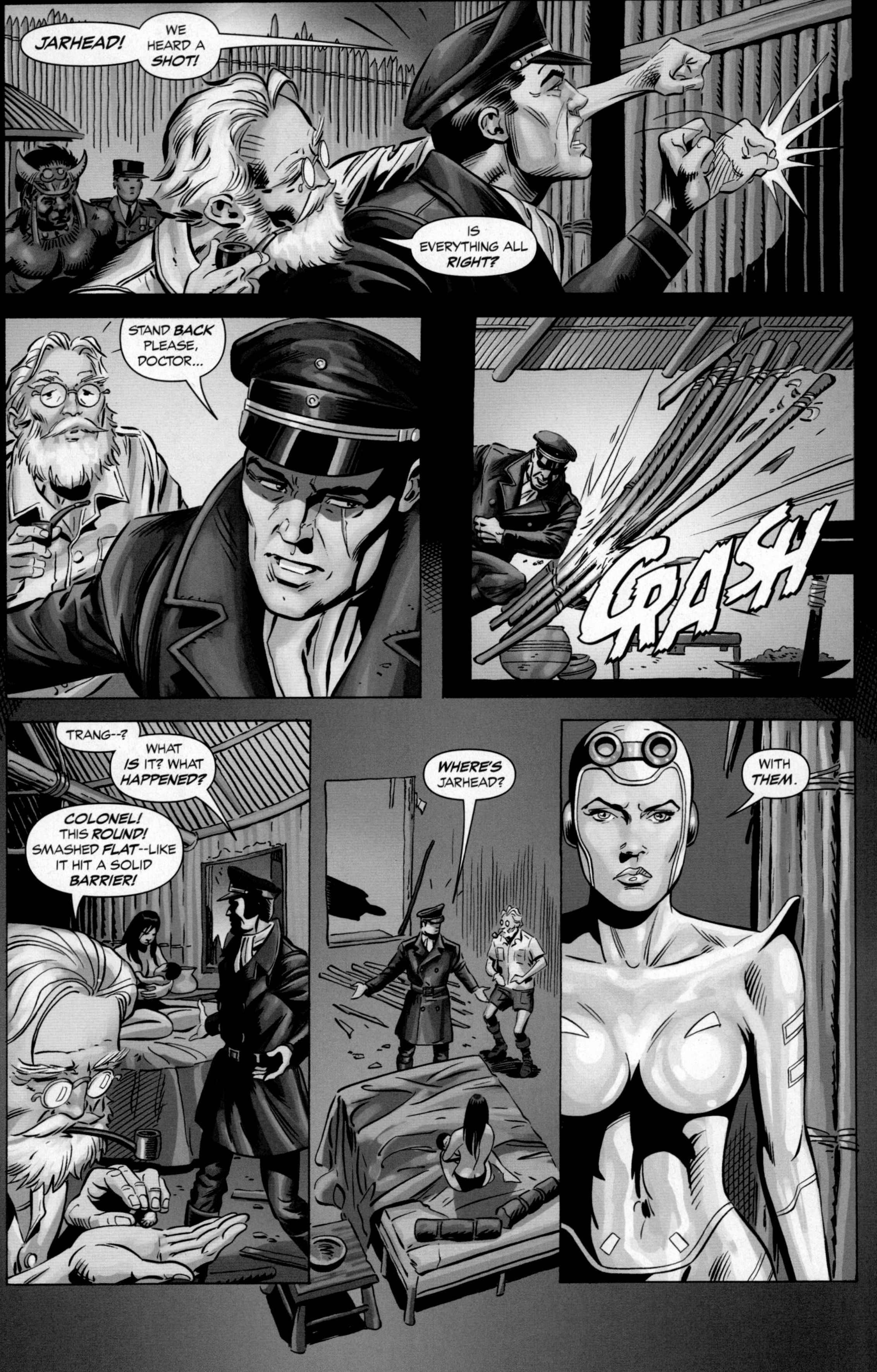
JARHEAD!
WE HEARD A SHOT!
IS EVERYTHING ALL RIGHT?
STAND BACK PLEASE, DOCTOR...
CRASH
TRANG--?
WHAT IS IT? WHAT HAPPENED?
COLONEL! THIS ROUND! SMASHED FLAT--LIKE IT HIT A SOLID BARRIER!
WHERE'S JARHEAD?
WITH THEM.

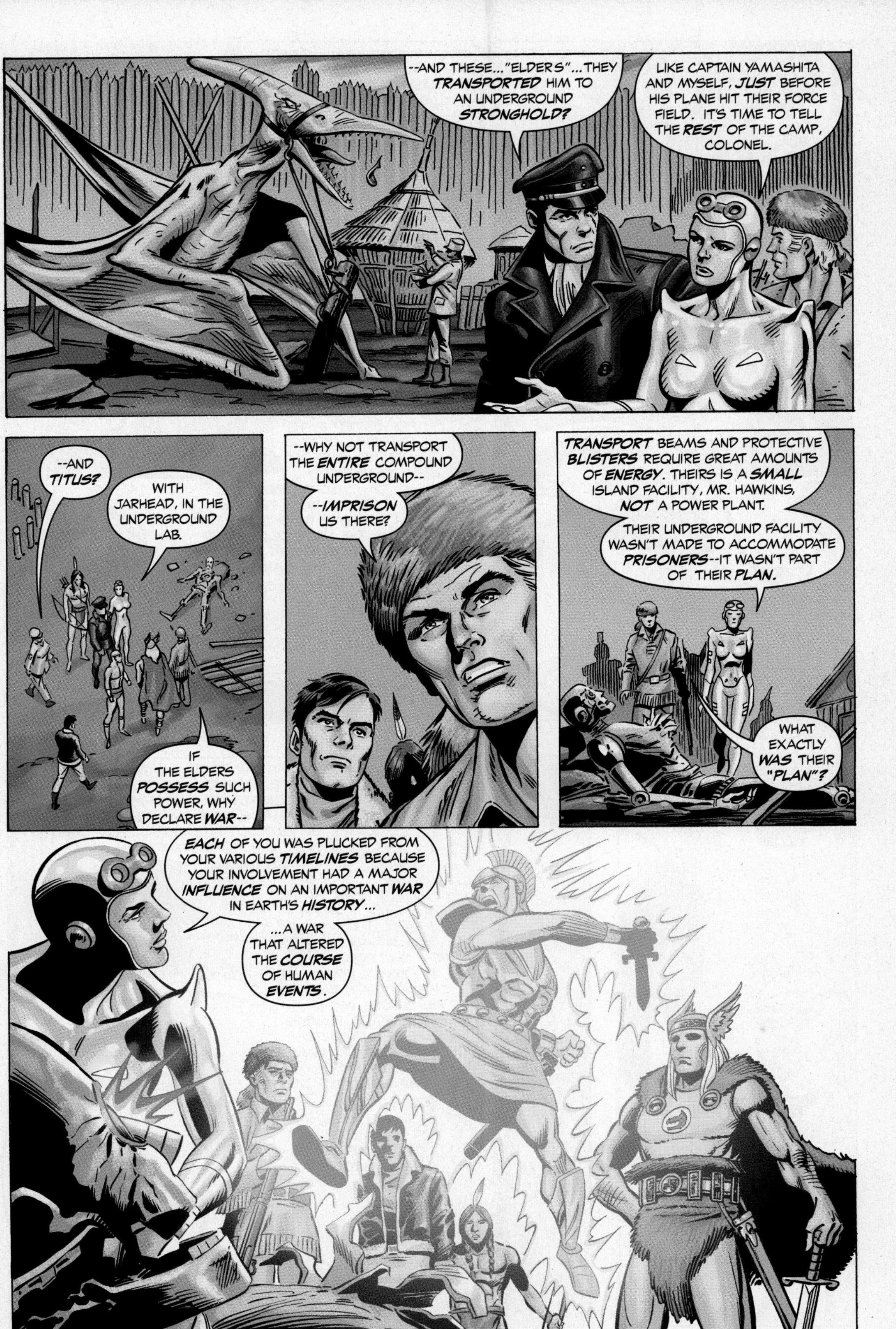
--AND THESE..."ELDERS"...THEY TRANSPORTED HIM TO AN UNDERGROUND STRONGHOLD?
LIKE CAPTAIN YAMASHITA AND MYSELF, JUST BEFORE HIS PLANE HIT THEIR FORCE FIELD. IT'S TIME TO TELL THE REST OF THE CAMP, COLONEL.
--AND TITUS?
WITH JARHEAD, IN THE UNDERGROUND LAB.
IF THE ELDERS POSSESS SUCH POWER, WHY DECLARE WAR--
--WHY NOT TRANSPORT THE ENTIRE COMPOUND UNDERGROUND--
--IMPRISON US THERE?
TRANSPORT BEAMS AND PROTECTIVE BLISTERS REQUIRE GREAT AMOUNTS OF ENERGY. THEIRS IS A SMALL ISLAND FACILITY, MR. HAWKINS, NOT A POWER PLANT.
THEIR UNDERGROUND FACILITY WASN'T MADE TO ACCOMMODATE PRISONERS--IT WASN'T PART OF THEIR PLAN.
WHAT EXACTLY WAS THEIR "PLAN"?
EACH OF YOU WAS PLUCKED FROM YOUR VARIOUS TIMELINES BECAUSE YOUR INVOLVEMENT HAD A MAJOR INFLUENCE ON AN IMPORTANT WAR IN EARTH'S HISTORY...
...A WAR THAT ALTERED THE COURSE OF HUMAN EVENTS.

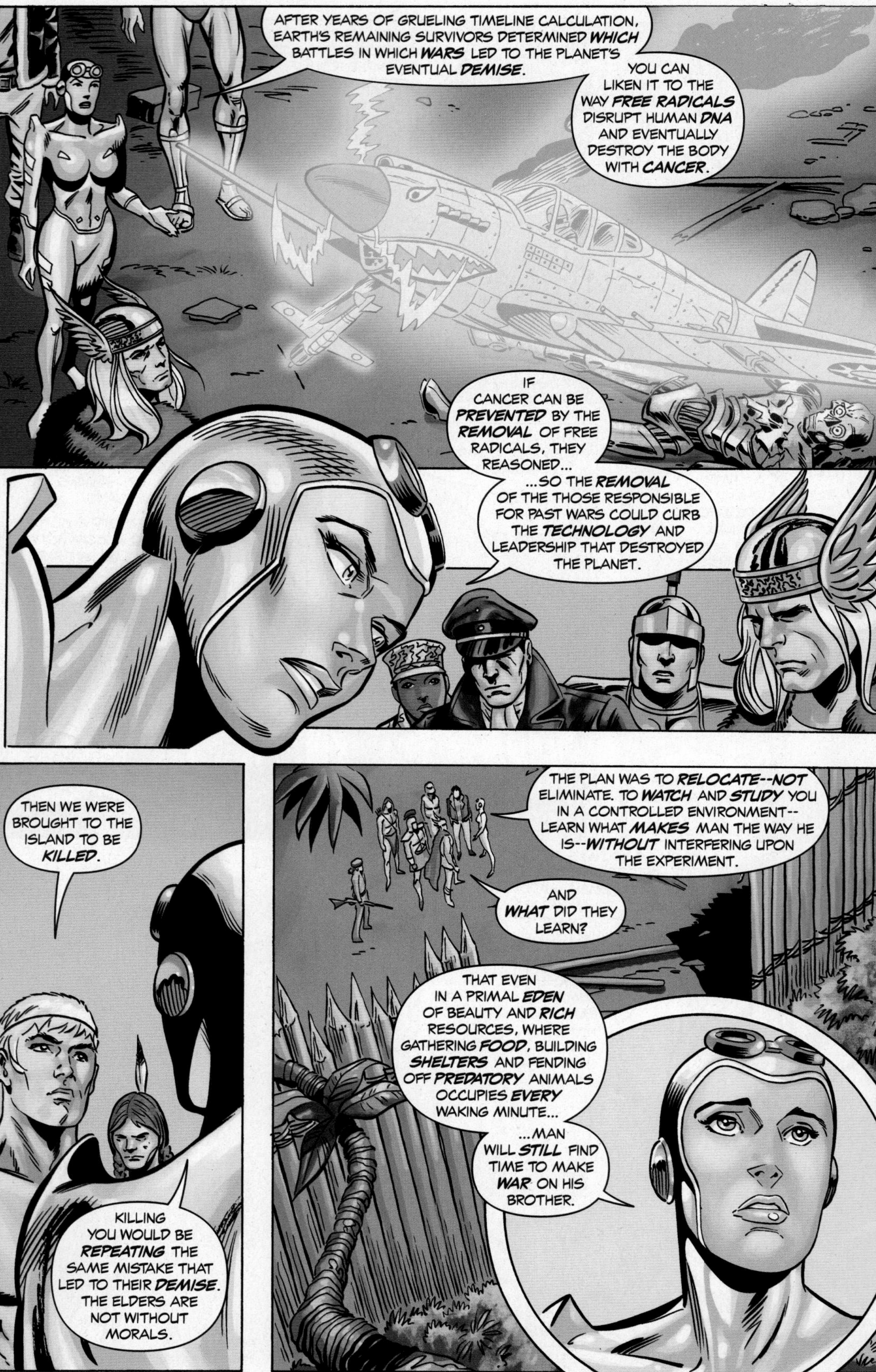
AFTER YEARS OF GRUELING TIMELINE CALCULATION, EARTH'S REMAINING SURVIVORS DETERMINED WHICH BATTLES IN WHICH WARS LED TO THE PLANET'S EVENTUAL DEMISE.
YOU CAN LIKEN IT TO THE WAY FREE RADICALS DISRUPT HUMAN DNA AND EVENTUALLY DESTROY THE BODY WITH CANCER.
IF CANCER CAN BE PREVENTED BY THE REMOVAL OF FREE RADICALS, THEY REASONED...
...SO THE REMOVAL OF THE THOSE RESPONSIBLE FOR PAST WARS COULD CURB THE TECHNOLOGY AND LEADERSHIP THAT DESTROYED THE PLANET.
THEN WE WERE BROUGHT TO THE ISLAND TO BE KILLED.
KILLING YOU WOULD BE REPEATING THE SAME MISTAKE THAT LED TO THEIR DEMISE. THE ELDERS ARE NOT WITHOUT MORALS.
THE PLAN WAS TO RELOCATE--NOT ELIMINATE. TO WATCH AND STUDY YOU IN A CONTROLLED ENVIRONMENT--LEARN WHAT MAKES MAN THE WAY HE IS--WITHOUT INTERFERING UPON THE EXPERIMENT.
AND WHAT DID THEY LEARN?
THAT EVEN IN A PRIMAL EDEN OF BEAUTY AND RICH RESOURCES, WHERE GATHERING FOOD, BUILDING SHELTERS AND FENDING OFF PREDATORY ANIMALS OCCUPIES EVERY WAKING MINUTE...
...MAN WILL STILL FIND TIME TO MAKE WAR ON HIS BROTHER.

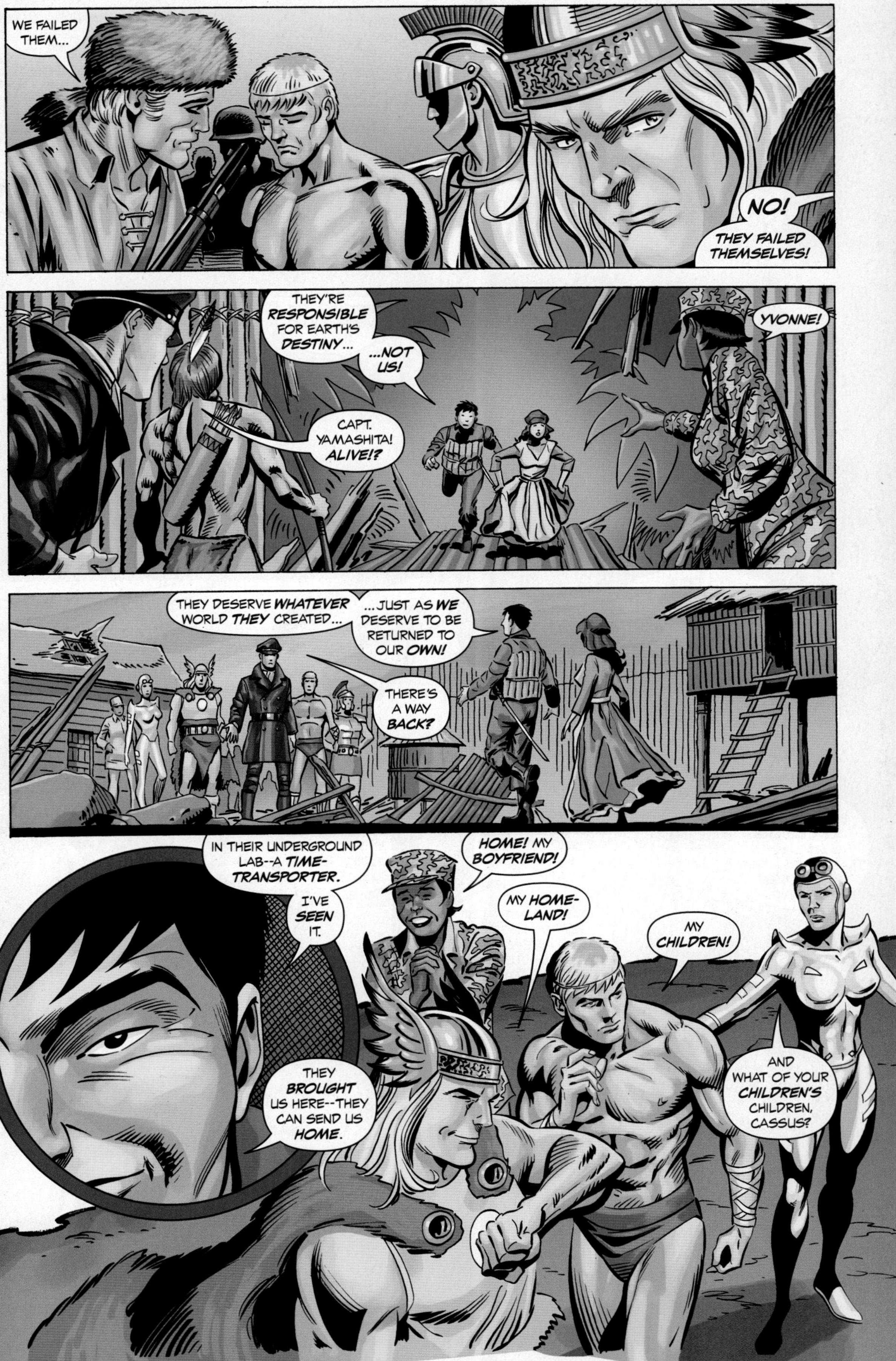
WE FAILED THEM...
NO!
THEY FAILED THEMSELVES!
THEY'RE RESPONSIBLE FOR EARTH'S DESTINY...
...NOT US!
YVONNE!
CAPT. YAMASHITA! ALIVE!?
THEY DESERVE WHATEVER WORLD THEY CREATED...
...JUST AS WE DESERVE TO BE RETURNED TO OUR OWN!
THERE'S A WAY BACK?
IN THEIR UNDERGROUND LAB--A TIME-TRANSPORTER.
I'VE SEEN IT.
HOME! MY BOYFRIEND!
MY HOME-LAND!
MY CHILDREN!
THEY BROUGHT US HERE--THEY CAN SEND US HOME.
AND WHAT OF YOUR CHILDREN'S CHILDREN, CASSUS?

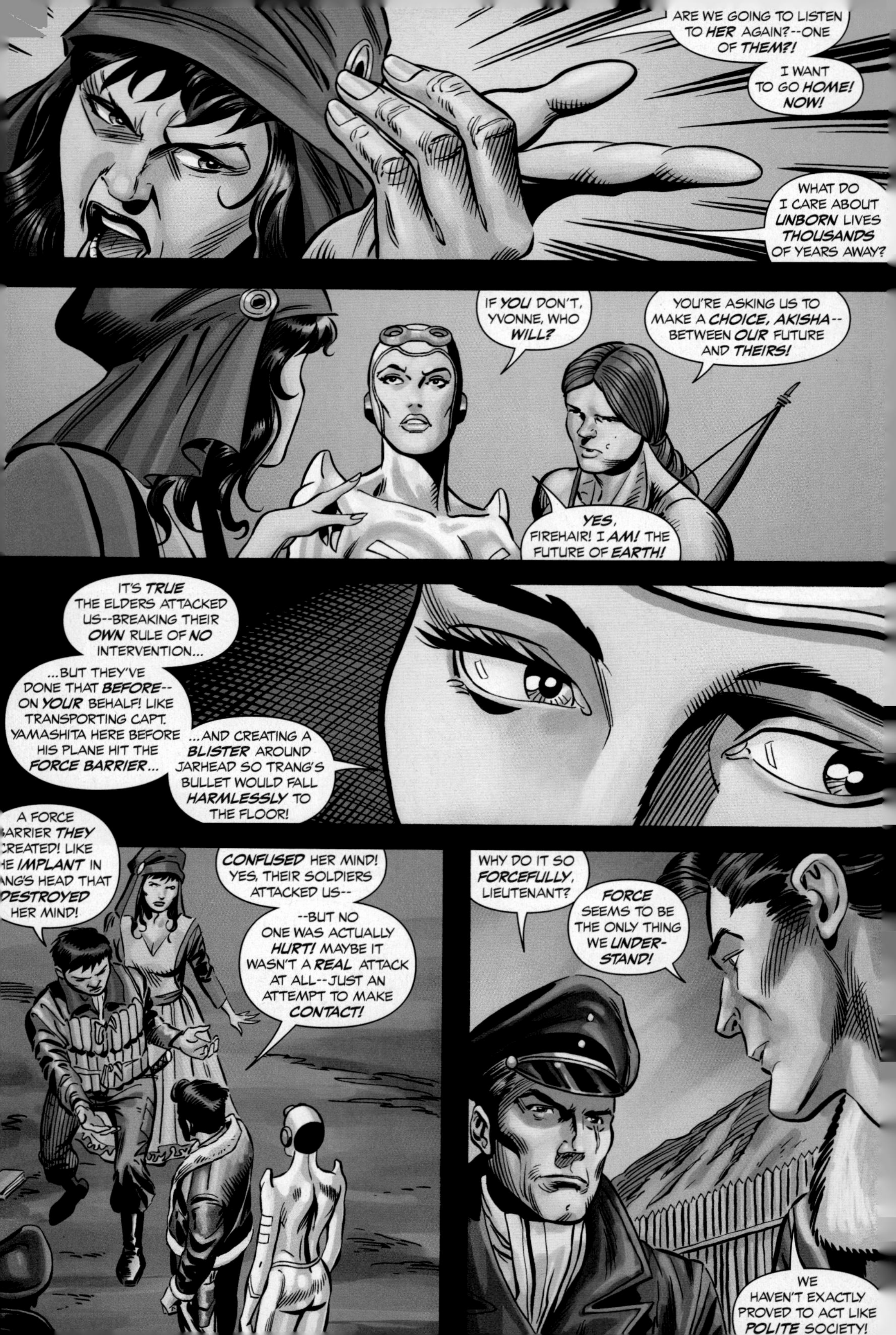

ARE WE GOING TO LISTEN TO HER AGAIN?--ONE OF THEM?!
I WANT TO GO HOME! NOW!
WHAT DO I CARE ABOUT UNBORN LIVES THOUSANDS OF YEARS AWAY?
IF YOU DON'T, YVONNE, WHO WILL?
YOU'RE ASKING US TO MAKE A CHOICE, AKISHA-- BETWEEN OUR FUTURE AND THEIRS!
YES, FIREHAIR! I AM! THE FUTURE OF EARTH!
IT'S TRUE THE ELDERS ATTACKED US--BREAKING THEIR OWN RULE OF NO INTERVENTION...
...BUT THEY'VE DONE THAT BEFORE-- ON YOUR BEHALF! LIKE TRANSPORTING CAPT. YAMASHITA HERE BEFORE HIS PLANE HIT THE FORCE BARRIER...
...AND CREATING A BLISTER AROUND JARHEAD SO TRANG'S BULLET WOULD FALL HARMLESSLY TO THE FLOOR!
A FORCE BARRIER THEY CREATED! LIKE HE IMPLANT IN ANG'S HEAD THAT DESTROYED HER MIND!
CONFUSED HER MIND! YES, THEIR SOLDIERS ATTACKED US--
--BUT NO ONE WAS ACTUALLY HURT! MAYBE IT WASN'T A REAL ATTACK AT ALL--JUST AN ATTEMPT TO MAKE CONTACT!
WHY DO IT SO FORCEFULLY, LIEUTENANT?
FORCE SEEMS TO BE THE ONLY THING WE UNDER-STAND!
WE HAVEN'T EXACTLY PROVED TO ACT LIKE POLITE SOCIETY!

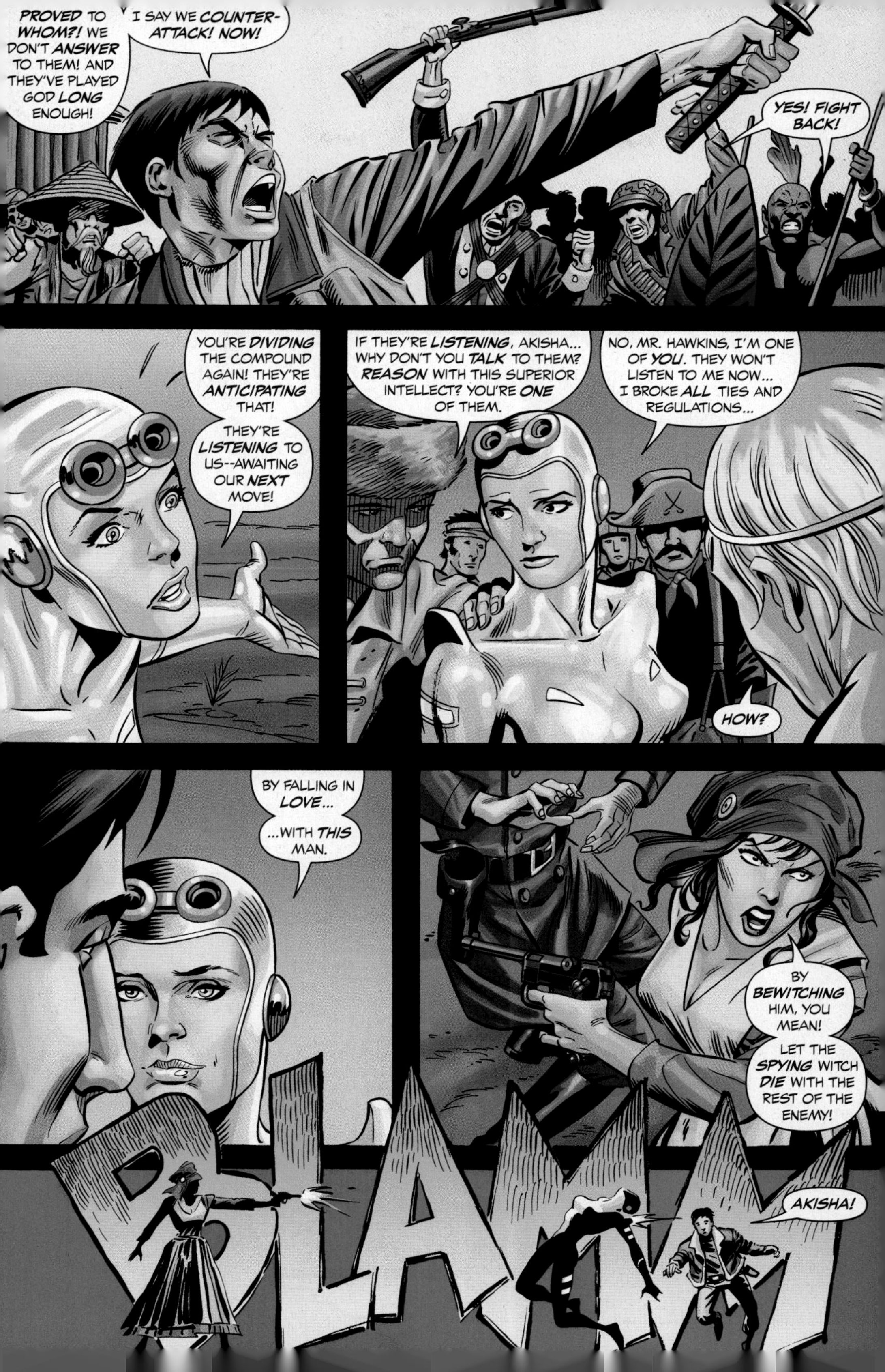

PROVED TO WHOM?! WE DON'T ANSWER TO THEM! AND THEY'VE PLAYED GOD LONG ENOUGH!
I SAY WE COUNTER-ATTACK! NOW!
YES! FIGHT BACK!
YOU'RE DIVIDING THE COMPOUND AGAIN! THEY'RE ANTICIPATING THAT!
THEY'RE LISTENING TO US--AWAITING OUR NEXT MOVE!
IF THEY'RE LISTENING, AKISHA... WHY DON'T YOU TALK TO THEM? REASON WITH THIS SUPERIOR INTELLECT? YOU'RE ONE OF THEM.
NO, MR. HAWKINS, I'M ONE OF YOU. THEY WON'T LISTEN TO ME NOW... I BROKE ALL TIES AND REGULATIONS...
HOW?
BY FALLING IN LOVE...
...WITH THIS MAN.
BY BEWITCHING HIM, YOU MEAN!
LET THE SPYING WITCH DIE WITH THE REST OF THE ENEMY!
BLAMM
AKISHA!

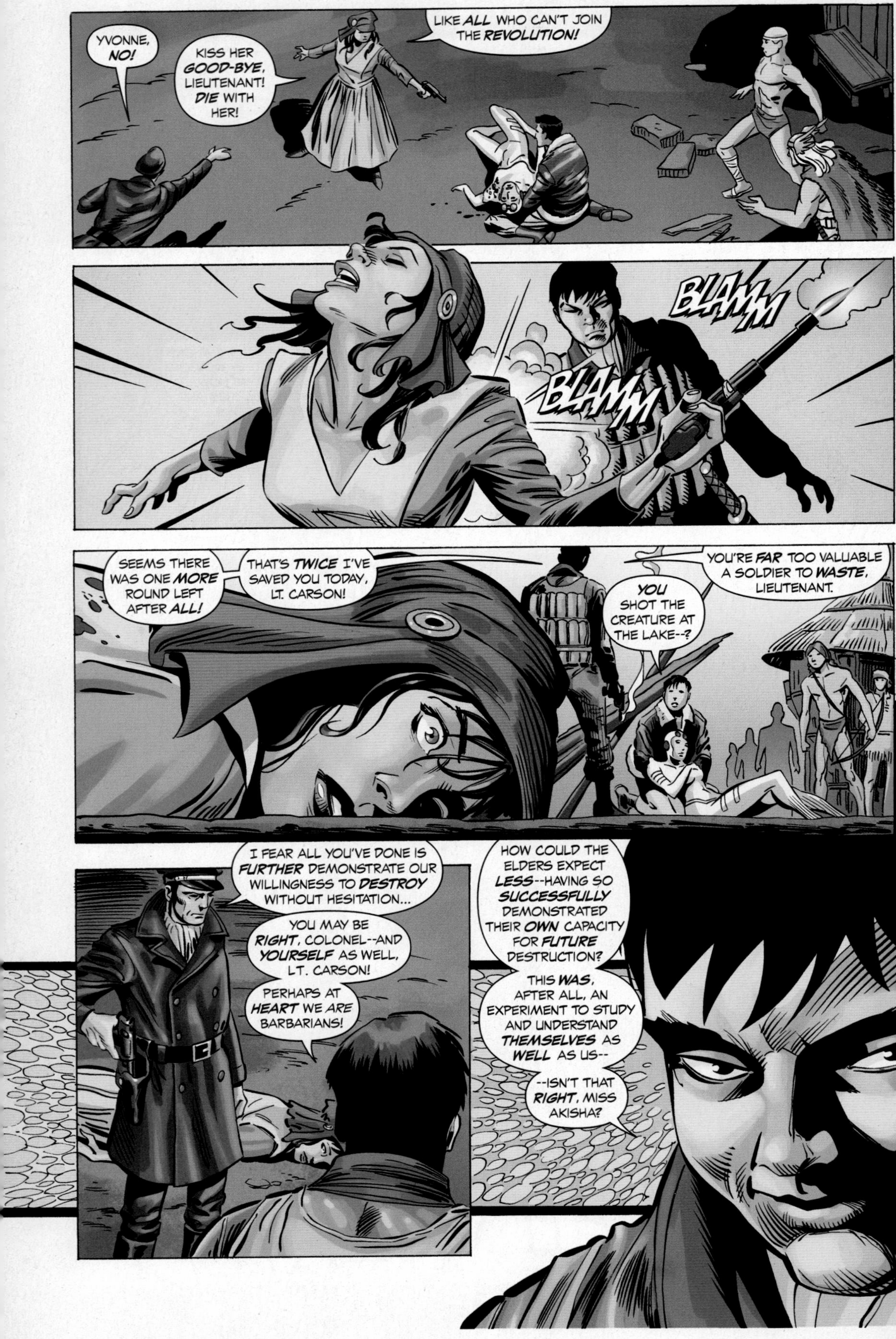

YVONNE, NO!
KISS HER GOOD-BYE, LIEUTENANT! DIE WITH HER!
LIKE ALL WHO CAN'T JOIN THE REVOLUTION!
BLAMM
BLAMM
SEEMS THERE WAS ONE MORE ROUND LEFT AFTER ALL!
THAT'S TWICE I'VE SAVED YOU TODAY, LT. CARSON!
YOU SHOT THE CREATURE AT THE LAKE--?
YOU'RE FAR TOO VALUABLE A SOLDIER TO WASTE, LIEUTENANT.
I FEAR ALL YOU'VE DONE IS FURTHER DEMONSTRATE OUR WILLINGNESS TO DESTROY WITHOUT HESITATION...
YOU MAY BE RIGHT, COLONEL--AND YOURSELF AS WELL, LT. CARSON!
PERHAPS AT HEART WE ARE BARBARIANS!
HOW COULD THE ELDERS EXPECT LESS--HAVING SO SUCCESSFULLY DEMONSTRATED THEIR OWN CAPACITY FOR FUTURE DESTRUCTION?
THIS WAS, AFTER ALL, AN EXPERIMENT TO STUDY AND UNDERSTAND THEMSELVES AS WELL AS US--
--ISN'T THAT RIGHT, MISS AKISHA?

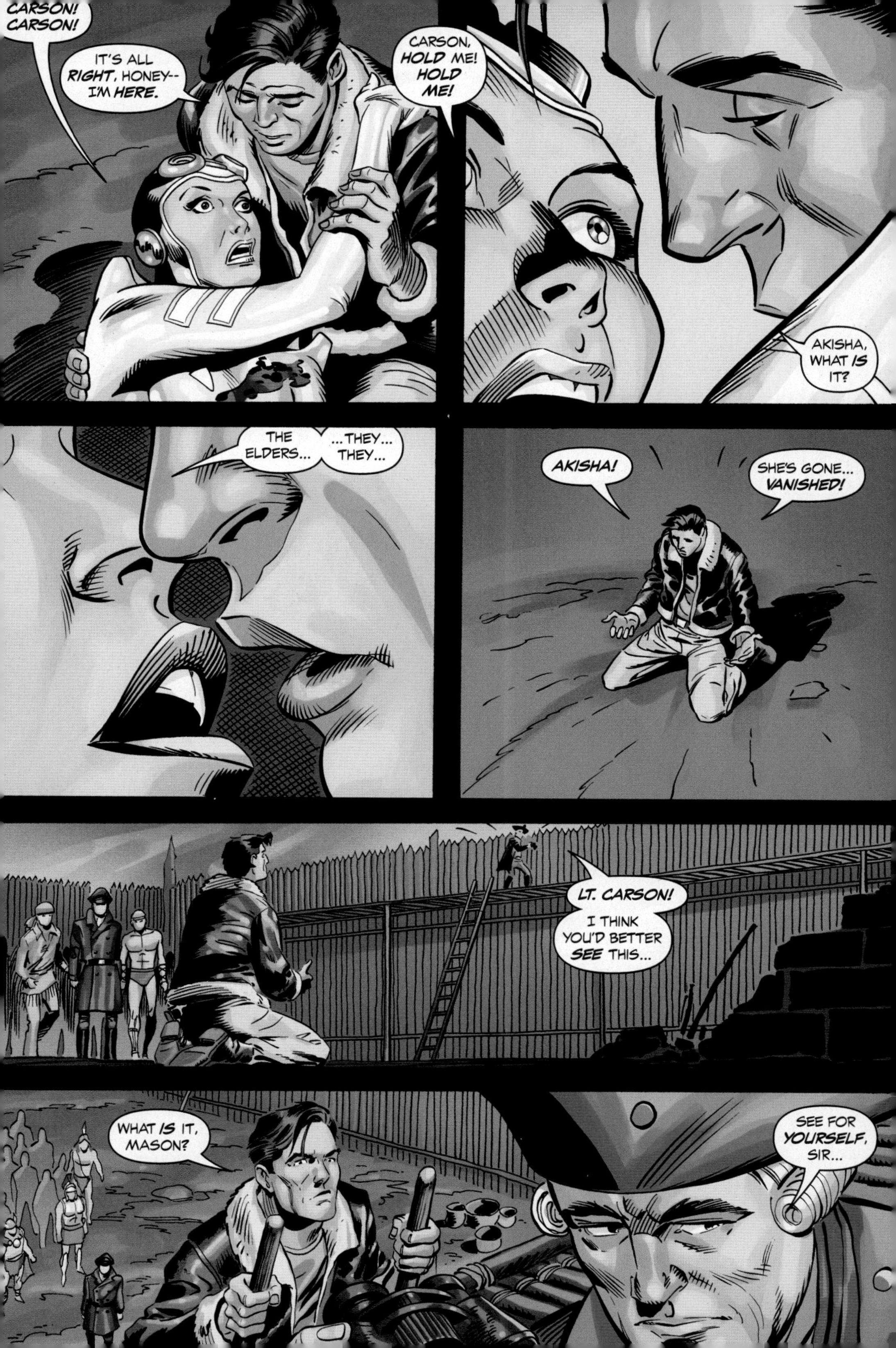
CARSON! CARSON!
IT'S ALL RIGHT, HONEY-- I'M HERE.
CARSON, HOLD ME! HOLD ME!
AKISHA, WHAT IS IT?
THE ELDERS...
...THEY... THEY...
AKISHA!
SHE'S GONE... VANISHED!
LT. CARSON!
I THINK YOU'D BETTER SEE THIS...
WHAT IS IT, MASON?
SEE FOR YOURSELF, SIR...

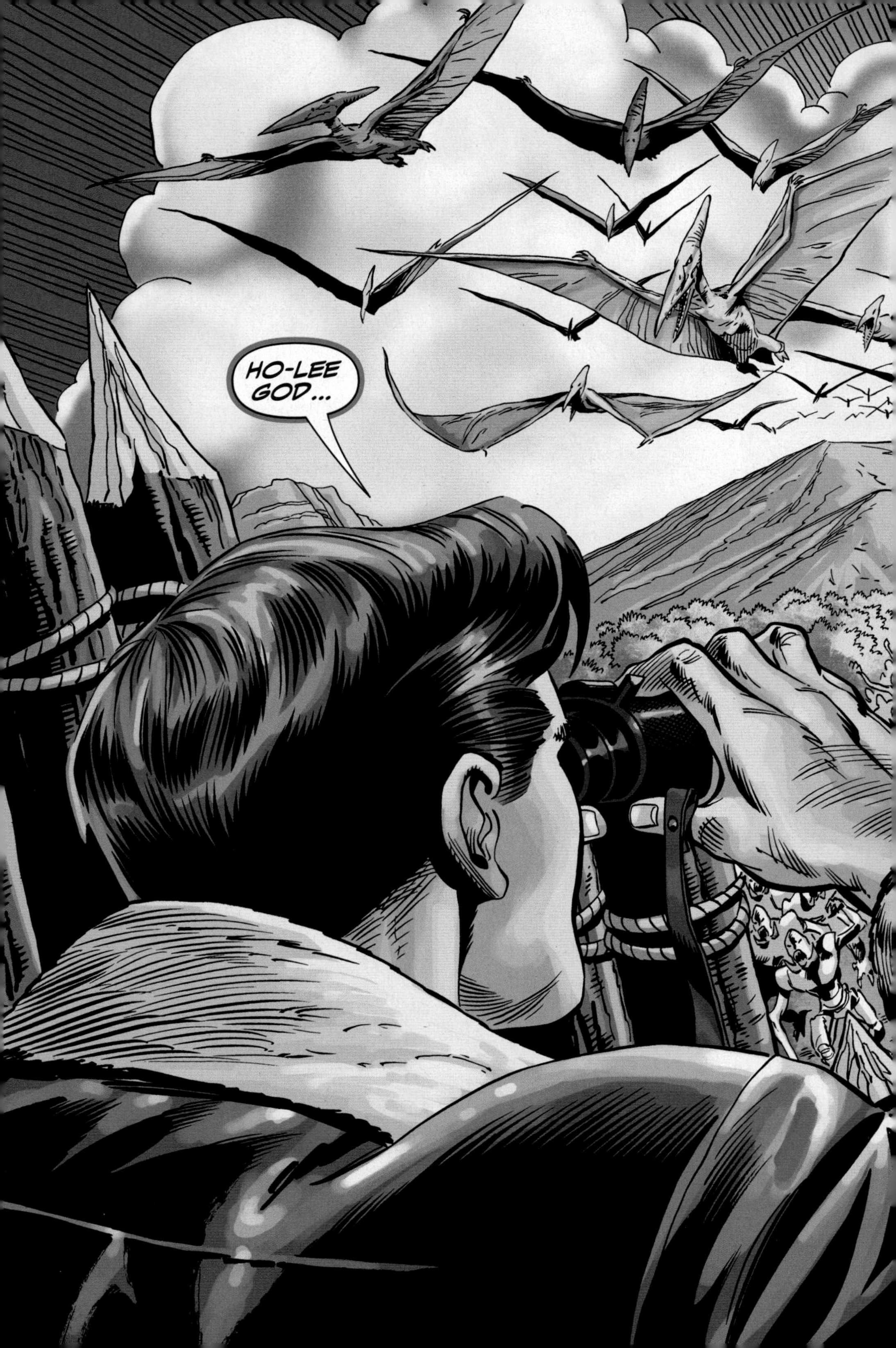
HO-LEE GOD...

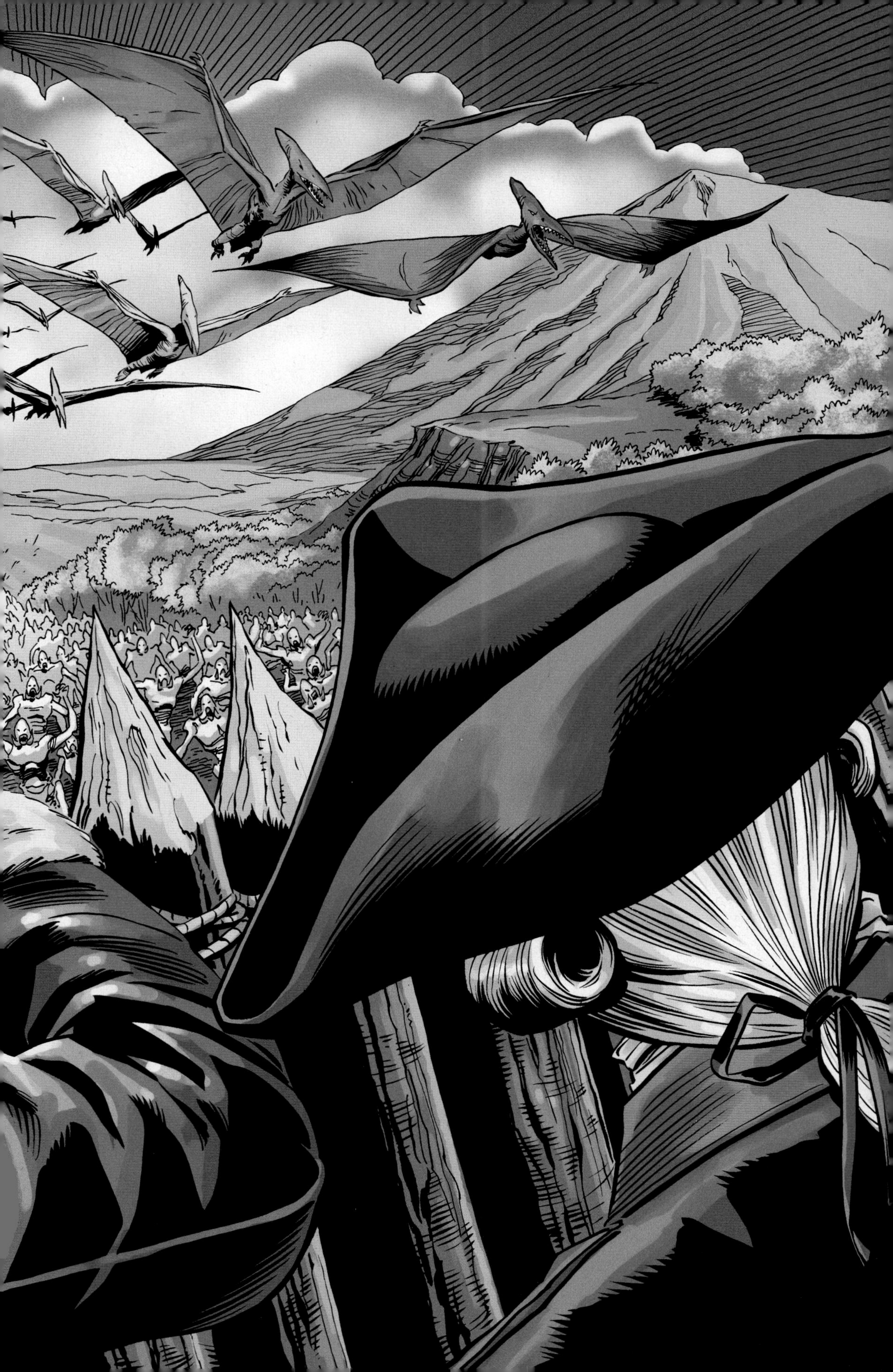

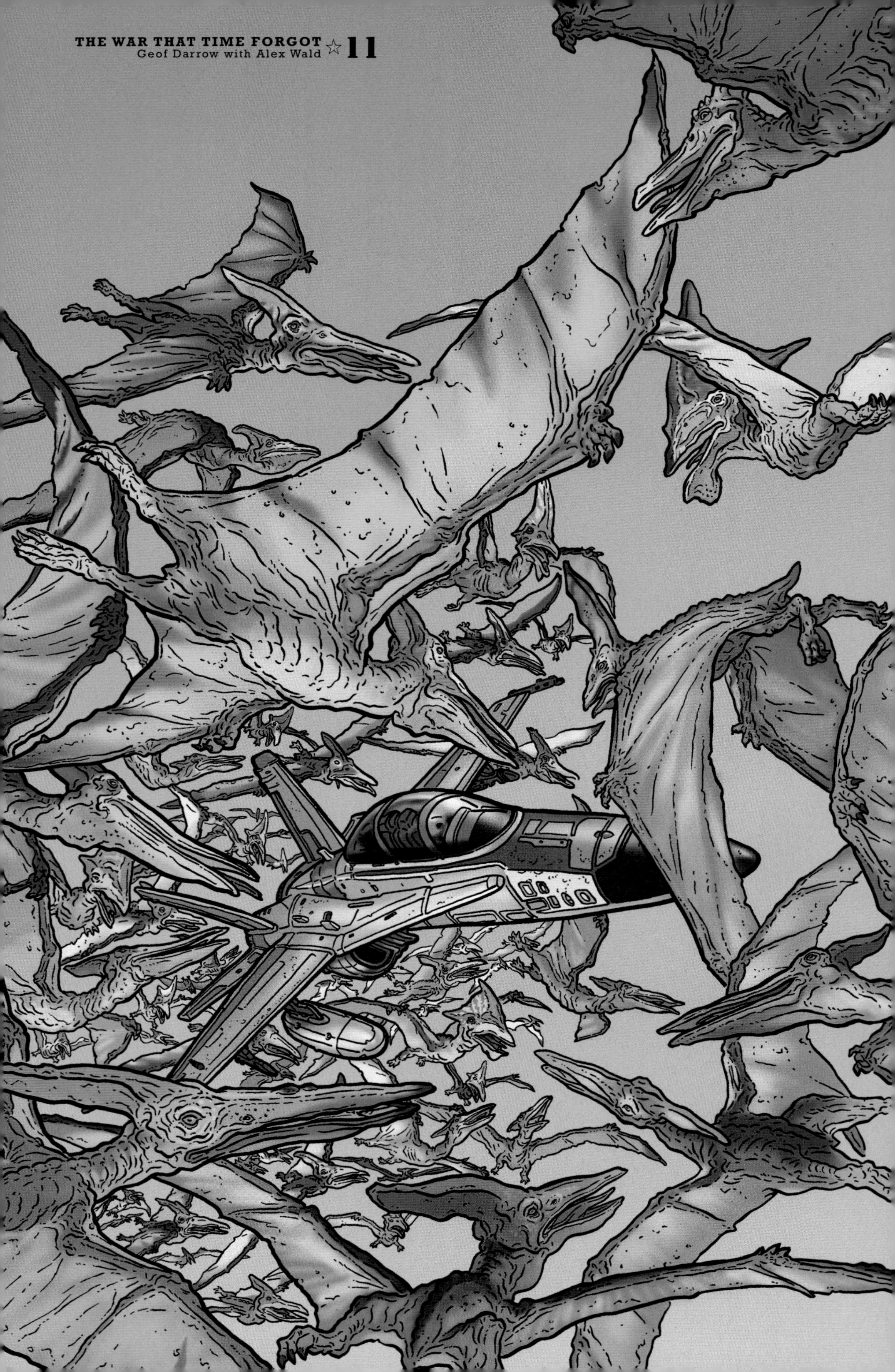

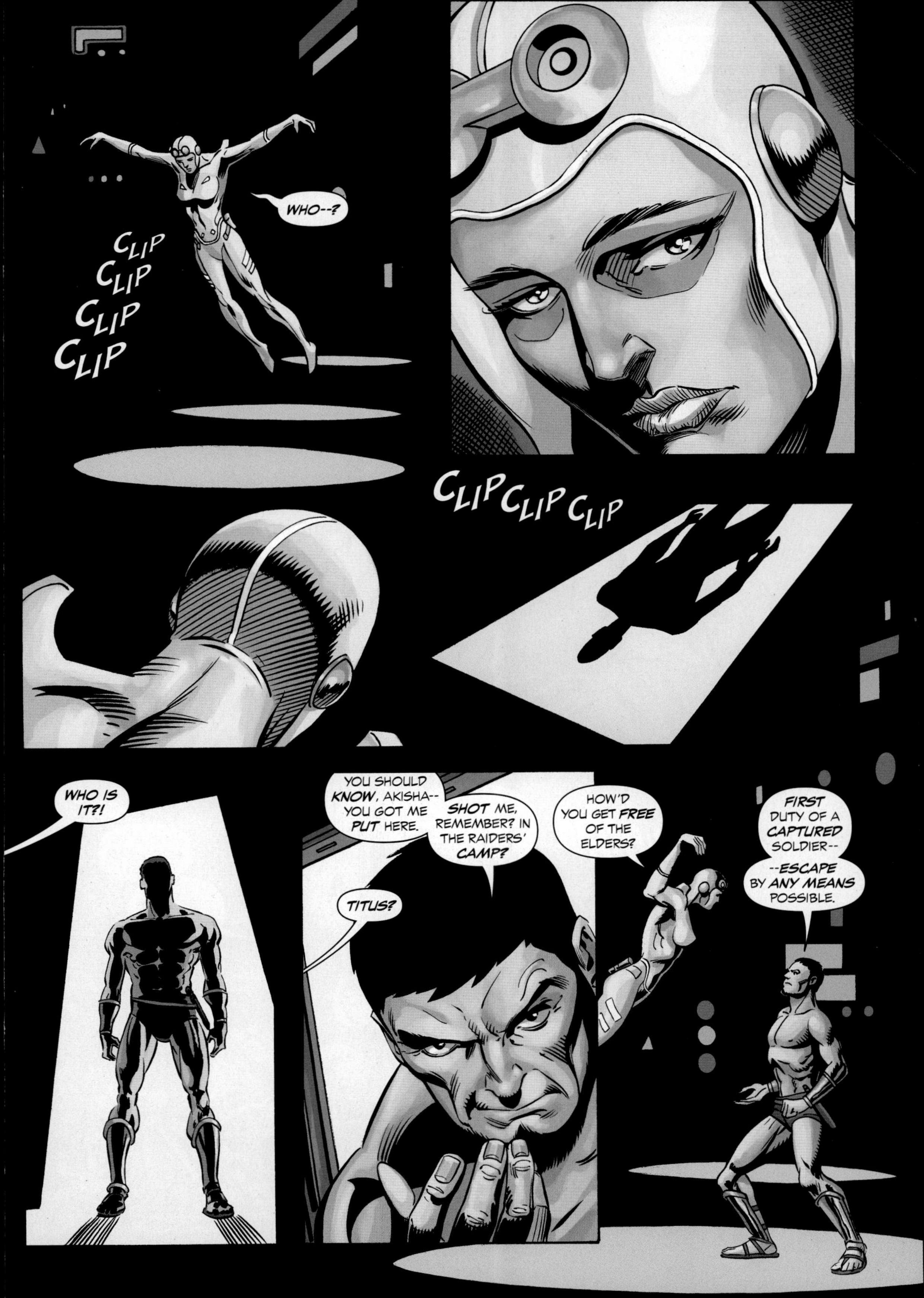
WHO--?
CLIP CLIP CLIP CLIP
CLIP CLIP CLIP
WHO IS IT?!
YOU SHOULD KNOW, AKISHA-- YOU GOT ME PUT HERE.
SHOT ME, REMEMBER? IN THE RAIDERS' CAMP?
TITUS?
HOW'D YOU GET FREE OF THE ELDERS?
FIRST DUTY OF A CAPTURED SOLDIER--
--ESCAPE BY ANY MEANS POSSIBLE.

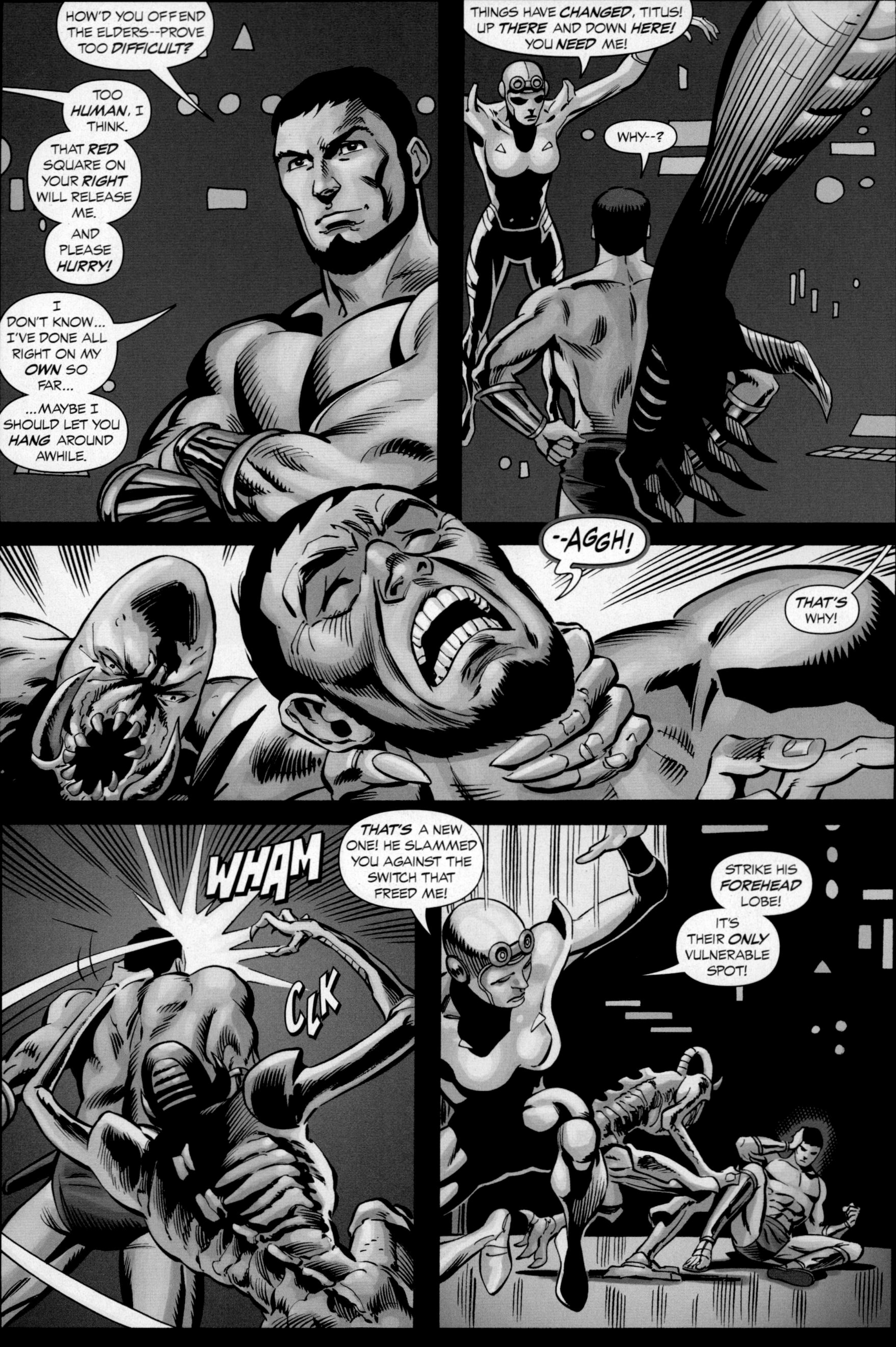
HOW'D YOU OFFEND THE ELDERS--PROVE TOO DIFFICULT?
TOO HUMAN, I THINK.
THAT RED SQUARE ON YOUR RIGHT WILL RELEASE ME.
AND PLEASE HURRY!
I DON'T KNOW... I'VE DONE ALL RIGHT ON MY OWN SO FAR...
...MAYBE I SHOULD LET YOU HANG AROUND AWHILE.
THINGS HAVE CHANGED, TITUS! UP THERE AND DOWN HERE! YOU NEED ME!
WHY--?
--AGGH!
THAT'S WHY!
WHAM
CLK
THAT'S A NEW ONE! HE SLAMMED YOU AGAINST THE SWITCH THAT FREED ME!
STRIKE HIS FOREHEAD LOBE!
IT'S THEIR ONLY VULNERABLE SPOT!

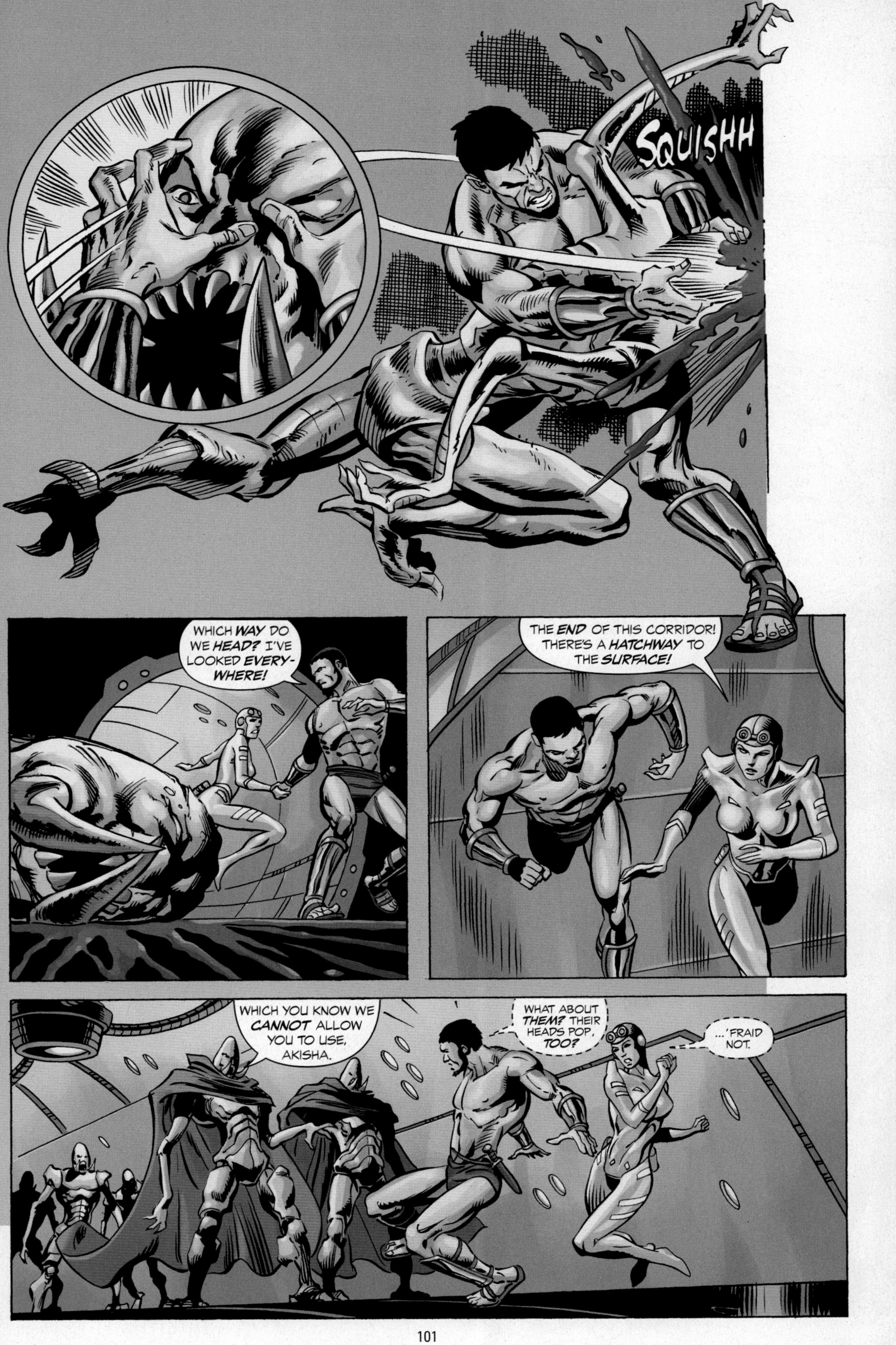
SQUISHH
WHICH WAY DO WE HEAD? I'VE LOOKED EVERY-WHERE!
THE END OF THIS CORRIDOR! THERE'S A HATCHWAY TO THE SURFACE!
WHICH YOU KNOW WE CANNOT ALLOW YOU TO USE, AKISHA.
WHAT ABOUT THEM? THEIR HEADS POP, TOO?
...'FRAID NOT.

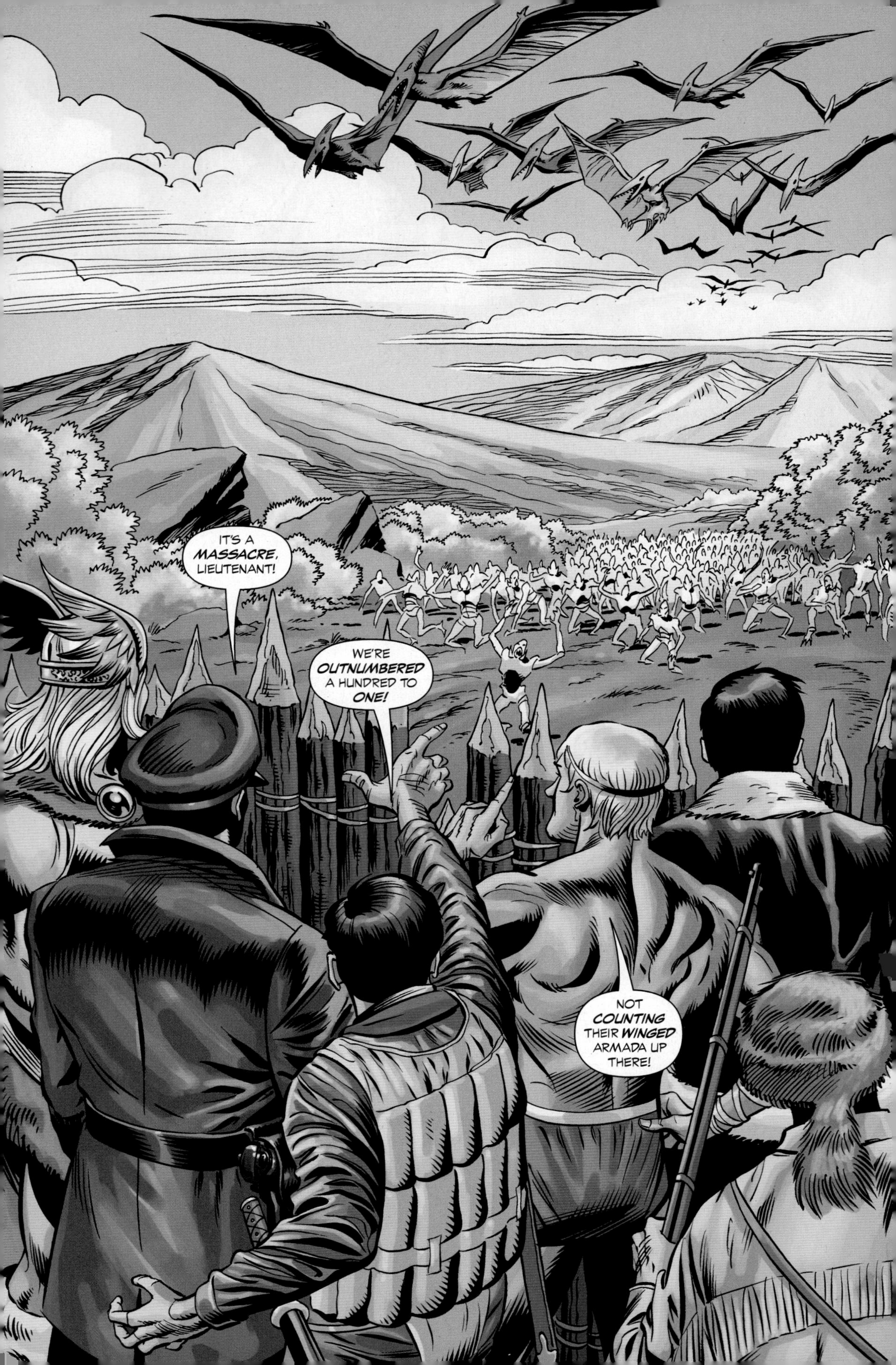
IT'S A MASSACRE, LIEUTENANT!
WE'RE OUTNUMBERED A HUNDRED TO ONE!
NOT COUNTING THEIR WINGED ARMADA UP THERE!

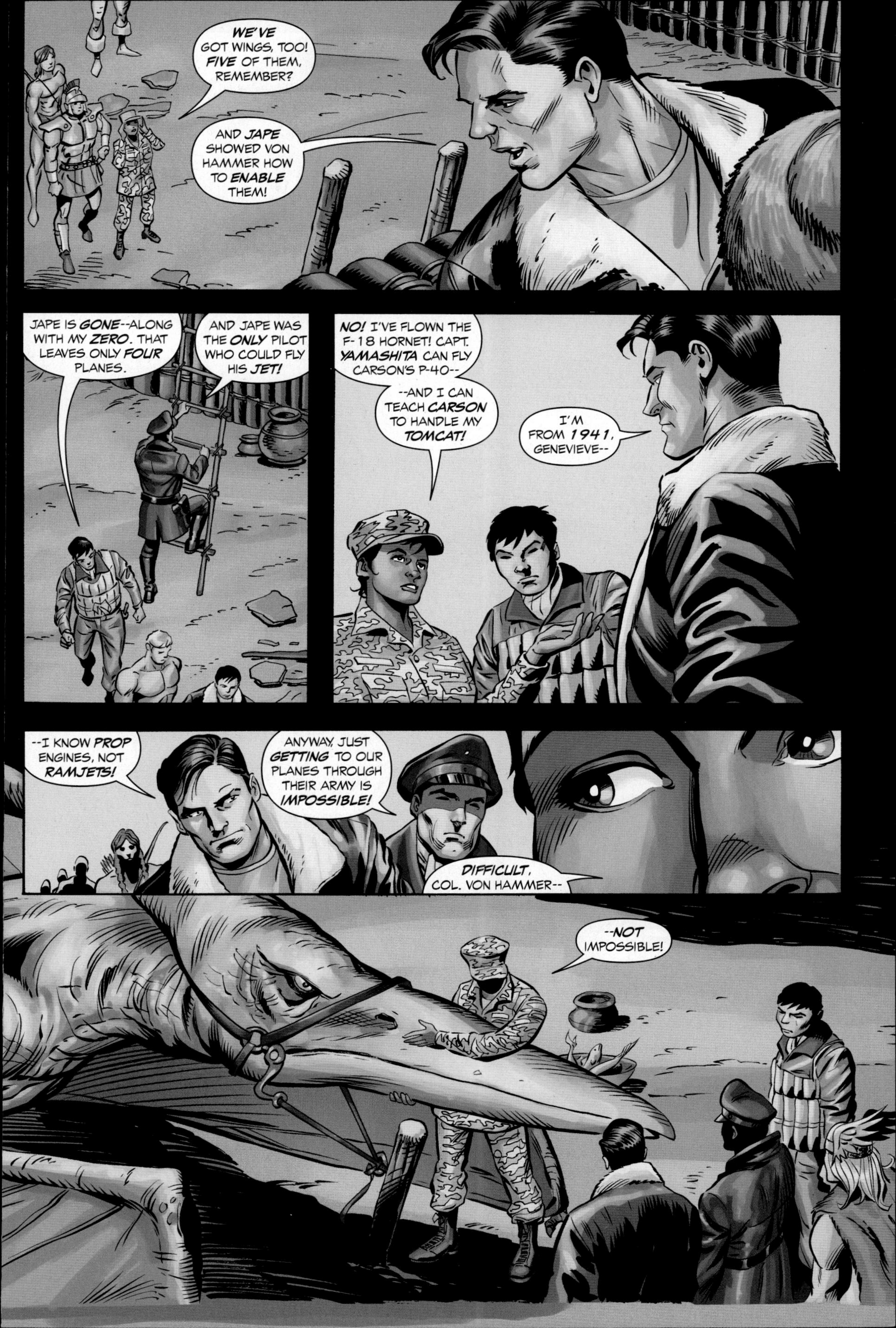
WE'VE GOT WINGS, TOO! FIVE OF THEM, REMEMBER?
AND JAPE SHOWED VON HAMMER HOW TO ENABLE THEM!
JAPE IS GONE--ALONG WITH MY ZERO. THAT LEAVES ONLY FOUR PLANES.
AND JAPE WAS THE ONLY PILOT WHO COULD FLY HIS JET!
NO! I'VE FLOWN THE F-18 HORNET! CAPT. YAMASHITA CAN FLY CARSON'S P-40--
--AND I CAN TEACH CARSON TO HANDLE MY TOMCAT!
I'M FROM 1941, GENEVIEVE--
--I KNOW PROP ENGINES, NOT RAMJETS!
ANYWAY, JUST GETTING TO OUR PLANES THROUGH THEIR ARMY IS IMPOSSIBLE!
DIFFICULT, COL. VON HAMMER--
--NOT IMPOSSIBLE!

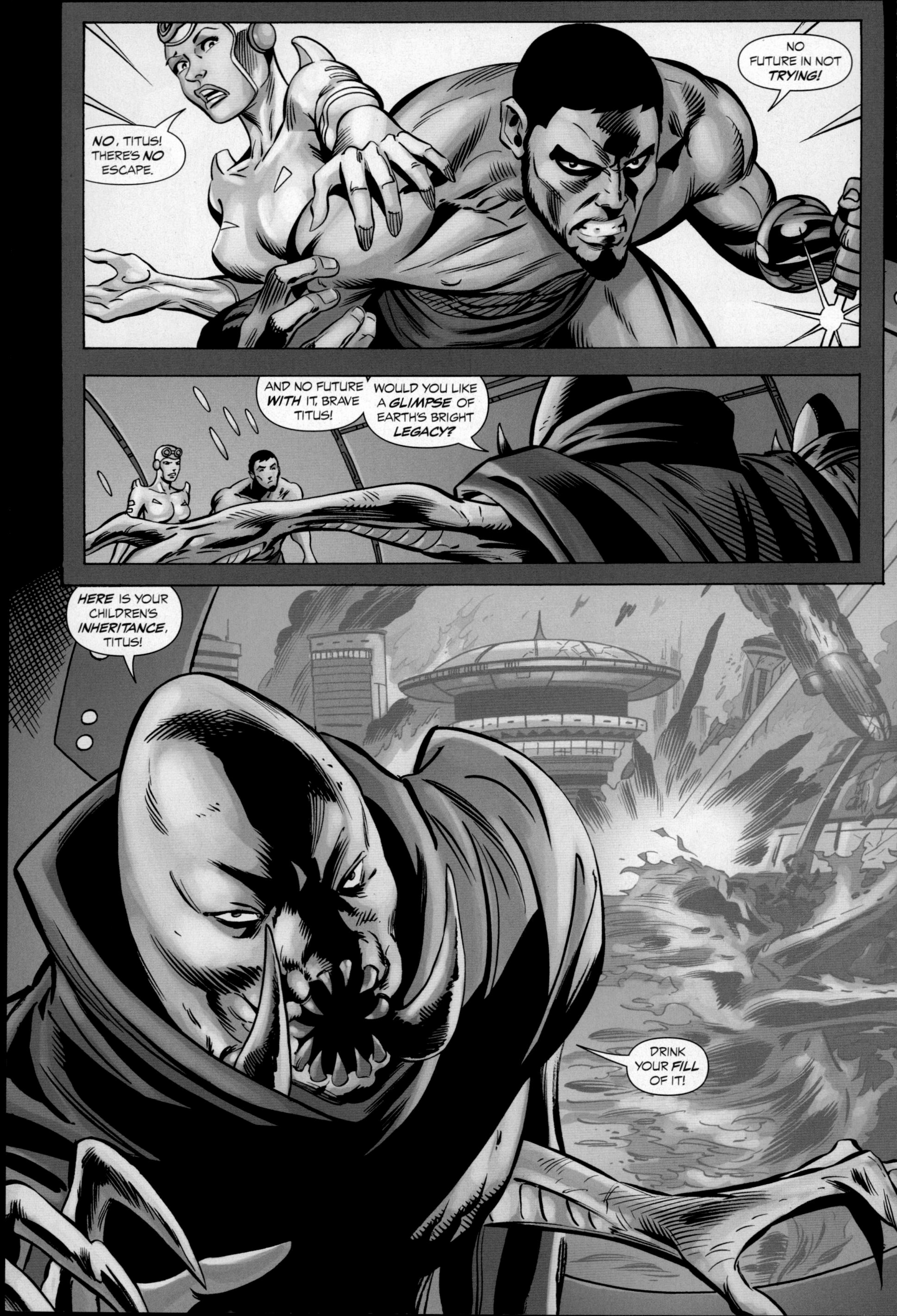
NO, TITUS! THERE'S NO ESCAPE.
NO FUTURE IN NOT TRYING!
AND NO FUTURE WITH IT, BRAVE TITUS!
WOULD YOU LIKE A GLIMPSE OF EARTH'S BRIGHT LEGACY?
HERE IS YOUR CHILDREN'S INHERITANCE, TITUS!
DRINK YOUR FILL OF IT!

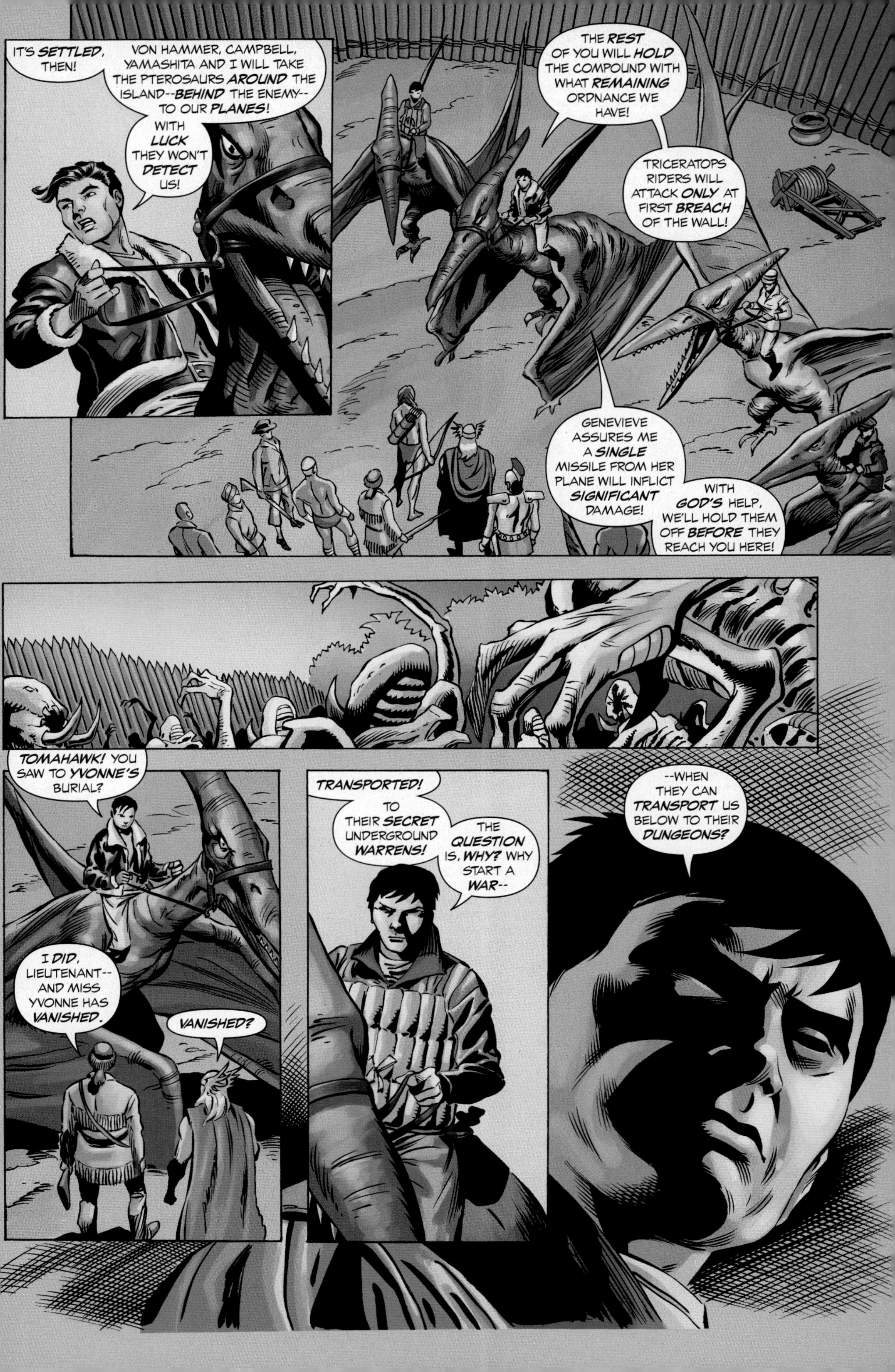
IT'S SETTLED, THEN!
VON HAMMER, CAMPBELL, YAMASHITA AND I WILL TAKE THE PTEROSAURS AROUND THE ISLAND--BEHIND THE ENEMY--TO OUR PLANES!
WITH LUCK THEY WON'T DETECT US!
THE REST OF YOU WILL HOLD THE COMPOUND WITH WHAT REMAINING ORDNANCE WE HAVE!
TRICERATOPS RIDERS WILL ATTACK ONLY AT FIRST BREACH OF THE WALL!
GENEVIEVE ASSURES ME A SINGLE MISSILE FROM HER PLANE WILL INFLICT SIGNIFICANT DAMAGE!
WITH GOD'S HELP, WE'LL HOLD THEM OFF BEFORE THEY REACH YOU HERE!
TOMAHAWK! YOU SAW TO YVONNE'S BURIAL?
I DID, LIEUTENANT--AND MISS YVONNE HAS VANISHED.
VANISHED?
TRANSPORTED!
TO THEIR SECRET UNDERGROUND WARRENS!
THE QUESTION IS, WHY? WHY START A WAR--
--WHEN THEY CAN TRANSPORT US BELOW TO THEIR DUNGEONS?

--BECAUSE, THOUGH WE CAN TRANSPORT OUR *OWN* RACE WITHIN LIMITED RANGE OF OUR *MACHINES* FROM ANYWHERE ON THE ISLAND...

...LIKE *YVONNE* HERE-- YOU *EARLIER HOMO SAPIENS* LACK THE PROPER *METABOLISM* FOR TRANSPORT...

...UNLESS YOUR *BLOOD PRESSURE* IS *ACCELERATED*...EITHER BY NORMAL *ANXIETY, FEAR*...

...OR *INJECTED* ADRENALINE.

AKISHA'S *WEAPON*, FOR INSTANCE.

YVONNE IS *ALIVE* THEN?

HEALING. IT'S AGAINST OUR *LAWS* AND *ETHICS* TO HARM INTELLIGENT LIFE.

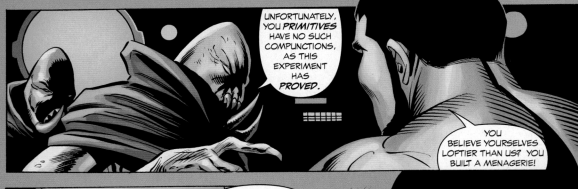

UNFORTUNATELY, YOU *PRIMITIVES* HAVE NO SUCH COMPUNCTIONS, AS THIS EXPERIMENT HAS *PROVED*.

YOU BELIEVE YOURSELVES *LOFTIER* THAN US? YOU BUILT A MENAGERIE!

WE MAKE *NO* EXCUSES. OUR HOPE WAS TO *SAVE* MANKIND-- *ALTER* EARTH'S *WAR-INFESTED* TIMELINE BY GATHERING YOU HERE.

IF YOU PROVED *CIVILIZED*... WE'D TAKE YOU BACK TO THE *FUTURE* WITH US. IF YOU *FAILED*--

--YOU'LL *LEAVE* US ON THIS ISLAND TO *ROT*.

EITHER WAY, YOUR TIMELINE IS ALL *TIDIED UP*. THAT'S JUST *GREAT*--FOR *YOU*!

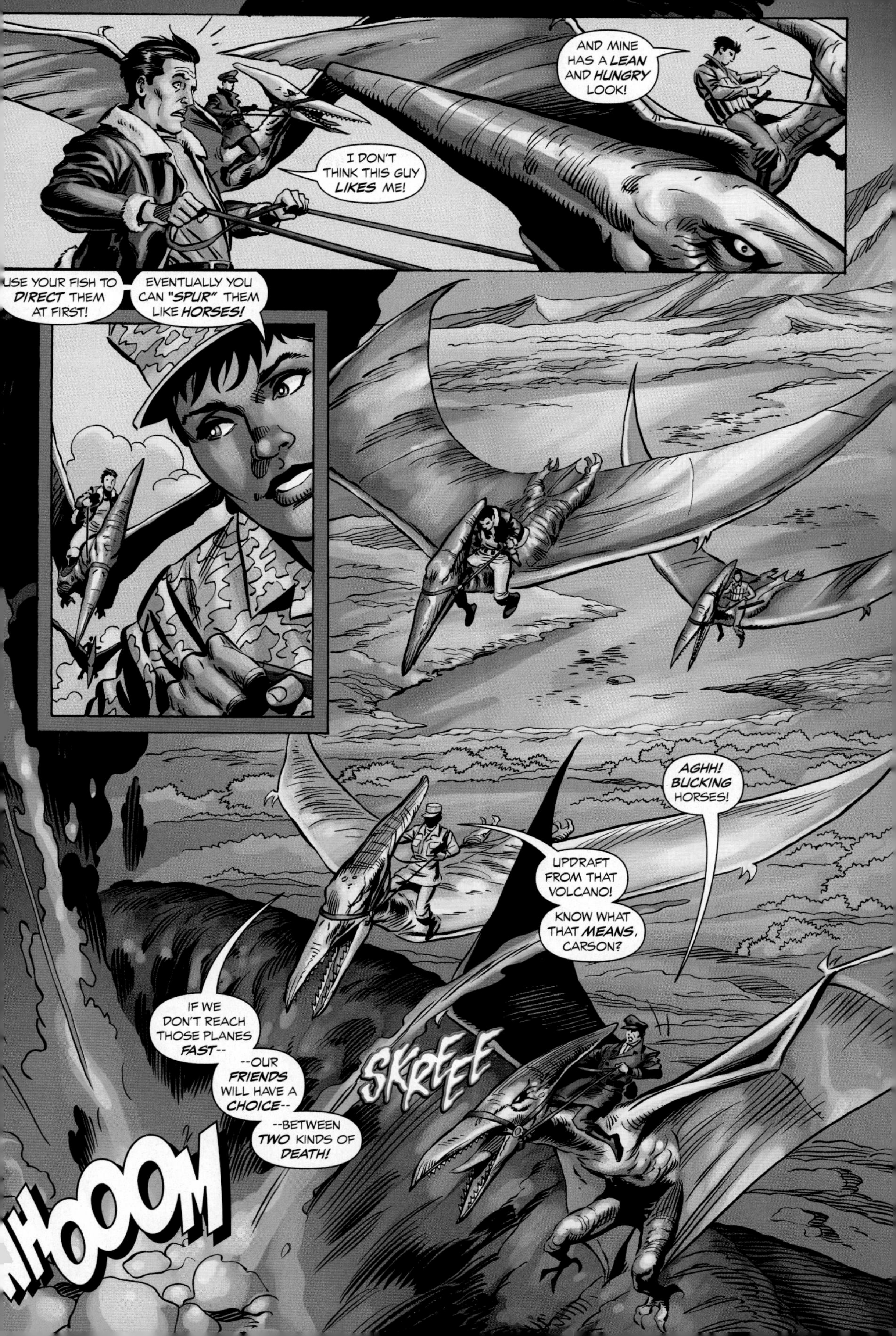

I DON'T THINK THIS GUY LIKES ME!
AND MINE HAS A LEAN AND HUNGRY LOOK!
USE YOUR FISH TO DIRECT THEM AT FIRST!
EVENTUALLY YOU CAN "SPUR" THEM LIKE HORSES!
AGHH! BUCKING HORSES!
UPDRAFT FROM THAT VOLCANO!
KNOW WHAT THAT MEANS, CARSON?
IF WE DON'T REACH THOSE PLANES FAST--
--OUR FRIENDS WILL HAVE A CHOICE--
--BETWEEN TWO KINDS OF DEATH!
SKREEE
WHOOOM

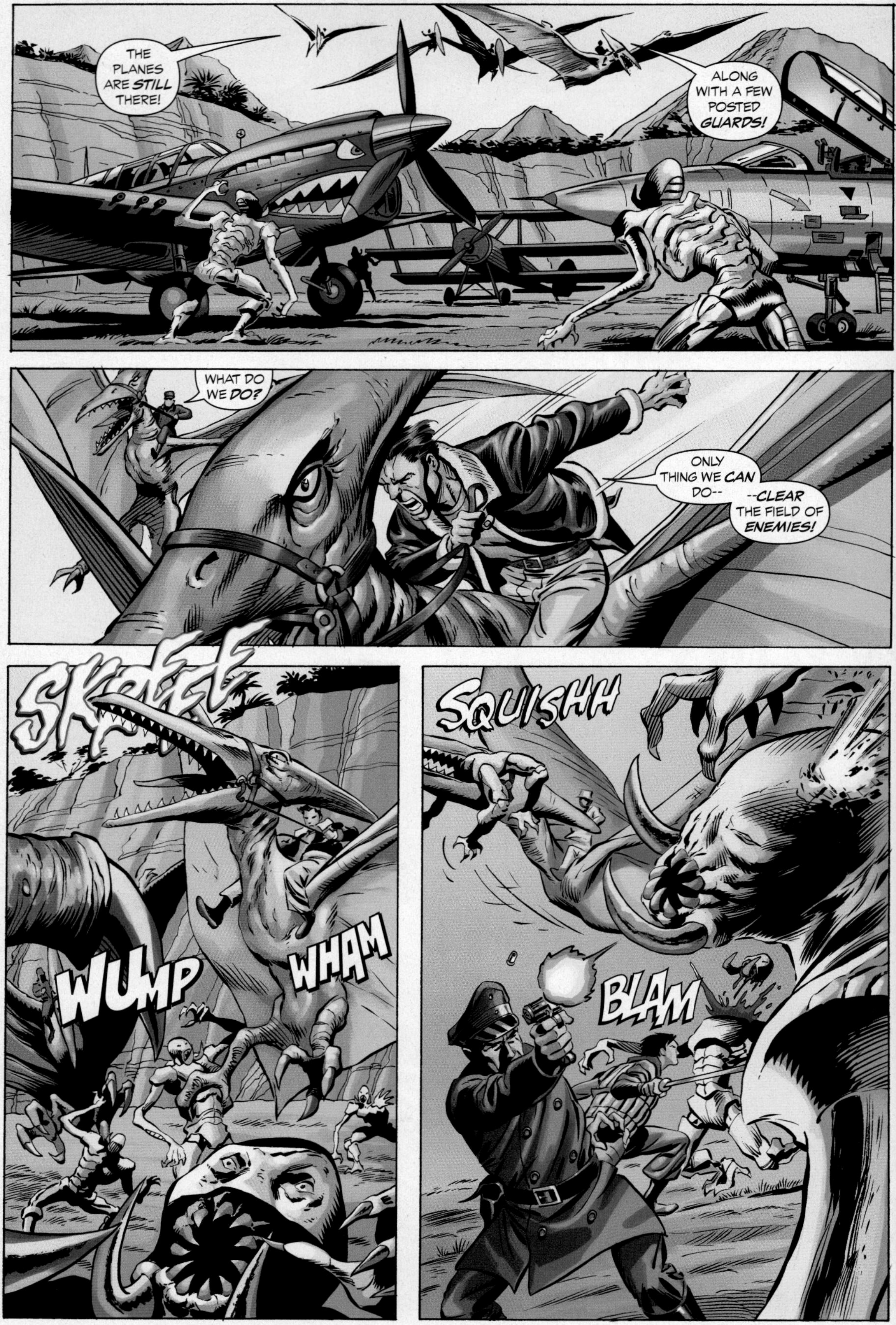
THE PLANES ARE STILL THERE!
ALONG WITH A FEW POSTED GUARDS!
WHAT DO WE DO?
ONLY THING WE CAN DO--
--CLEAR THE FIELD OF ENEMIES!
SQUISHH
WUMP
WHAM
BLAM

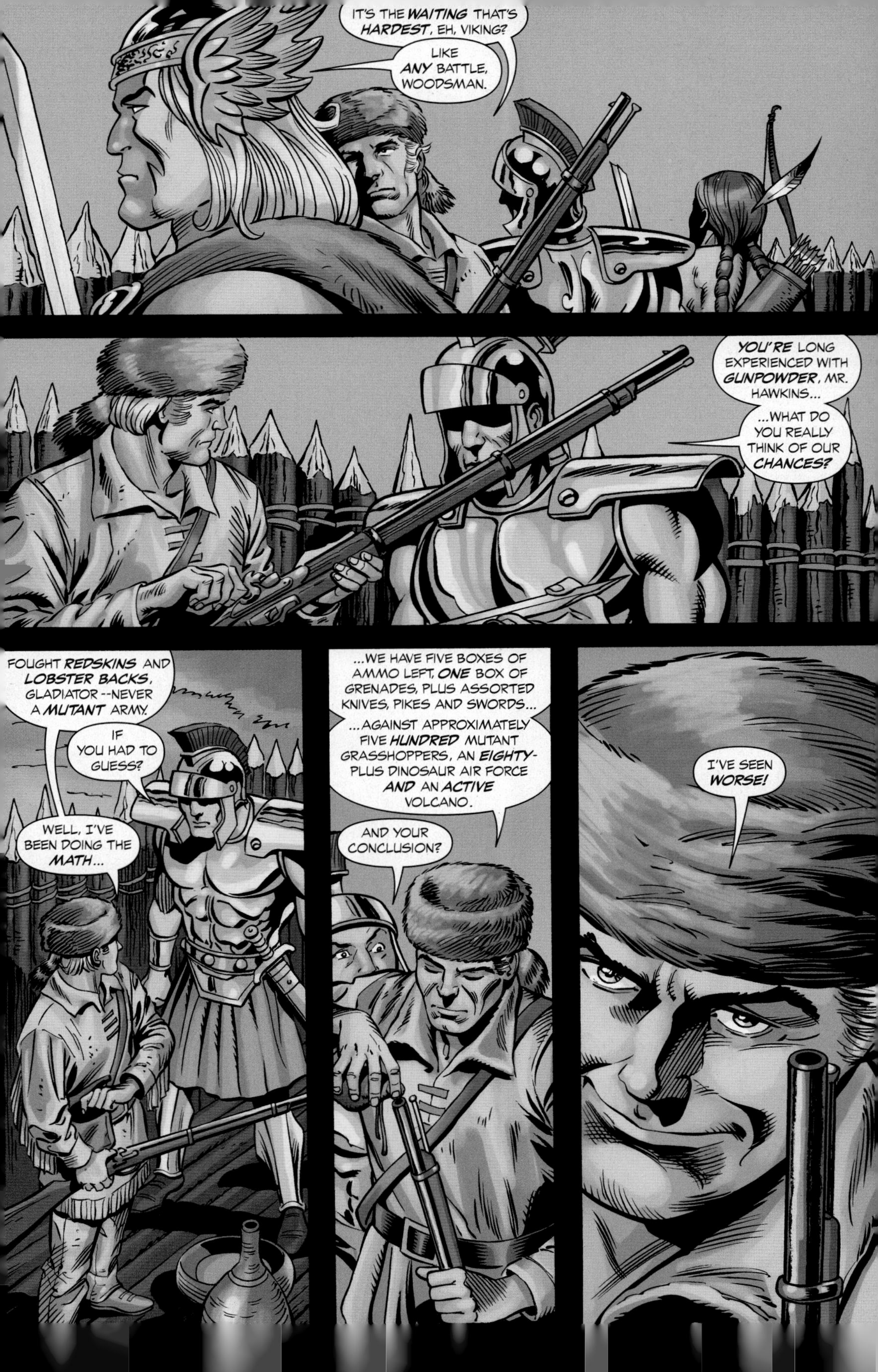
IT'S THE WAITING THAT'S HARDEST, EH, VIKING?
LIKE ANY BATTLE, WOODSMAN.
YOU'RE LONG EXPERIENCED WITH GUNPOWDER, MR. HAWKINS...
...WHAT DO YOU REALLY THINK OF OUR CHANCES?
FOUGHT REDSKINS AND LOBSTER BACKS, GLADIATOR --NEVER A MUTANT ARMY.
IF YOU HAD TO GUESS?
WELL, I'VE BEEN DOING THE MATH...
...WE HAVE FIVE BOXES OF AMMO LEFT, ONE BOX OF GRENADES, PLUS ASSORTED KNIVES, PIKES AND SWORDS...
...AGAINST APPROXIMATELY FIVE HUNDRED MUTANT GRASSHOPPERS, AN EIGHTY-PLUS DINOSAUR AIR FORCE AND AN ACTIVE VOLCANO.
AND YOUR CONCLUSION?
I'VE SEEN WORSE!

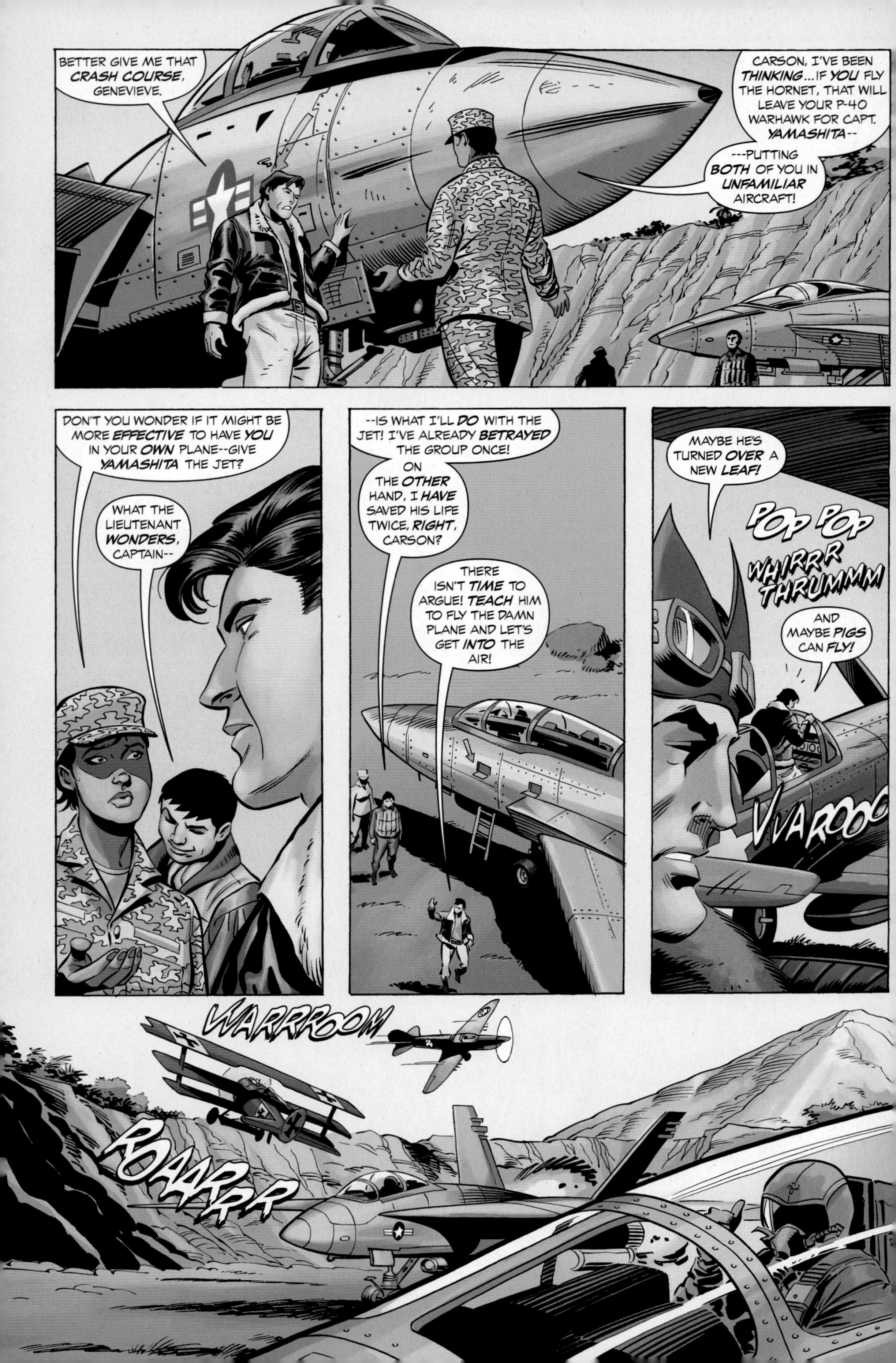

BETTER GIVE ME THAT CRASH COURSE, GENEVIEVE.
CARSON, I'VE BEEN THINKING...IF YOU FLY THE HORNET, THAT WILL LEAVE YOUR P-40 WARHAWK FOR CAPT. YAMASHITA--
---PUTTING BOTH OF YOU IN UNFAMILIAR AIRCRAFT!
DON'T YOU WONDER IF IT MIGHT BE MORE EFFECTIVE TO HAVE YOU IN YOUR OWN PLANE--GIVE YAMASHITA THE JET?
WHAT THE LIEUTENANT WONDERS, CAPTAIN--
--IS WHAT I'LL DO WITH THE JET! I'VE ALREADY BETRAYED THE GROUP ONCE!
ON THE OTHER HAND, I HAVE SAVED HIS LIFE TWICE, RIGHT, CARSON?
THERE ISN'T TIME TO ARGUE! TEACH HIM TO FLY THE DAMN PLANE AND LET'S GET INTO THE AIR!
MAYBE HE'S TURNED OVER A NEW LEAF!
POP POP
WHIRRR THRUMMM
AND MAYBE PIGS CAN FLY!
VVAROOO
WARRROOM
ROAARRR

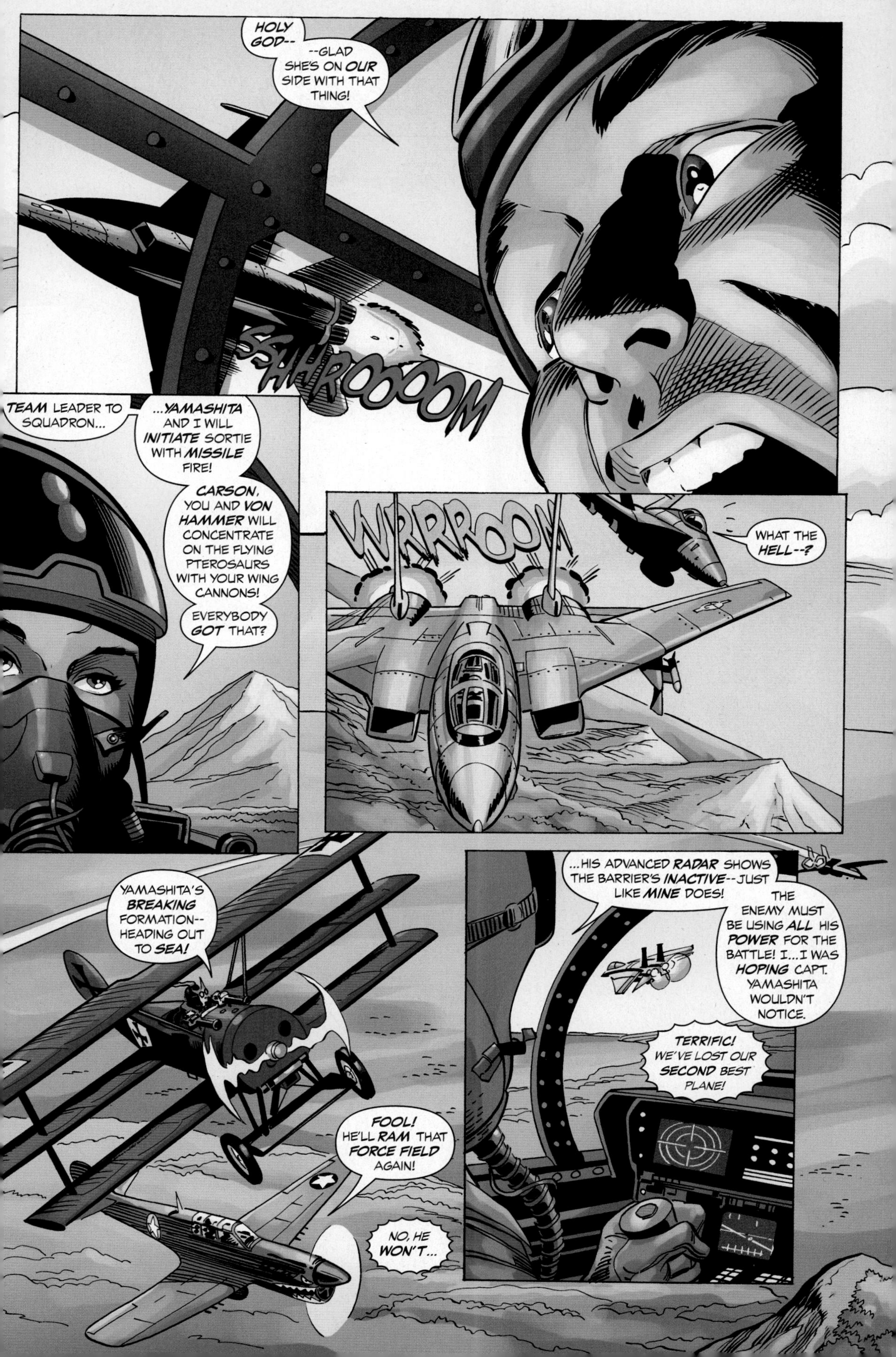
HOLY GOD--
--GLAD SHE'S ON OUR SIDE WITH THAT THING!
SSHHROOOOOM
TEAM LEADER TO SQUADRON...
...YAMASHITA AND I WILL INITIATE SORTIE WITH MISSILE FIRE!
CARSON, YOU AND VON HAMMER WILL CONCENTRATE ON THE FLYING PTEROSAURS WITH YOUR WING CANNONS!
EVERYBODY GOT THAT?
WRRROOM
WHAT THE HELL--?
YAMASHITA'S BREAKING FORMATION-- HEADING OUT TO SEA!
FOOL! HE'LL RAM THAT FORCE FIELD AGAIN!
NO, HE WON'T...
...HIS ADVANCED RADAR SHOWS THE BARRIER'S INACTIVE--JUST LIKE MINE DOES!
THE ENEMY MUST BE USING ALL HIS POWER FOR THE BATTLE! I...I WAS HOPING CAPT. YAMASHITA WOULDN'T NOTICE.
TERRIFIC! WE'VE LOST OUR SECOND BEST PLANE!

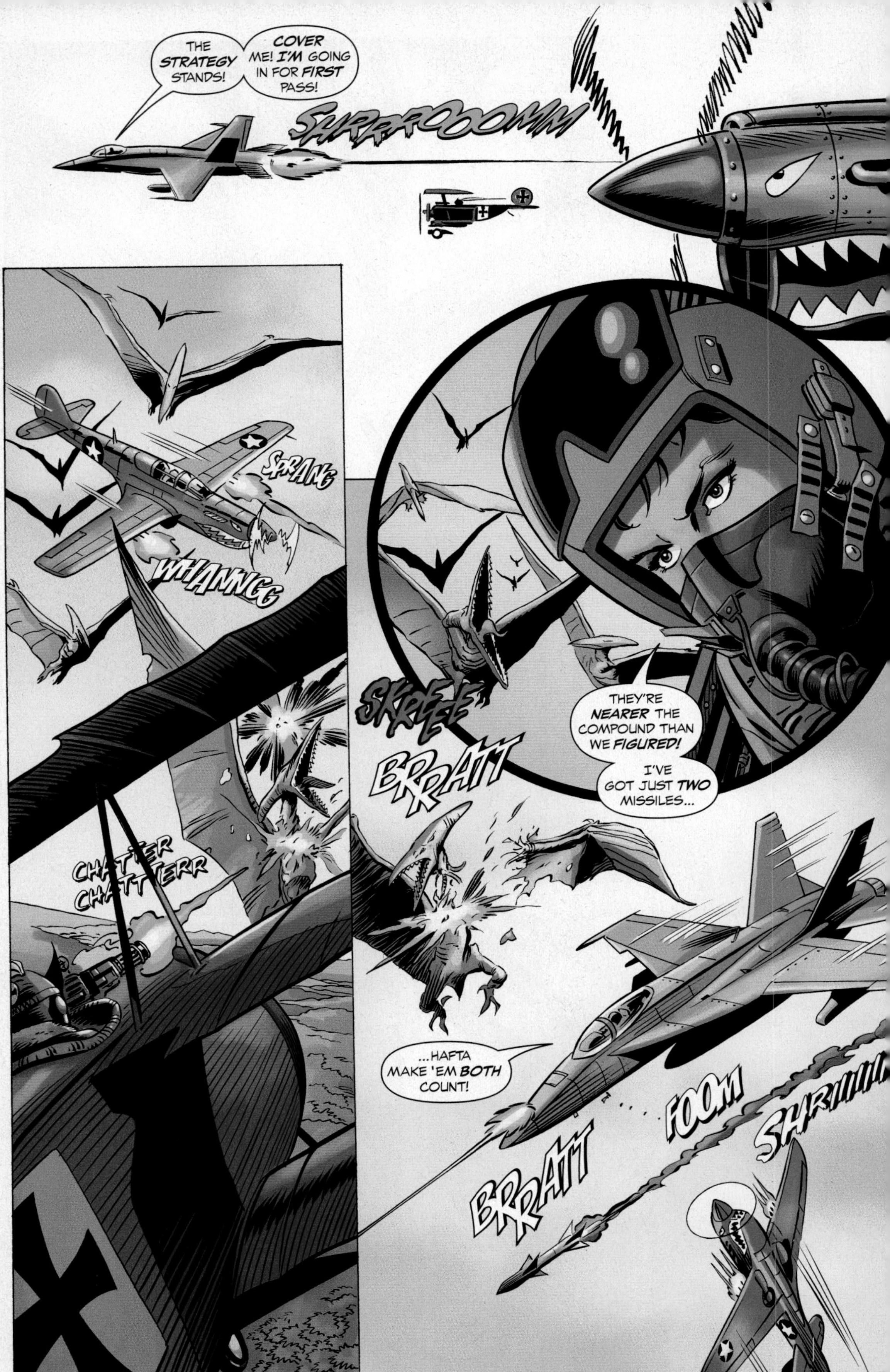
THE STRATEGY STANDS!
COVER ME! I'M GOING IN FOR FIRST PASS!
SHRRROOOOMM
SPRANG
WHANNGG
CHATTER CHATTERR
SKREEE
BRRATT
THEY'RE NEARER THE COMPOUND THAN WE FIGURED!
I'VE GOT JUST TWO MISSILES...
...HAFTA MAKE 'EM BOTH COUNT!
FOOM
SHRIIIII
BRRATT

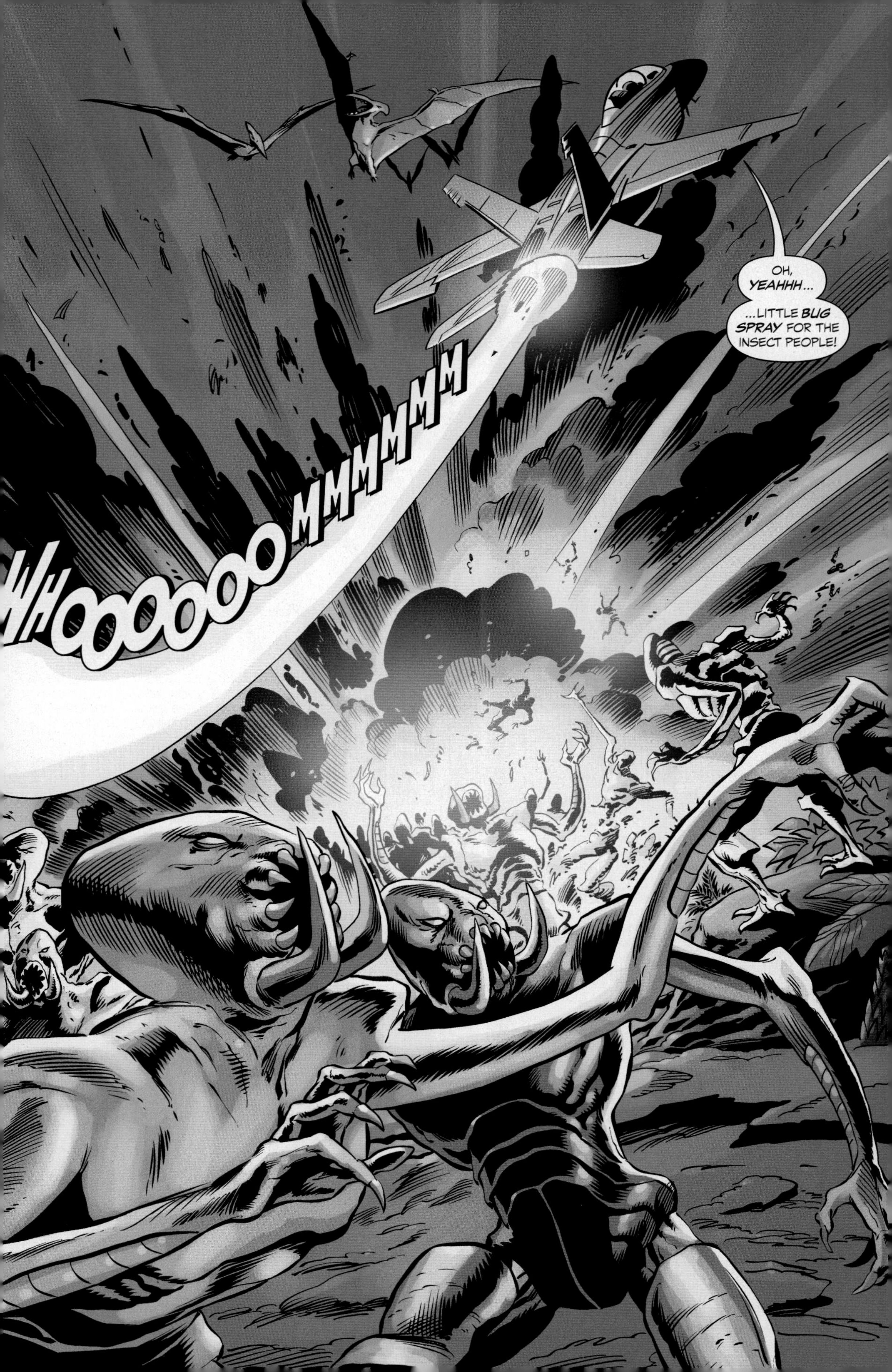

OH, YEAHHH...
...LITTLE BUG SPRAY FOR THE INSECT PEOPLE!
WHOOOOOOMMMMMMMM

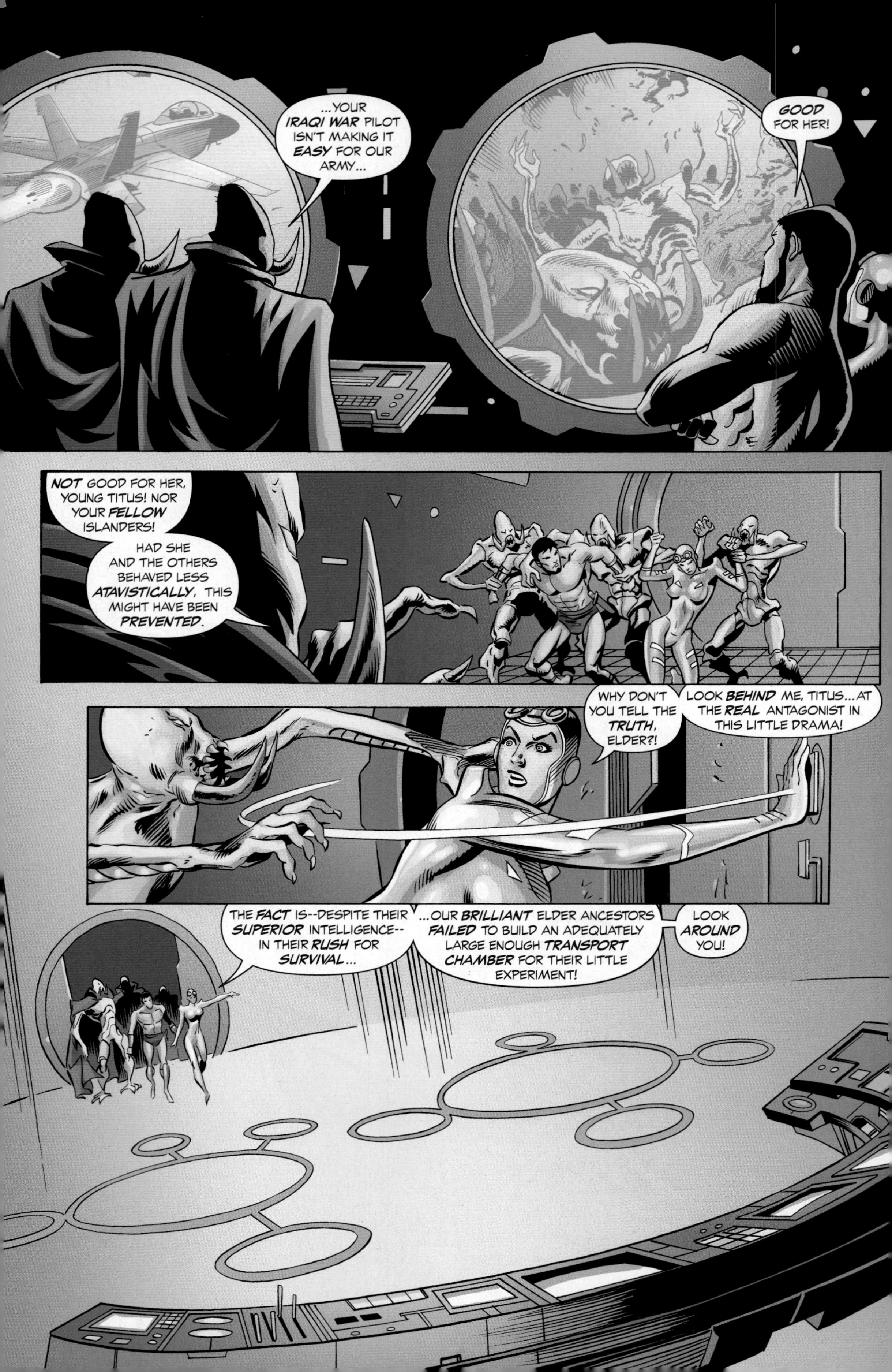
...YOUR IRAQI WAR PILOT ISN'T MAKING IT EASY FOR OUR ARMY...
GOOD FOR HER!
NOT GOOD FOR HER, YOUNG TITUS! NOR YOUR FELLOW ISLANDERS!
HAD SHE AND THE OTHERS BEHAVED LESS ATAVISTICALLY, THIS MIGHT HAVE BEEN PREVENTED.
WHY DON'T YOU TELL THE TRUTH, ELDER?!
LOOK BEHIND ME, TITUS...AT THE REAL ANTAGONIST IN THIS LITTLE DRAMA!
THE FACT IS--DESPITE THEIR SUPERIOR INTELLIGENCE-- IN THEIR RUSH FOR SURVIVAL...
...OUR BRILLIANT ELDER ANCESTORS FAILED TO BUILD AN ADEQUATELY LARGE ENOUGH TRANSPORT CHAMBER FOR THEIR LITTLE EXPERIMENT!
LOOK AROUND YOU!

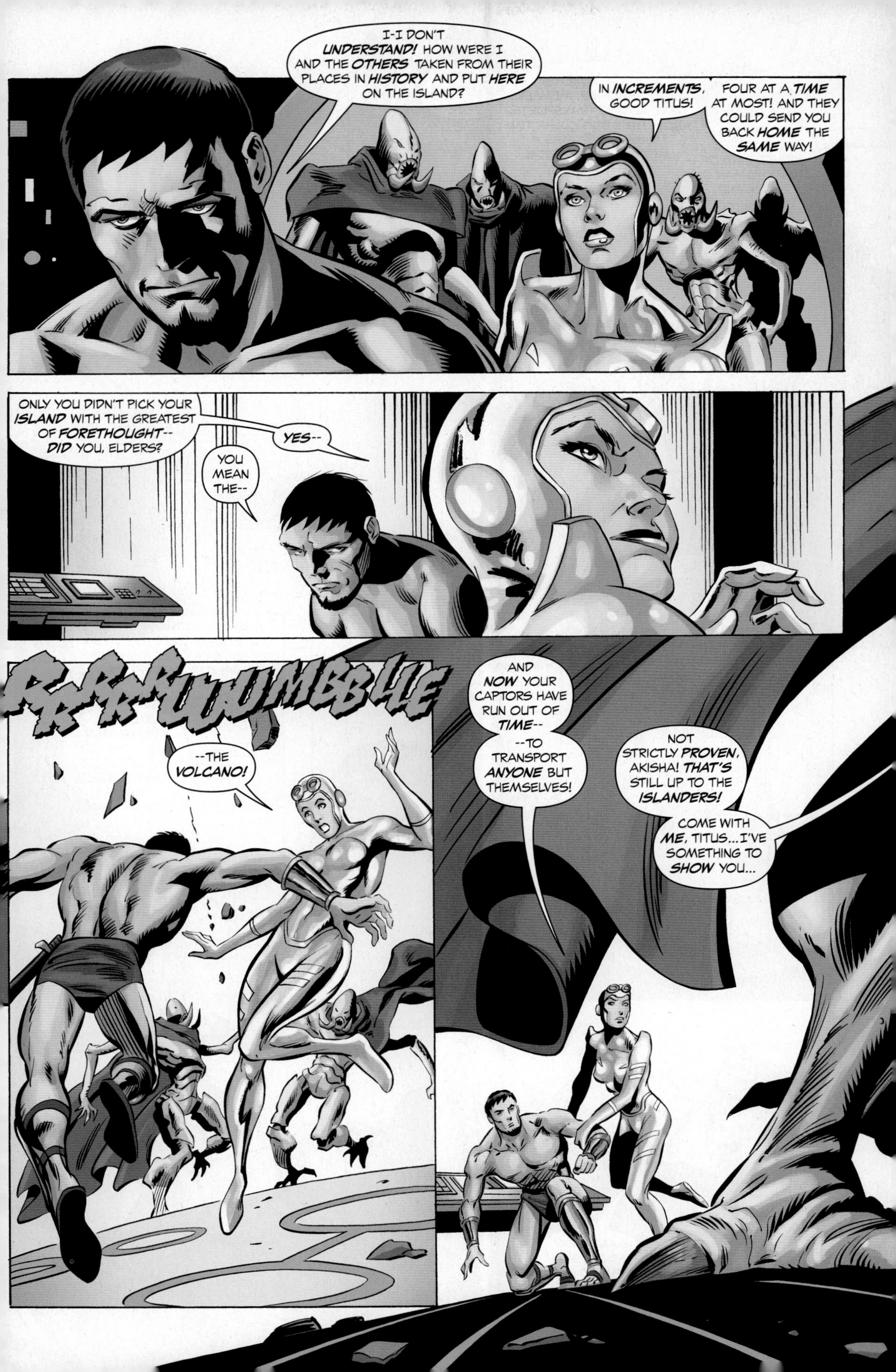
I-I DON'T UNDERSTAND! HOW WERE I AND THE OTHERS TAKEN FROM THEIR PLACES IN HISTORY AND PUT HERE ON THE ISLAND?
IN INCREMENTS, GOOD TITUS!
FOUR AT A TIME AT MOST! AND THEY COULD SEND YOU BACK HOME THE SAME WAY!
ONLY YOU DIDN'T PICK YOUR ISLAND WITH THE GREATEST OF FORETHOUGHT-- DID YOU, ELDERS?
YES--
YOU MEAN THE--
RRRRRUUUMBBLLE
--THE VOLCANO!
AND NOW YOUR CAPTORS HAVE RUN OUT OF TIME--
--TO TRANSPORT ANYONE BUT THEMSELVES!
NOT STRICTLY PROVEN, AKISHA! THAT'S STILL UP TO THE ISLANDERS!
COME WITH ME, TITUS...I'VE SOMETHING TO SHOW YOU...

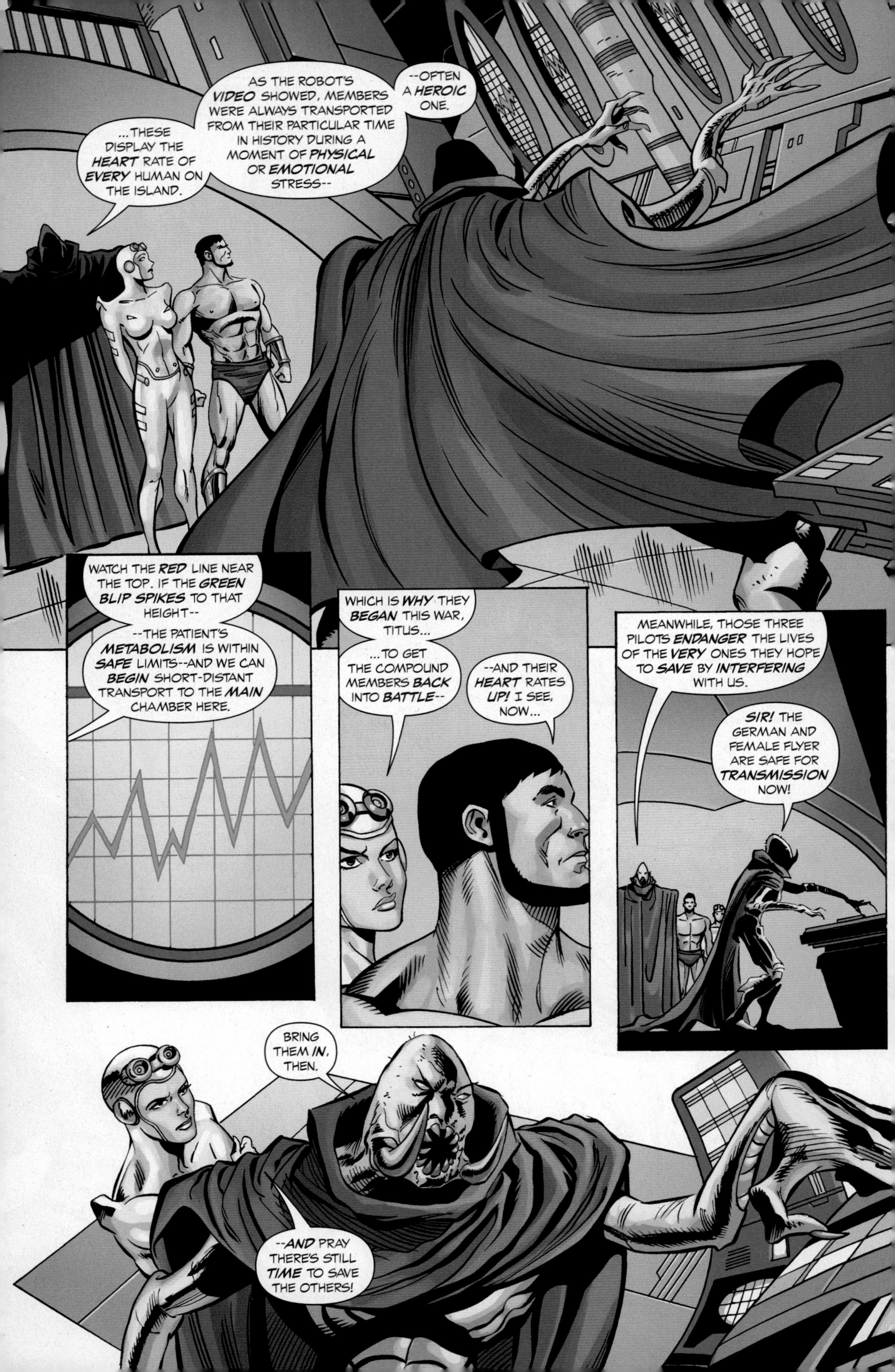
...THESE DISPLAY THE HEART RATE OF EVERY HUMAN ON THE ISLAND.
AS THE ROBOT'S VIDEO SHOWED, MEMBERS WERE ALWAYS TRANSPORTED FROM THEIR PARTICULAR TIME IN HISTORY DURING A MOMENT OF PHYSICAL OR EMOTIONAL STRESS--
--OFTEN A HEROIC ONE.
WATCH THE RED LINE NEAR THE TOP. IF THE GREEN BLIP SPIKES TO THAT HEIGHT--
--THE PATIENT'S METABOLISM IS WITHIN SAFE LIMITS--AND WE CAN BEGIN SHORT-DISTANT TRANSPORT TO THE MAIN CHAMBER HERE.
WHICH IS WHY THEY BEGAN THIS WAR, TITUS...
...TO GET THE COMPOUND MEMBERS BACK INTO BATTLE--
--AND THEIR HEART RATES UP! I SEE, NOW...
MEANWHILE, THOSE THREE PILOTS ENDANGER THE LIVES OF THE VERY ONES THEY HOPE TO SAVE BY INTERFERING WITH US.
SIR! THE GERMAN AND FEMALE FLYER ARE SAFE FOR TRANSMISSION NOW!
BRING THEM IN, THEN.
--AND PRAY THERE'S STILL TIME TO SAVE THE OTHERS!

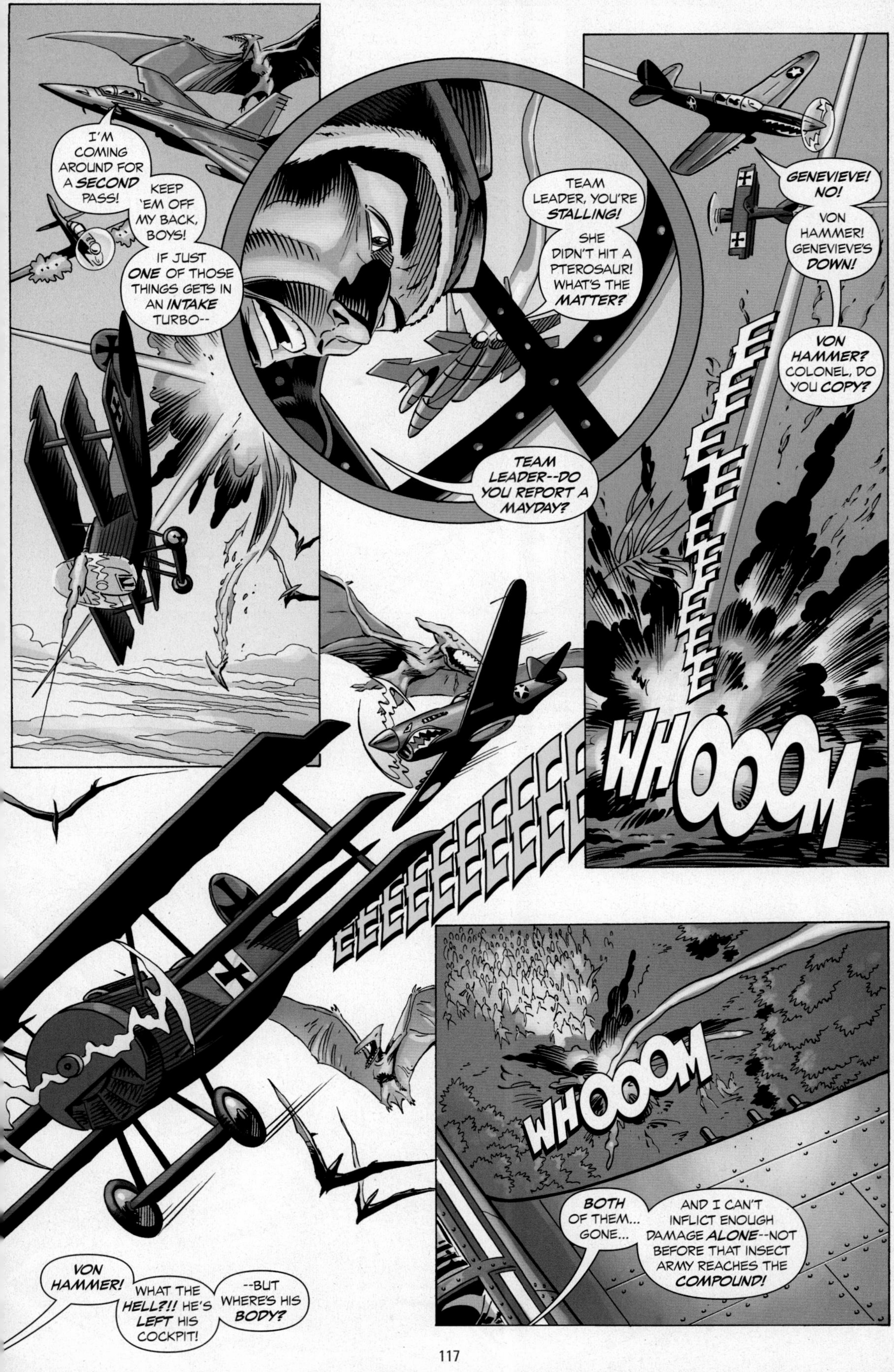

I'M COMING AROUND FOR A SECOND PASS!
KEEP 'EM OFF MY BACK, BOYS!
IF JUST ONE OF THOSE THINGS GETS IN AN INTAKE TURBO--
TEAM LEADER, YOU'RE STALLING!
SHE DIDN'T HIT A PTEROSAUR! WHAT'S THE MATTER?
TEAM LEADER--DO YOU REPORT A MAYDAY?
GENEVIEVE! NO!
VON HAMMER! GENEVIEVE'S DOWN!
VON HAMMER? COLONEL, DO YOU COPY?
EEEEEEEEEEEEEEEEEEEEEEEE
WHOOOM
VON HAMMER!
WHAT THE HELL?!! HE'S LEFT HIS COCKPIT!
--BUT WHERE'S HIS BODY?
WHOOOM
BOTH OF THEM... GONE...
AND I CAN'T INFLICT ENOUGH DAMAGE ALONE--NOT BEFORE THAT INSECT ARMY REACHES THE COMPOUND!

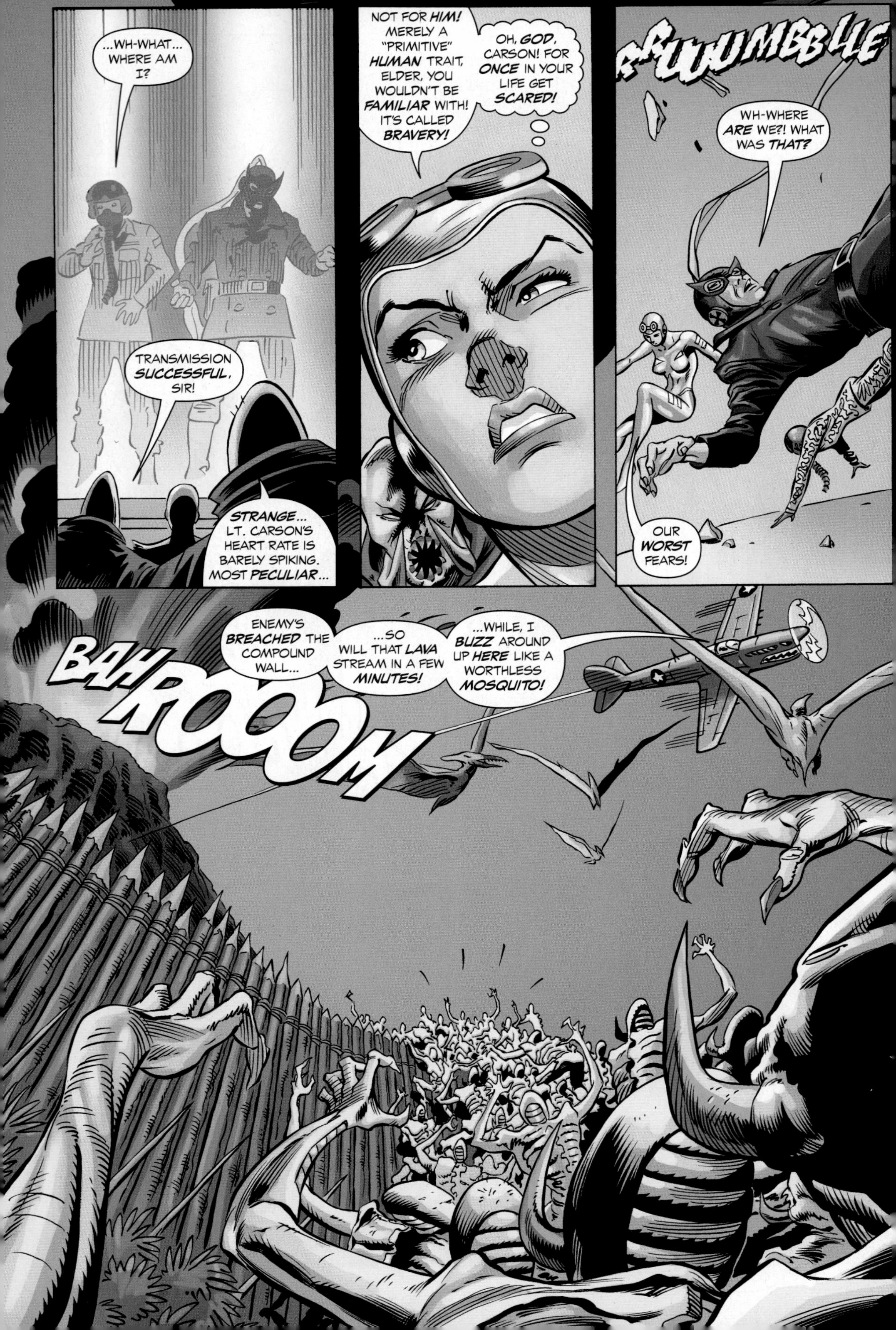
...WH-WHAT... WHERE AM I?
TRANSMISSION SUCCESSFUL, SIR!
STRANGE... LT. CARSON'S HEART RATE IS BARELY SPIKING. MOST PECULIAR...
NOT FOR HIM! MERELY A "PRIMITIVE" HUMAN TRAIT, ELDER, YOU WOULDN'T BE FAMILIAR WITH! IT'S CALLED BRAVERY!
OH, GOD, CARSON! FOR ONCE IN YOUR LIFE GET SCARED!
RRUUUMBBLLE
WH-WHERE ARE WE?! WHAT WAS THAT?
OUR WORST FEARS!
BAHROOOM
ENEMY'S BREACHED THE COMPOUND WALL...
...SO WILL THAT LAVA STREAM IN A FEW MINUTES!
...WHILE, I BUZZ AROUND UP HERE LIKE A WORTHLESS MOSQUITO!

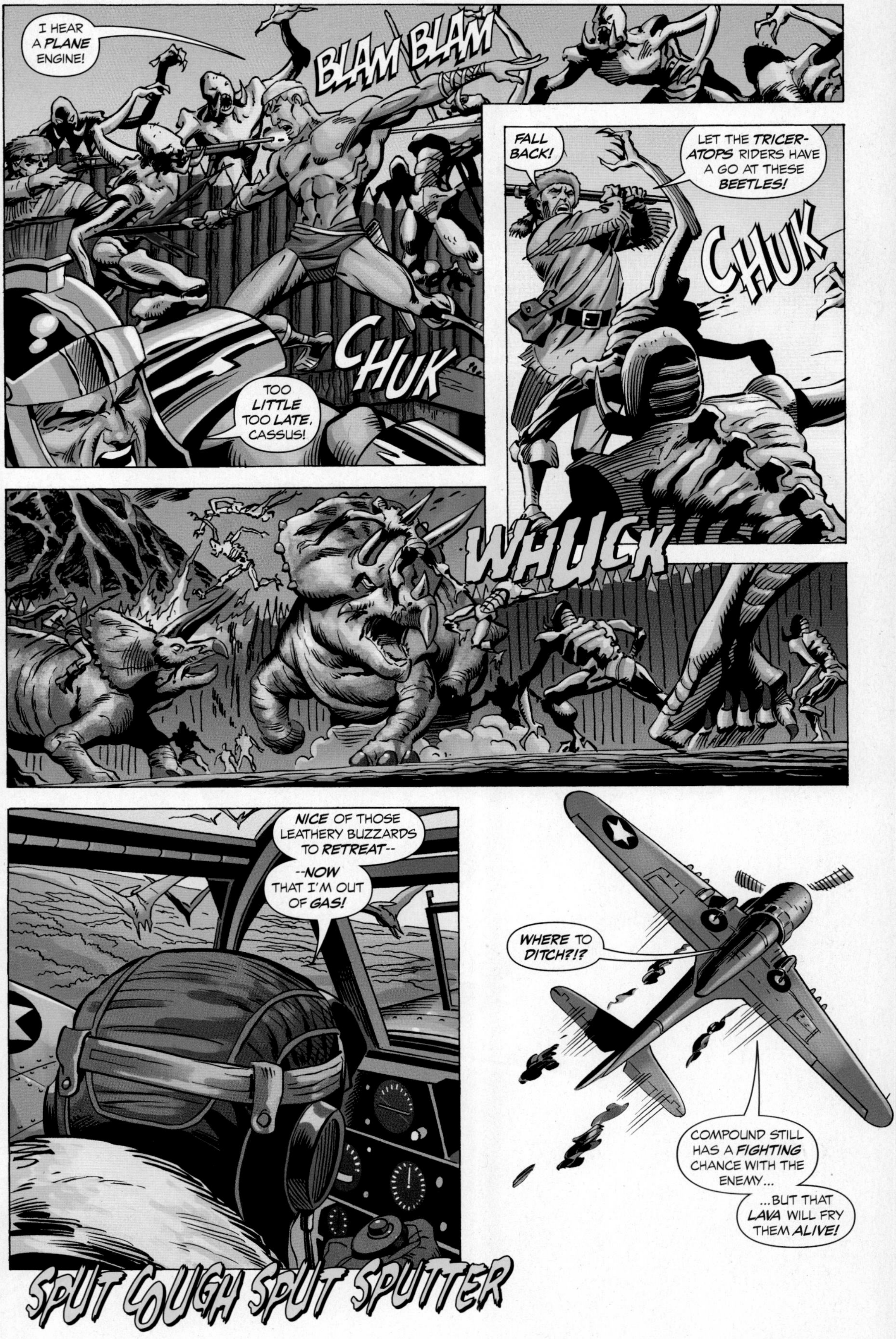
I HEAR A PLANE ENGINE!
BLAM BLAM
CHUK
TOO LITTLE TOO LATE, CASSUS!
FALL BACK!
LET THE TRICER-ATOPS RIDERS HAVE A GO AT THESE BEETLES!
CHUK
WHUCK
NICE OF THOSE LEATHERY BUZZARDS TO RETREAT--
--NOW THAT I'M OUT OF GAS!
SPUT COUGH SPUT SPUTTER
WHERE TO DITCH?!?
COMPOUND STILL HAS A FIGHTING CHANCE WITH THE ENEMY...
...BUT THAT LAVA WILL FRY THEM ALIVE!

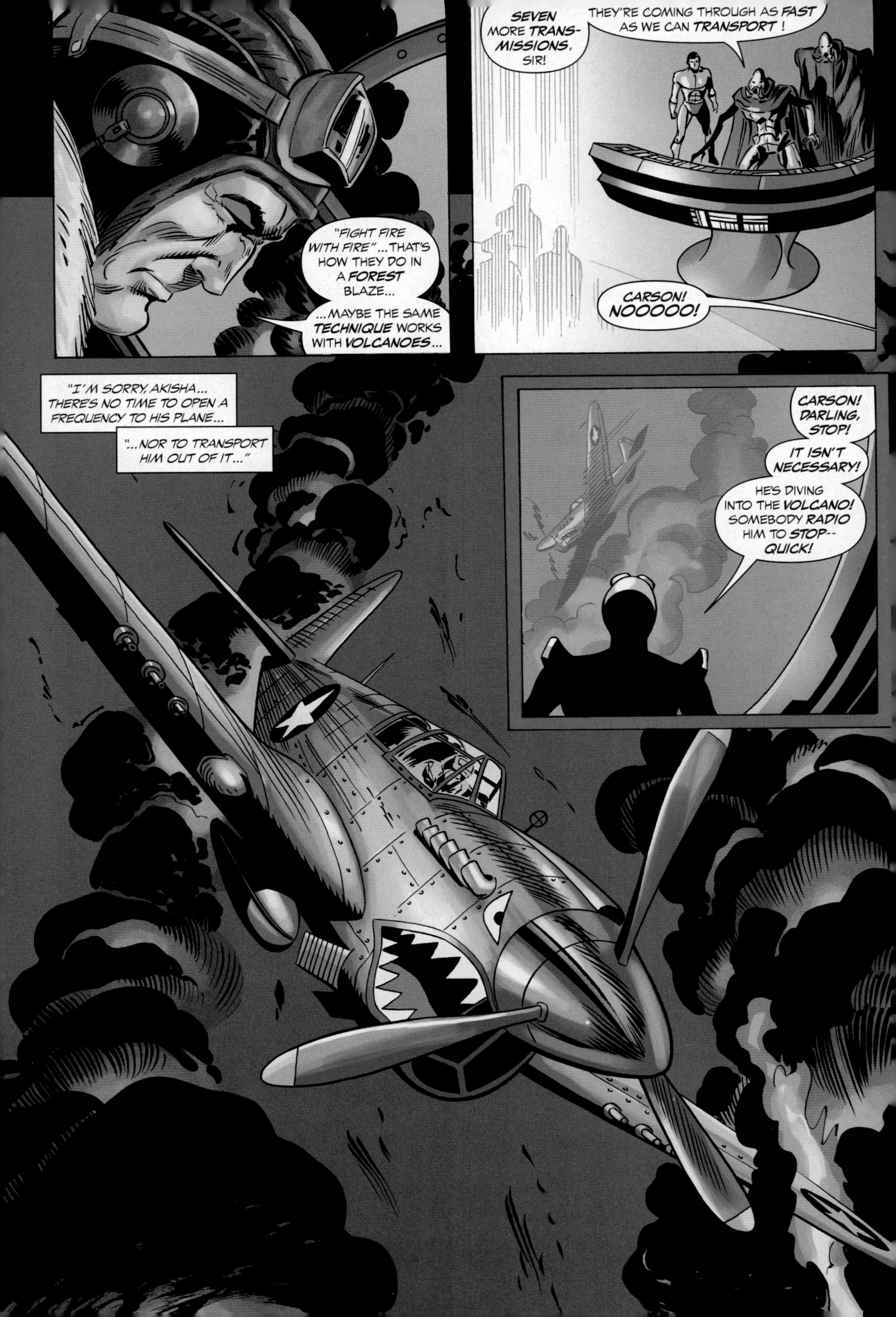
"FIGHT FIRE WITH FIRE"...THAT'S HOW THEY DO IN A FOREST BLAZE...
...MAYBE THE SAME TECHNIQUE WORKS WITH VOLCANOES...
SEVEN MORE TRANS-MISSIONS, SIR!
THEY'RE COMING THROUGH AS FAST AS WE CAN TRANSPORT!
CARSON! NOOOOO!
"I'M SORRY, AKISHA... THERE'S NO TIME TO OPEN A FREQUENCY TO HIS PLANE...
"...NOR TO TRANSPORT HIM OUT OF IT..."
CARSON! DARLING, STOP!
IT ISN'T NECESSARY!
HE'S DIVING INTO THE VOLCANO! SOMEBODY RADIO HIM TO STOP-- QUICK!

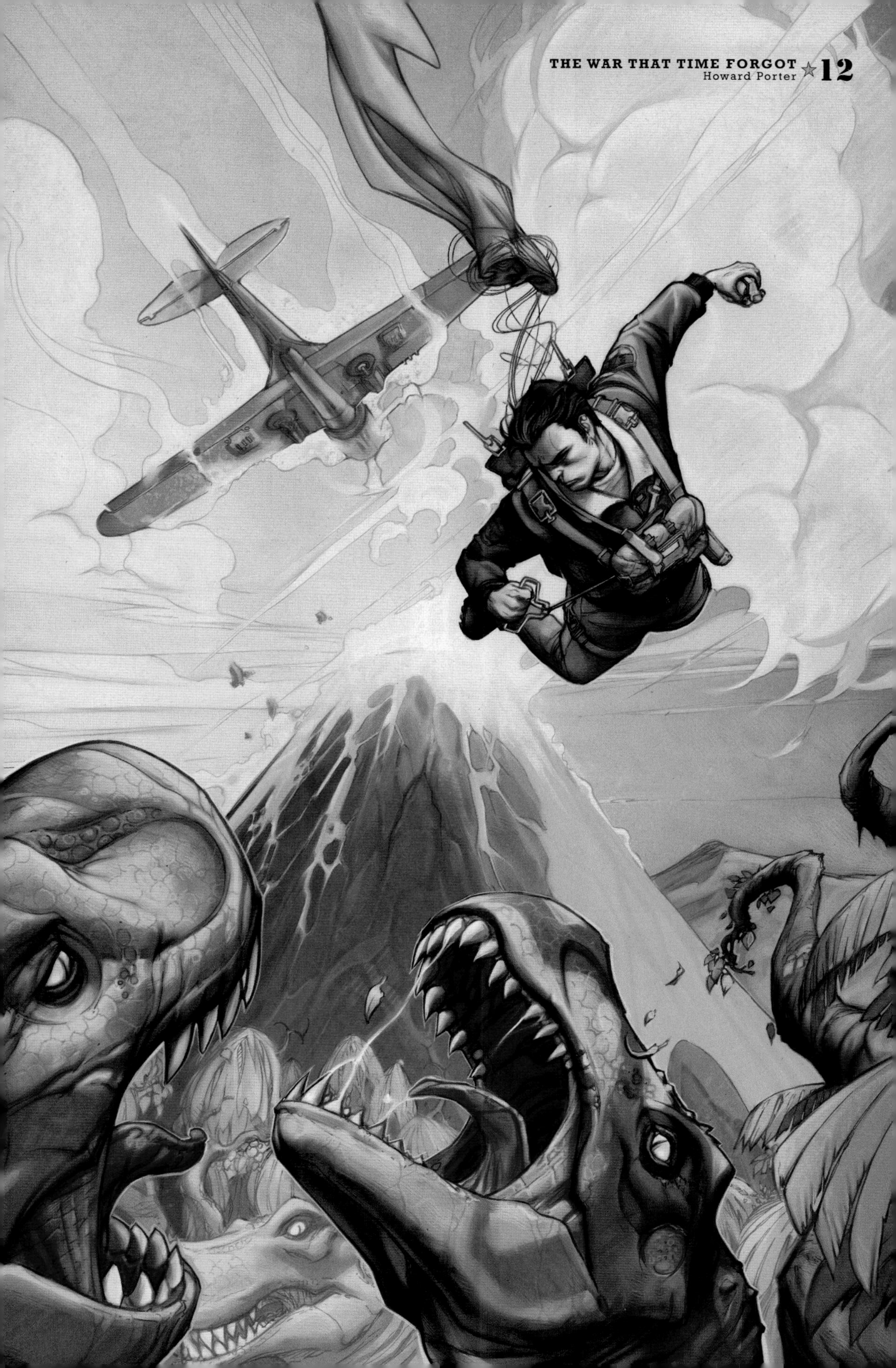

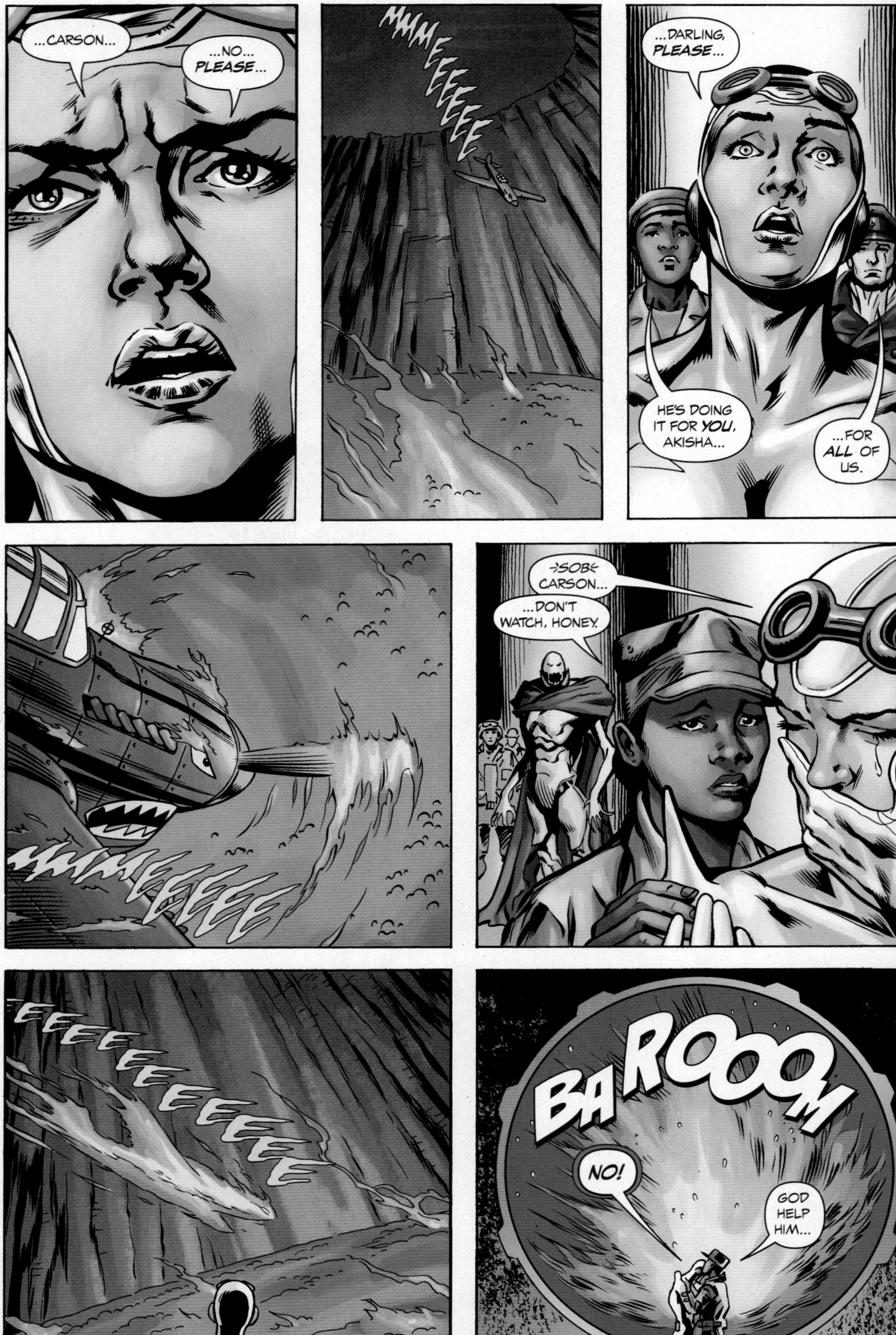
...CARSON...
...NO... PLEASE...
MMMEEEEEE
...DARLING, PLEASE...
HE'S DOING IT FOR YOU, AKISHA...
...FOR ALL OF US.
MMMEEEEEE
-SOB- CARSON...
...DON'T WATCH, HONEY.
EEEEEEEEEEEEEEEE
BAROOOM
NO!
GOD HELP HIM...

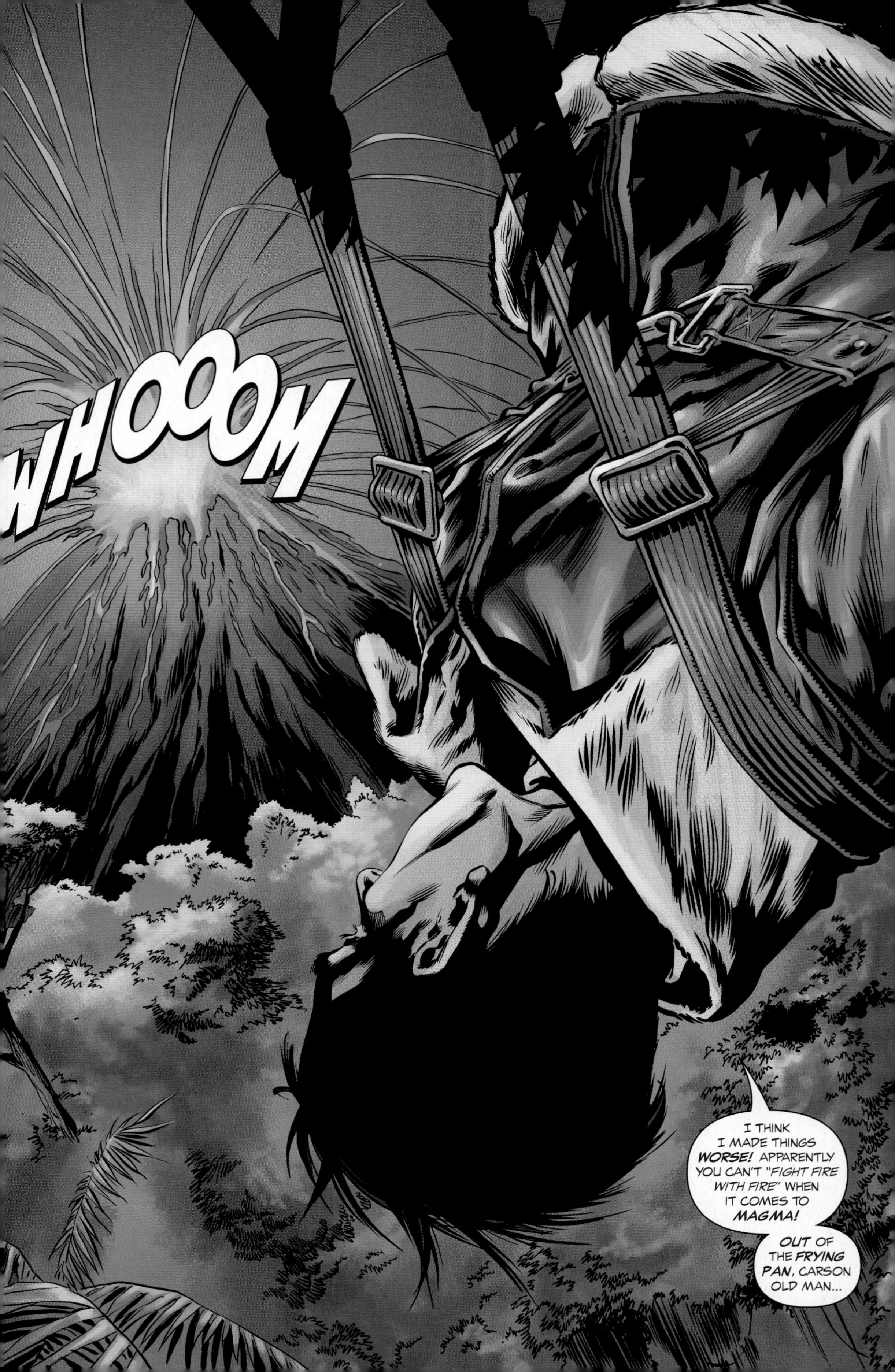
WHOOOM
I THINK I MADE THINGS WORSE! APPARENTLY YOU CAN'T "FIGHT FIRE WITH FIRE" WHEN IT COMES TO MAGMA!
OUT OF THE FRYING PAN, CARSON OLD MAN...

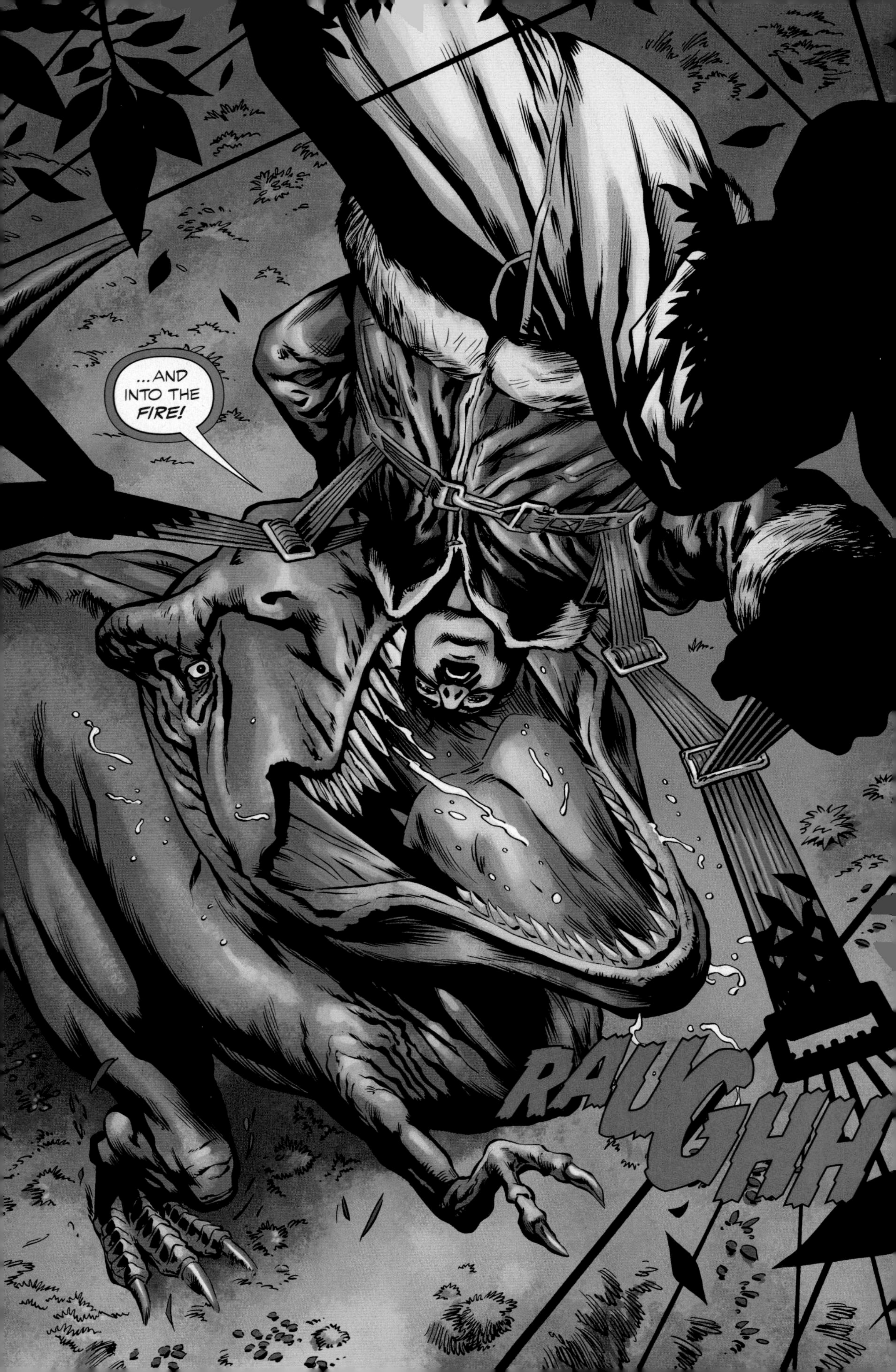
...AND INTO THE FIRE!
RAUGHH

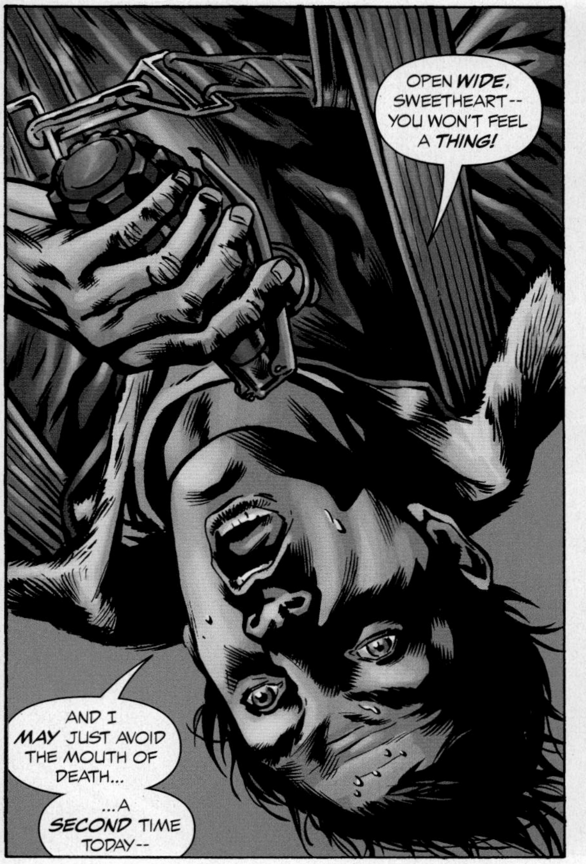
OPEN WIDE, SWEETHEART-- YOU WON'T FEEL A THING!
AND I MAY JUST AVOID THE MOUTH OF DEATH...
...A SECOND TIME TODAY--

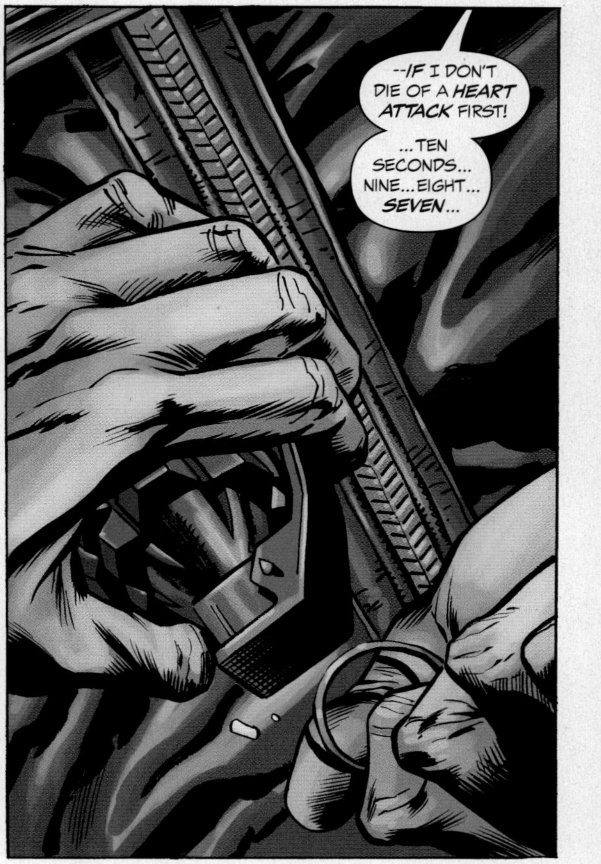
--IF I DON'T DIE OF A HEART ATTACK FIRST!
...TEN SECONDS... NINE...EIGHT... SEVEN...

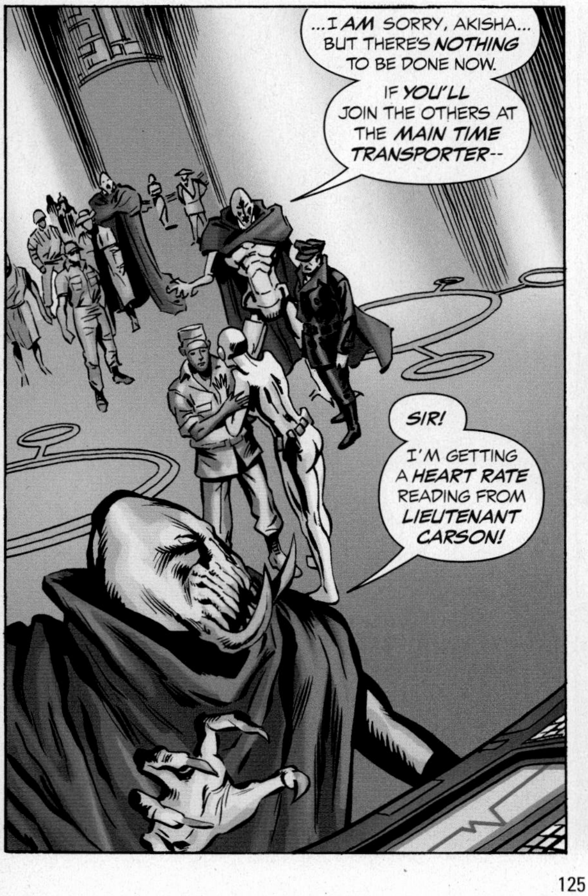
...I AM SORRY, AKISHA... BUT THERE'S NOTHING TO BE DONE NOW.
IF YOU'LL JOIN THE OTHERS AT THE MAIN TIME TRANSPORTER--
SIR!
I'M GETTING A HEART RATE READING FROM LIEUTENANT CARSON!

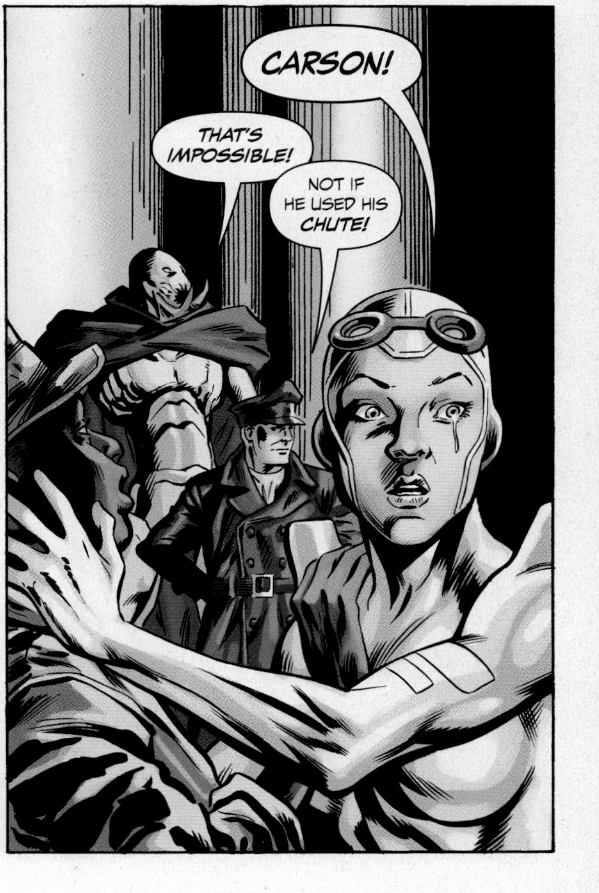
CARSON!
THAT'S IMPOSSIBLE!
NOT IF HE USED HIS CHUTE!

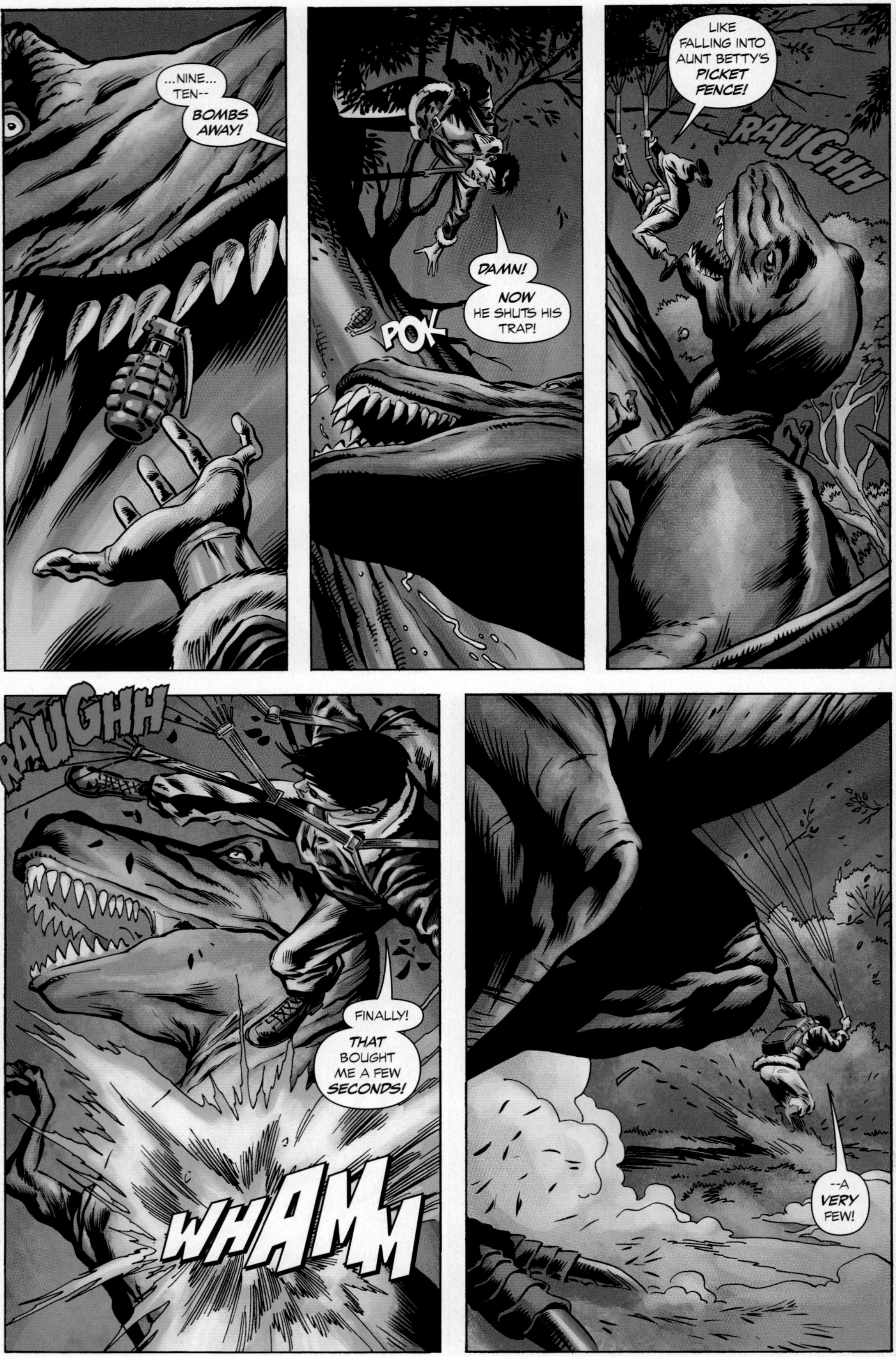
...NINE... TEN-- BOMBS AWAY!
DAMN! NOW HE SHUTS HIS TRAP!
POK
LIKE FALLING INTO AUNT BETTY'S PICKET FENCE!
RAUGHH
RAUGHH
FINALLY! THAT BOUGHT ME A FEW SECONDS!
WHAMM
--A VERY FEW!

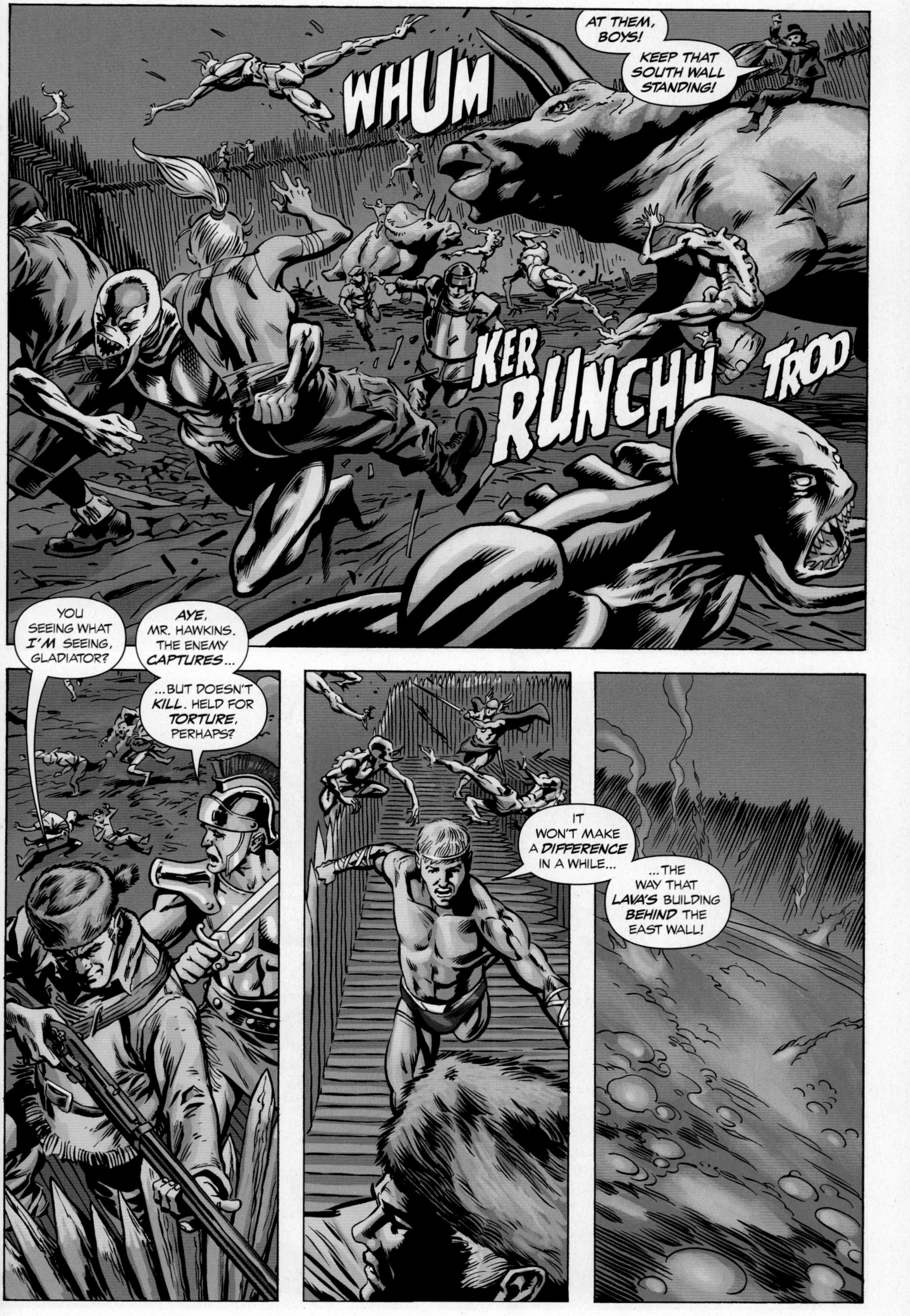
AT THEM, BOYS!
KEEP THAT SOUTH WALL STANDING!
WHUM
KER RUNCHU
TROD
YOU SEEING WHAT I'M SEEING, GLADIATOR?
AYE, MR. HAWKINS. THE ENEMY CAPTURES...
...BUT DOESN'T KILL. HELD FOR TORTURE, PERHAPS?
IT WON'T MAKE A DIFFERENCE IN A WHILE...
...THE WAY THAT LAVA'S BUILDING BEHIND THE EAST WALL!

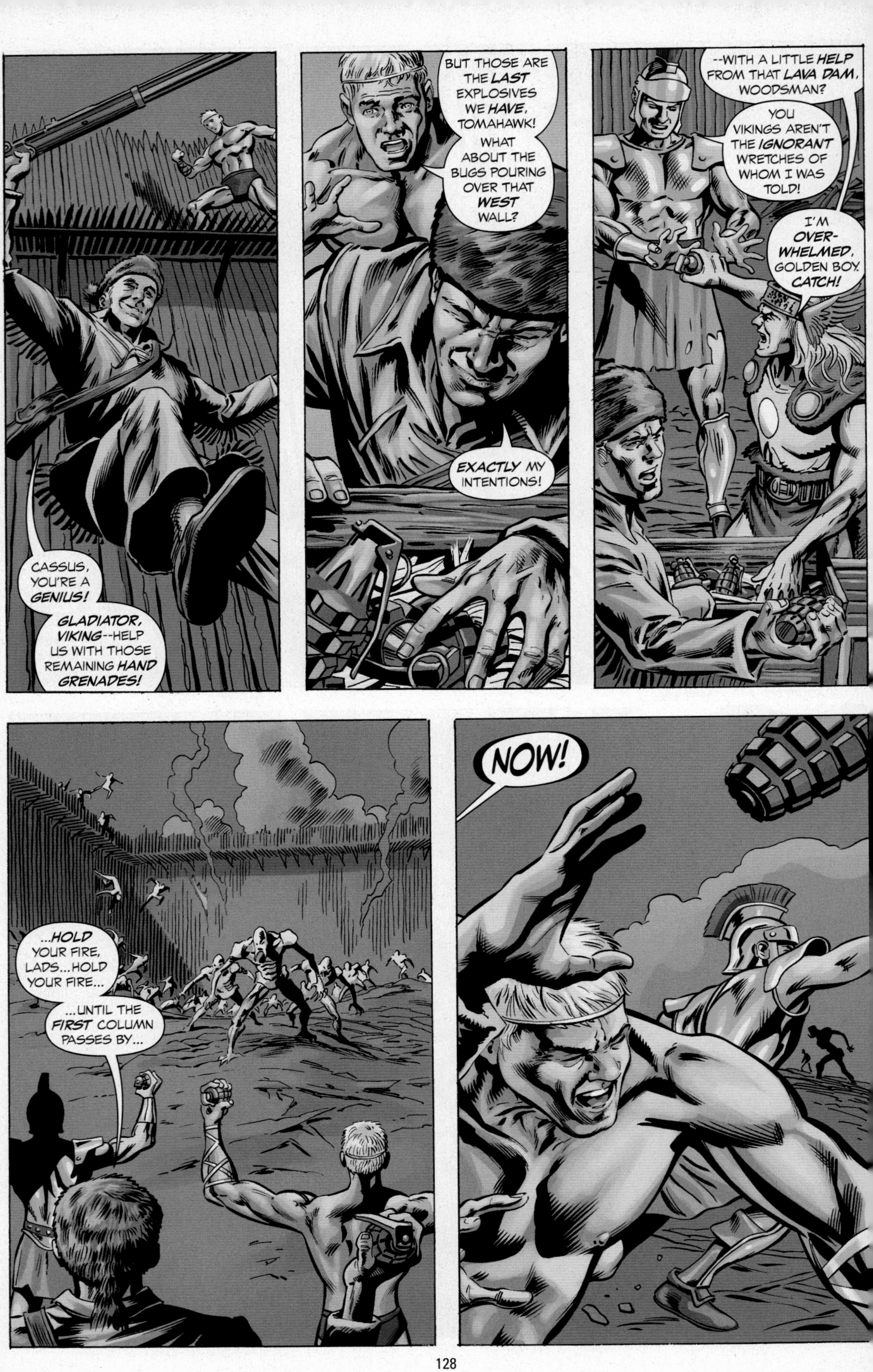
BUT THOSE ARE THE LAST EXPLOSIVES WE HAVE, TOMAHAWK!
WHAT ABOUT THE BUGS POURING OVER THAT WEST WALL?
EXACTLY MY INTENTIONS!
CASSUS, YOU'RE A GENIUS!
GLADIATOR, VIKING--HELP US WITH THOSE REMAINING HAND GRENADES!
--WITH A LITTLE HELP FROM THAT LAVA DAM, WOODSMAN?
YOU VIKINGS AREN'T THE IGNORANT WRETCHES OF WHOM I WAS TOLD!
I'M OVER-WHELMED, GOLDEN BOY. CATCH!
...HOLD YOUR FIRE, LADS...HOLD YOUR FIRE...
...UNTIL THE FIRST COLUMN PASSES BY...
NOW!

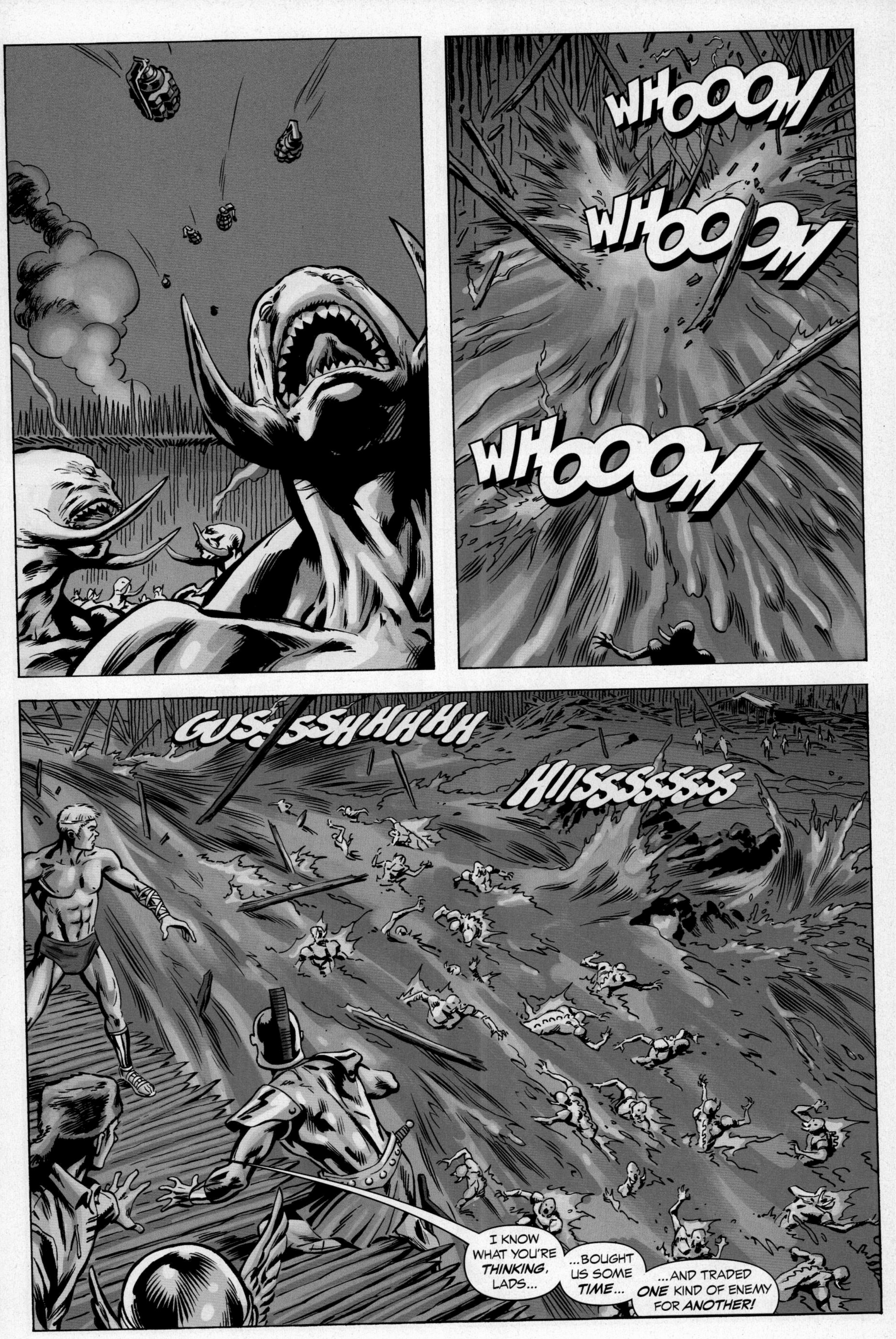
WHOOOM
WHOOOOM
WHOOOM
GUSSSSHHHHH
HIISSSSSSSS
I KNOW WHAT YOU'RE *THINKING,* LADS...
...BOUGHT US SOME *TIME...*
...AND TRADED *ONE* KIND OF ENEMY FOR *ANOTHER!*

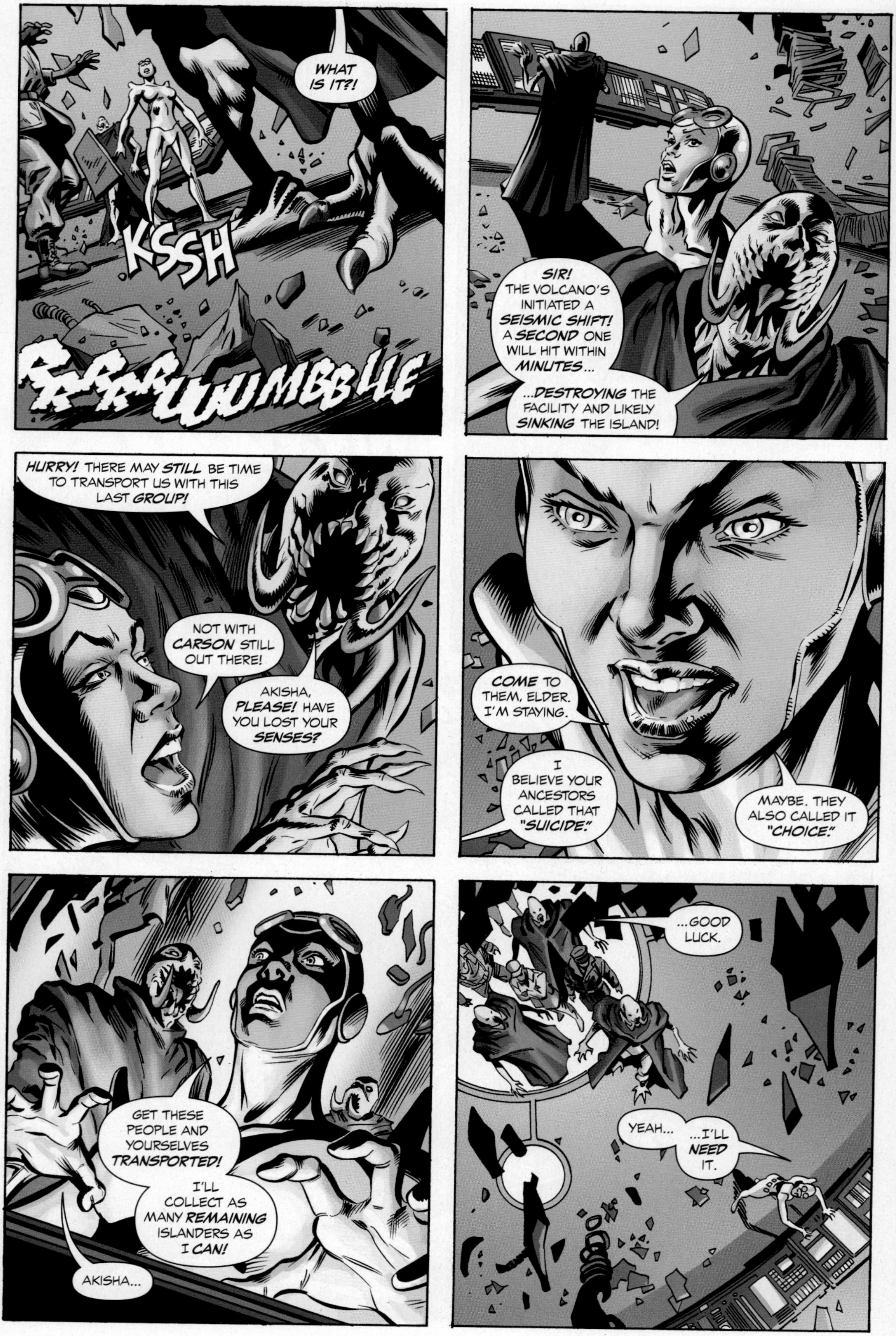

WHAT IS IT?!
KSSH
RRRRUUUMBBLLE
SIR! THE VOLCANO'S INITIATED A SEISMIC SHIFT! A SECOND ONE WILL HIT WITHIN MINUTES...
...DESTROYING THE FACILITY AND LIKELY SINKING THE ISLAND!
HURRY! THERE MAY STILL BE TIME TO TRANSPORT US WITH THIS LAST GROUP!
NOT WITH CARSON STILL OUT THERE!
AKISHA, PLEASE! HAVE YOU LOST YOUR SENSES?
COME TO THEM, ELDER. I'M STAYING.
I BELIEVE YOUR ANCESTORS CALLED THAT "SUICIDE."
MAYBE. THEY ALSO CALLED IT "CHOICE."
GET THESE PEOPLE AND YOURSELVES TRANSPORTED!
I'LL COLLECT AS MANY REMAINING ISLANDERS AS I CAN!
AKISHA...
...GOOD LUCK.
YEAH...
...I'LL NEED IT.

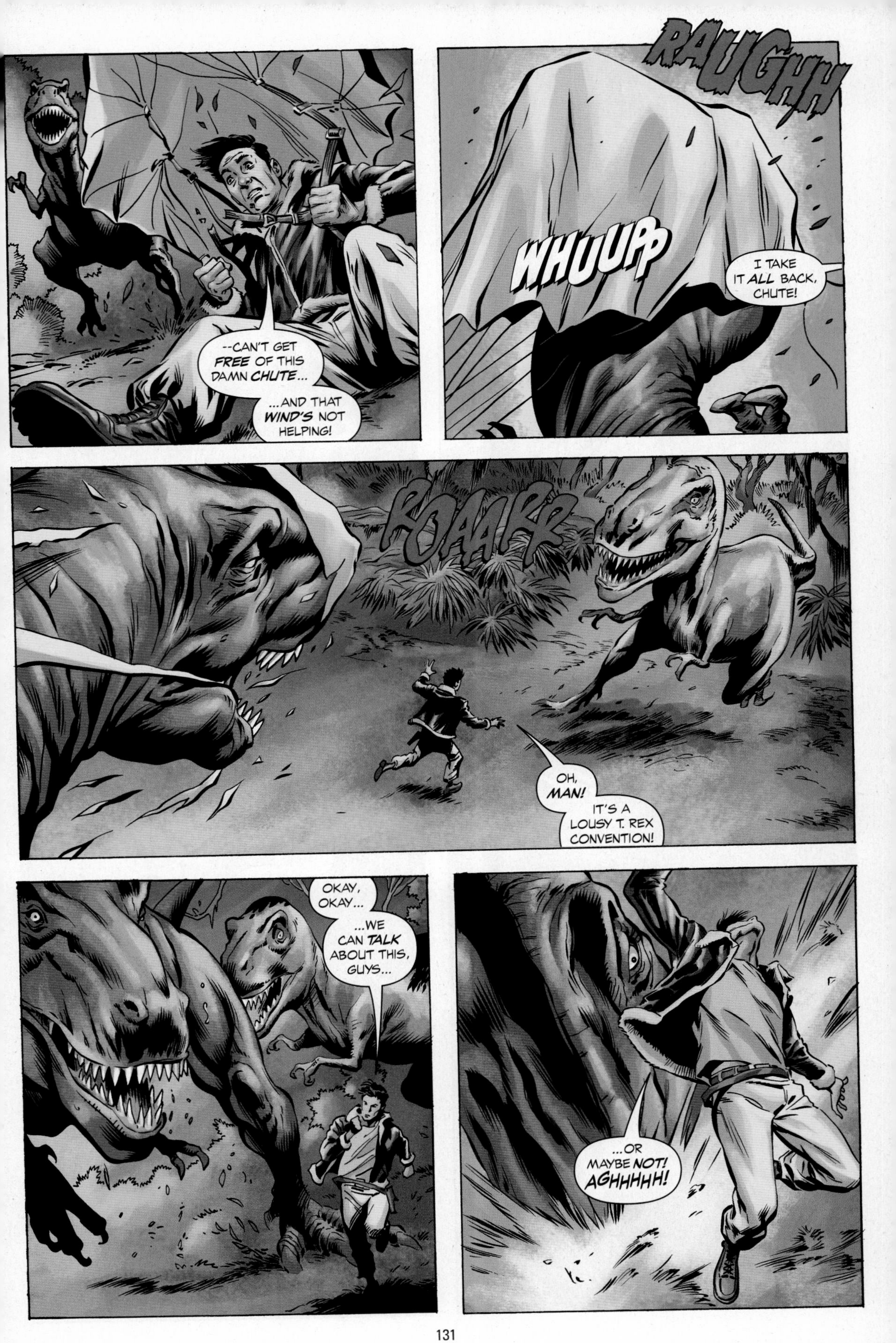
--CAN'T GET FREE OF THIS DAMN CHUTE...
...AND THAT WIND'S NOT HELPING!
RAUGHH
WHUUPP
I TAKE IT ALL BACK, CHUTE!
ROAARR
OH, MAN!
IT'S A LOUSY T. REX CONVENTION!
OKAY, OKAY...
...WE CAN TALK ABOUT THIS, GUYS...
...OR MAYBE NOT! AGHHHHH!

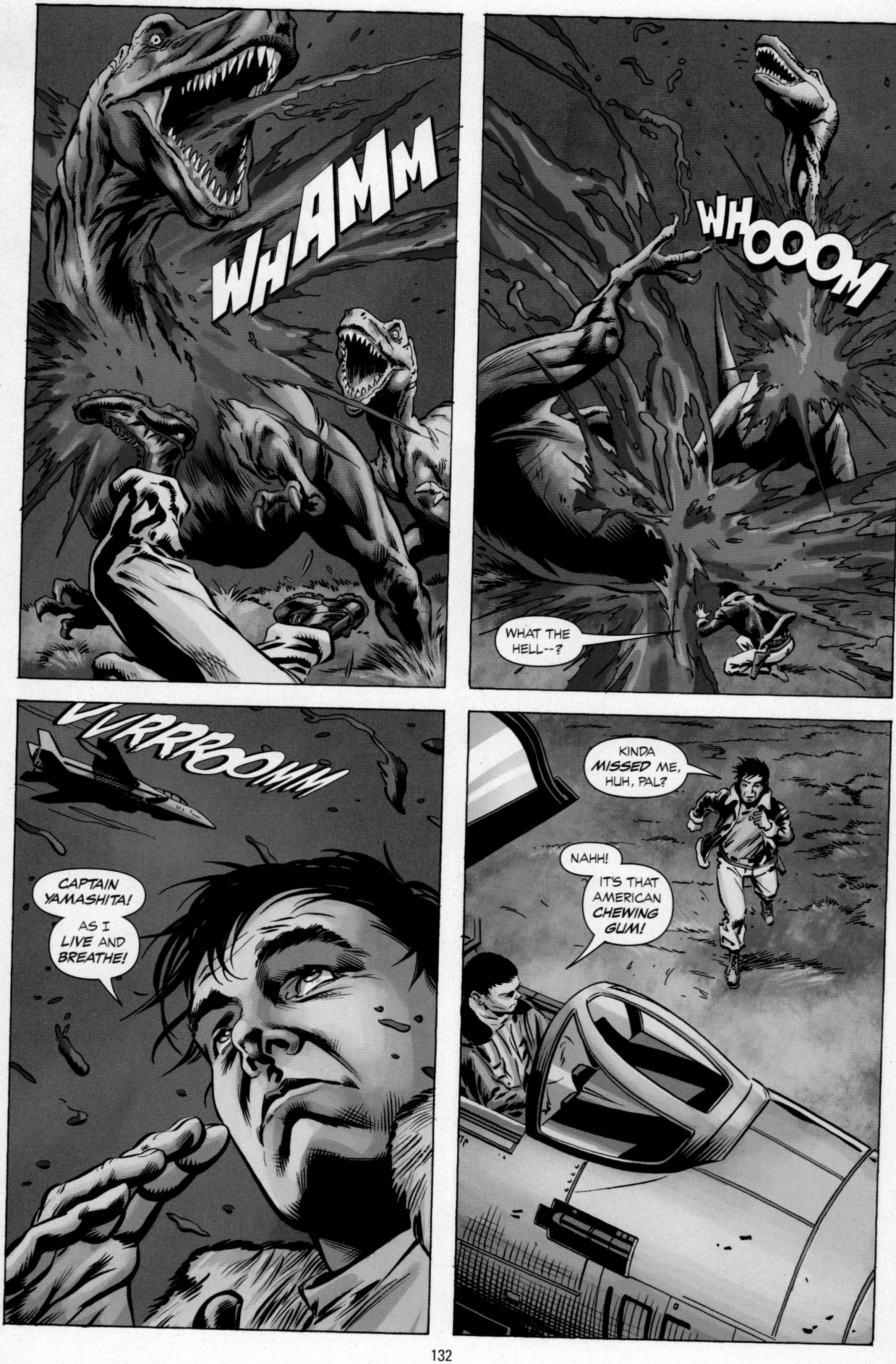
WHAMM
WHOOOM
WHAT THE HELL--?
VVRRROOMM
CAPTAIN YAMASHITA!
AS I LIVE AND BREATHE!
KINDA MISSED ME, HUH, PAL?
NAHH!
IT'S THAT AMERICAN CHEWING GUM!

TOMAHAWK!

WE MAY HAVE A CHANCE *OUT* OF THIS COMPOUND YET!

AYE--WE *SEE* THEM, FIREHAIR!

MUTANTS *FINALLY* LEARNED TO *FEAR* THE LAVA!

...UH...MY *FELLOWS*?

...I *DON'T* THINK THAT'S WHAT THEY'RE *AFRAID* OF!

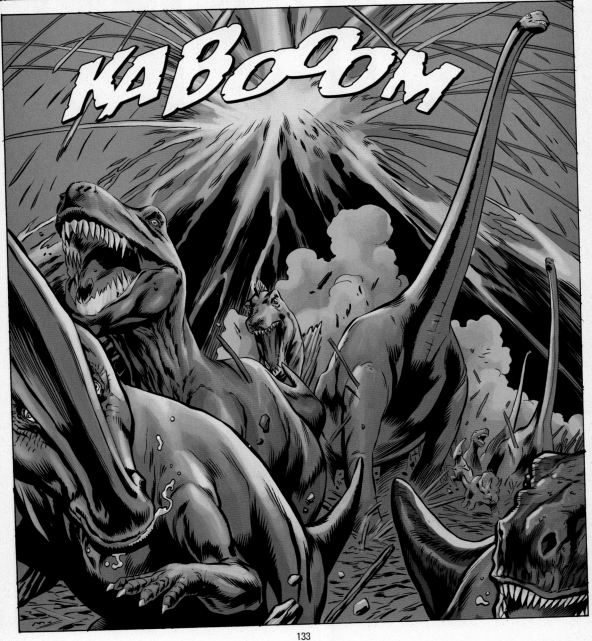

KABOOOM

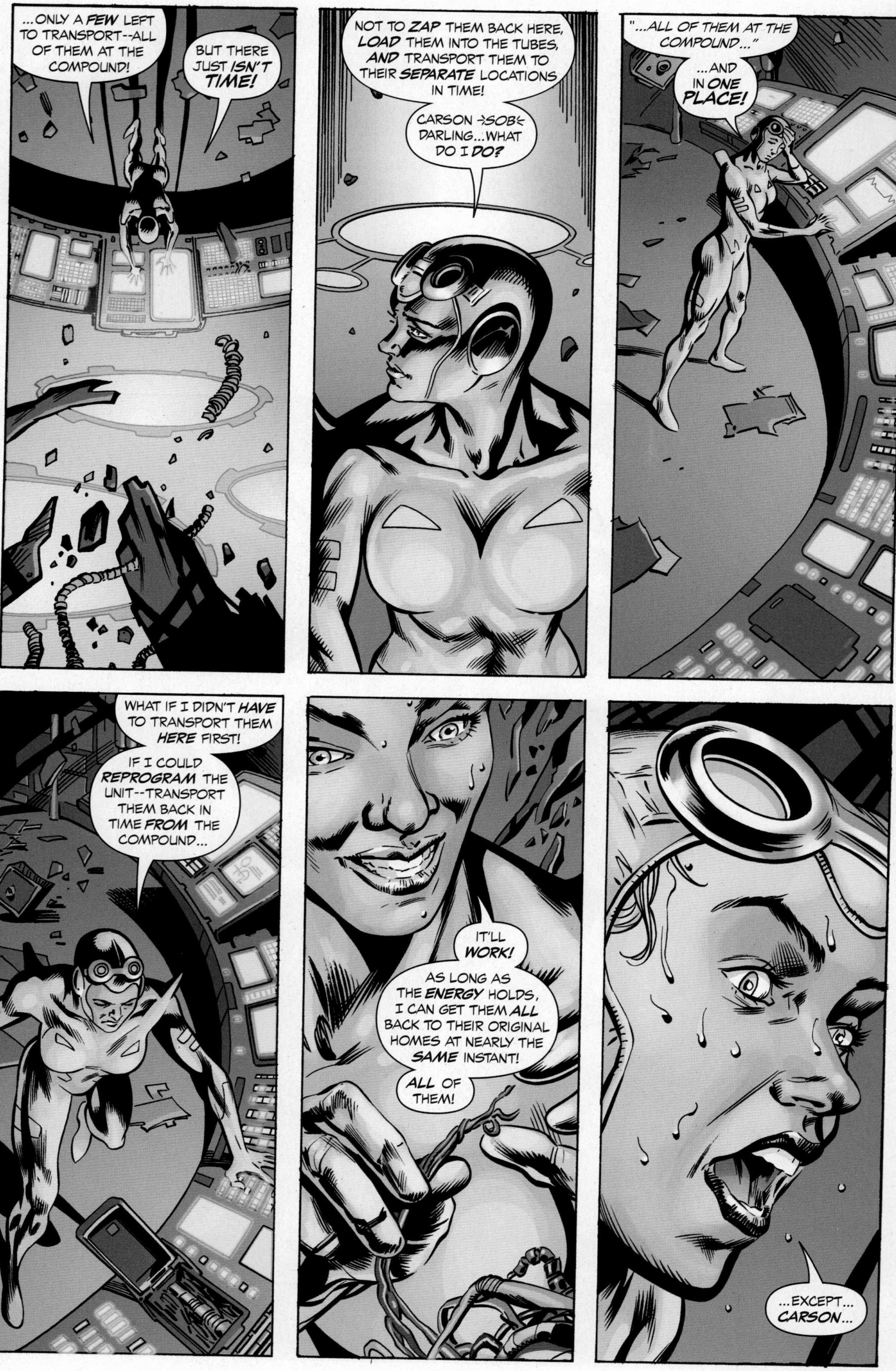
...ONLY A FEW LEFT TO TRANSPORT--ALL OF THEM AT THE COMPOUND!
BUT THERE JUST ISN'T TIME!
NOT TO ZAP THEM BACK HERE, LOAD THEM INTO THE TUBES, AND TRANSPORT THEM TO THEIR SEPARATE LOCATIONS IN TIME!
CARSON -SOB- DARLING...WHAT DO I DO?
"...ALL OF THEM AT THE COMPOUND..."
...AND IN ONE PLACE!
WHAT IF I DIDN'T HAVE TO TRANSPORT THEM HERE FIRST!
IF I COULD REPROGRAM THE UNIT--TRANSPORT THEM BACK IN TIME FROM THE COMPOUND...
IT'LL WORK!
AS LONG AS THE ENERGY HOLDS, I CAN GET THEM ALL BACK TO THEIR ORIGINAL HOMES AT NEARLY THE SAME INSTANT!
ALL OF THEM!
...EXCEPT... CARSON...

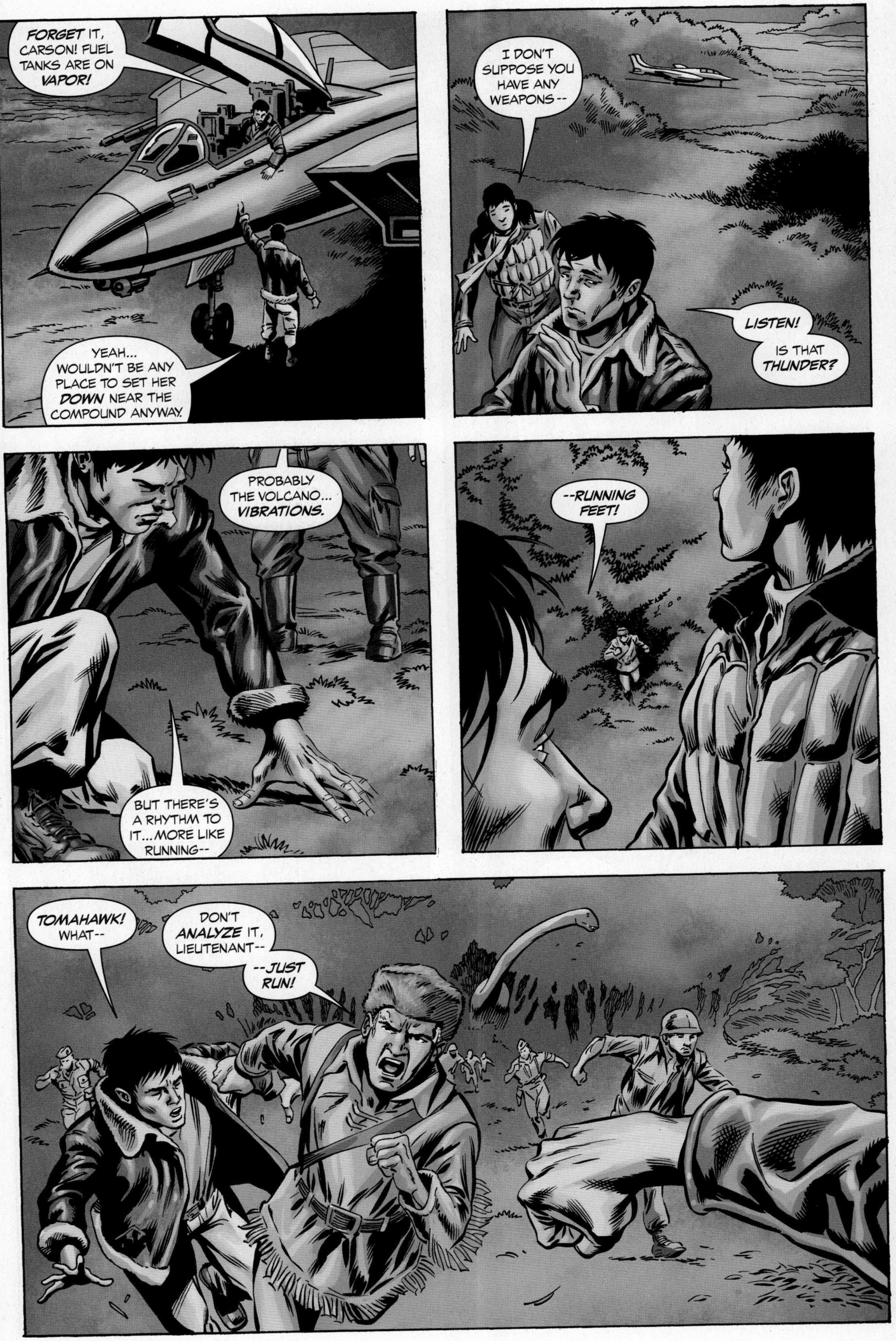
FORGET IT, CARSON! FUEL TANKS ARE ON VAPOR!
YEAH... WOULDN'T BE ANY PLACE TO SET HER DOWN NEAR THE COMPOUND ANYWAY.
I DON'T SUPPOSE YOU HAVE ANY WEAPONS --
LISTEN!
IS THAT THUNDER?
PROBABLY THE VOLCANO... VIBRATIONS.
BUT THERE'S A RHYTHM TO IT...MORE LIKE RUNNING--
--RUNNING FEET!
TOMAHAWK! WHAT--
DON'T ANALYZE IT, LIEUTENANT--
--JUST RUN!

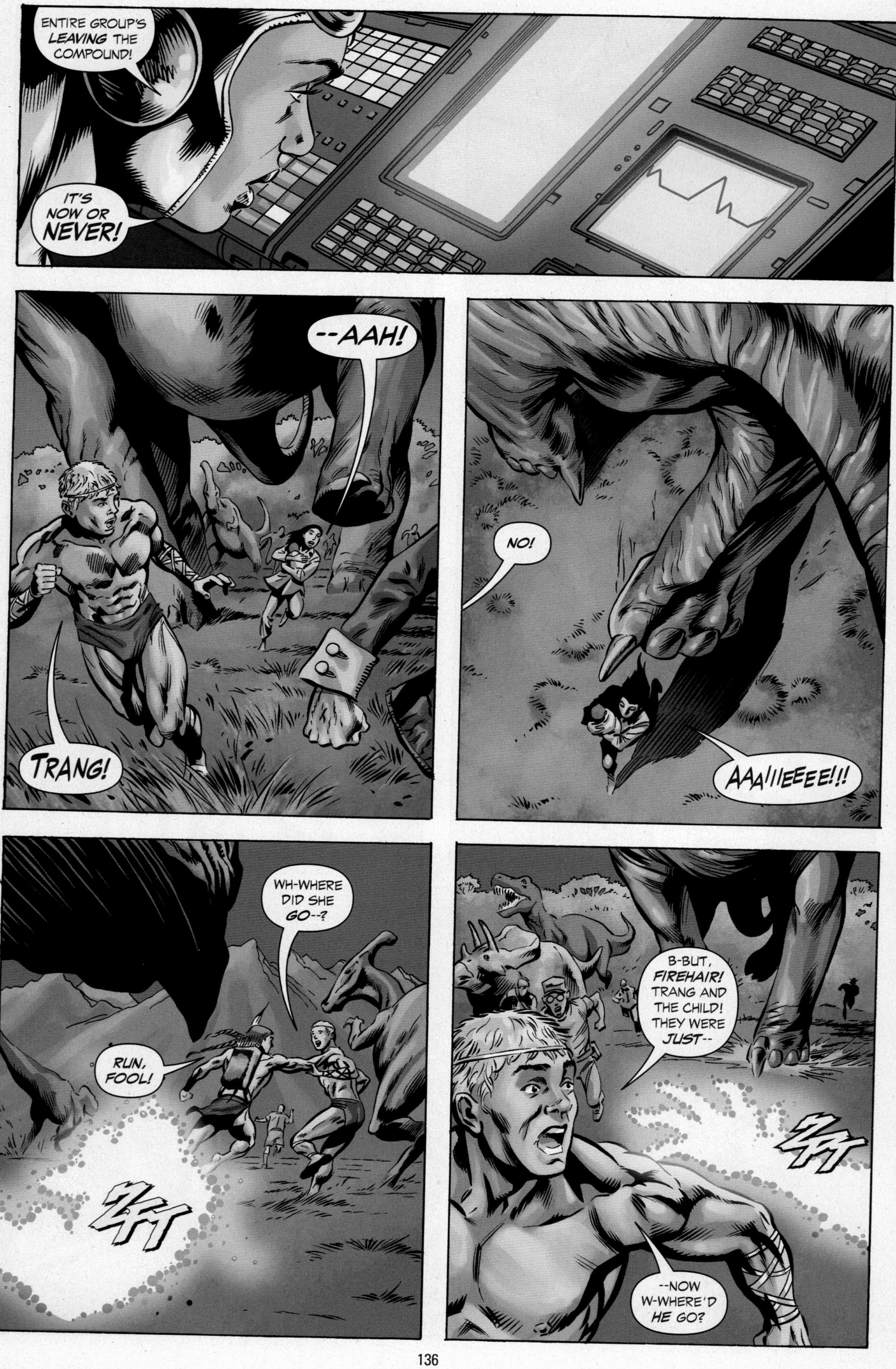
ENTIRE GROUP'S LEAVING THE COMPOUND!
IT'S NOW OR NEVER!
--AAH!
TRANG!
NO!
AAAIIIEEEE!!!
WH-WHERE DID SHE GO--?
RUN, FOOL!
ZFT
B-BUT, FIREHAIR! TRANG AND THE CHILD! THEY WERE JUST--
ZFT
--NOW W-WHERE'D HE GO?

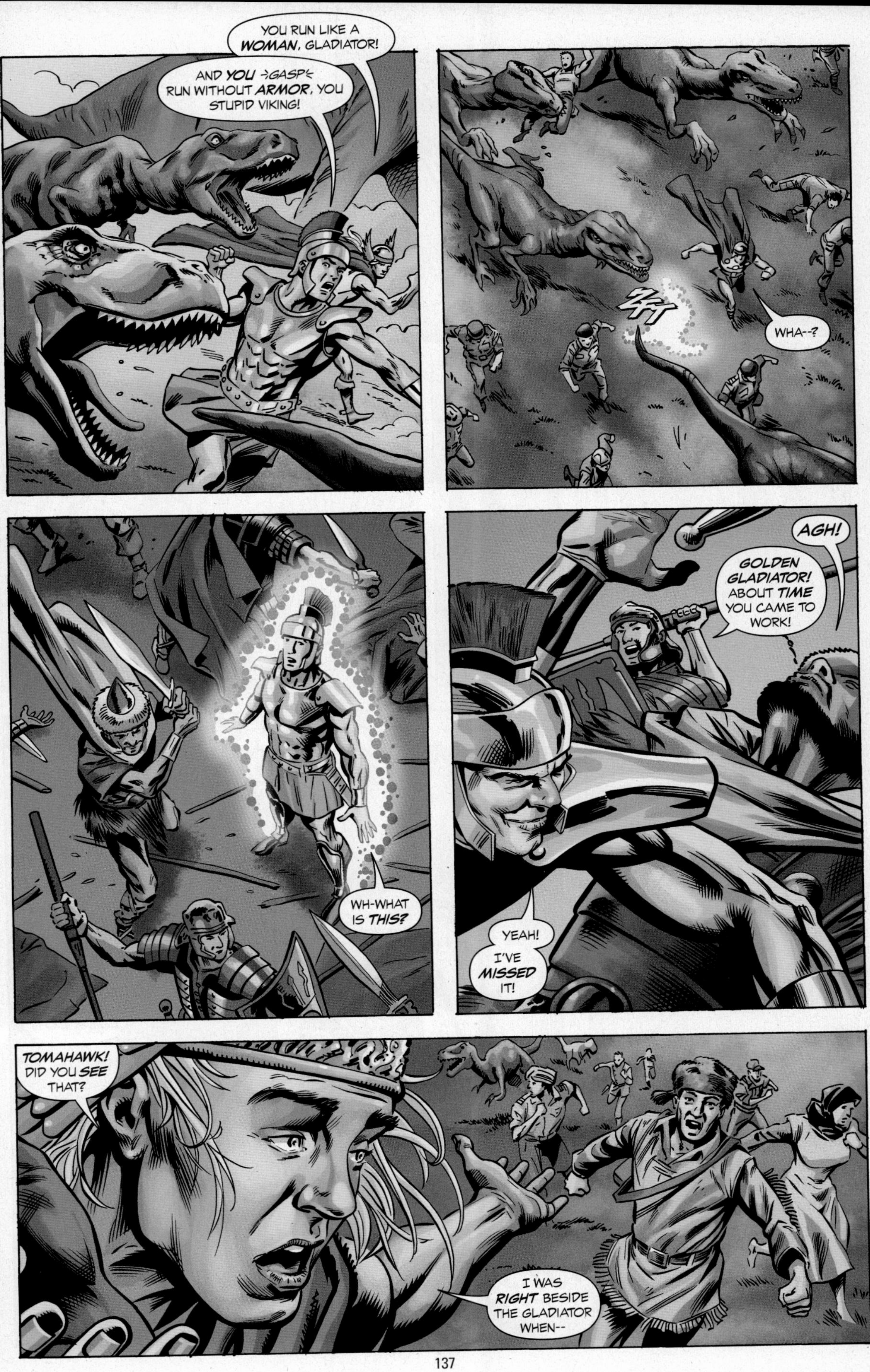
YOU RUN LIKE A WOMAN, GLADIATOR!
AND YOU ~GASP~ RUN WITHOUT ARMOR, YOU STUPID VIKING!
ZZT
WHA--?
WH-WHAT IS THIS?
AGH!
GOLDEN GLADIATOR! ABOUT TIME YOU CAME TO WORK!
YEAH! I'VE MISSED IT!
TOMAHAWK! DID YOU SEE THAT?
I WAS RIGHT BESIDE THE GLADIATOR WHEN--

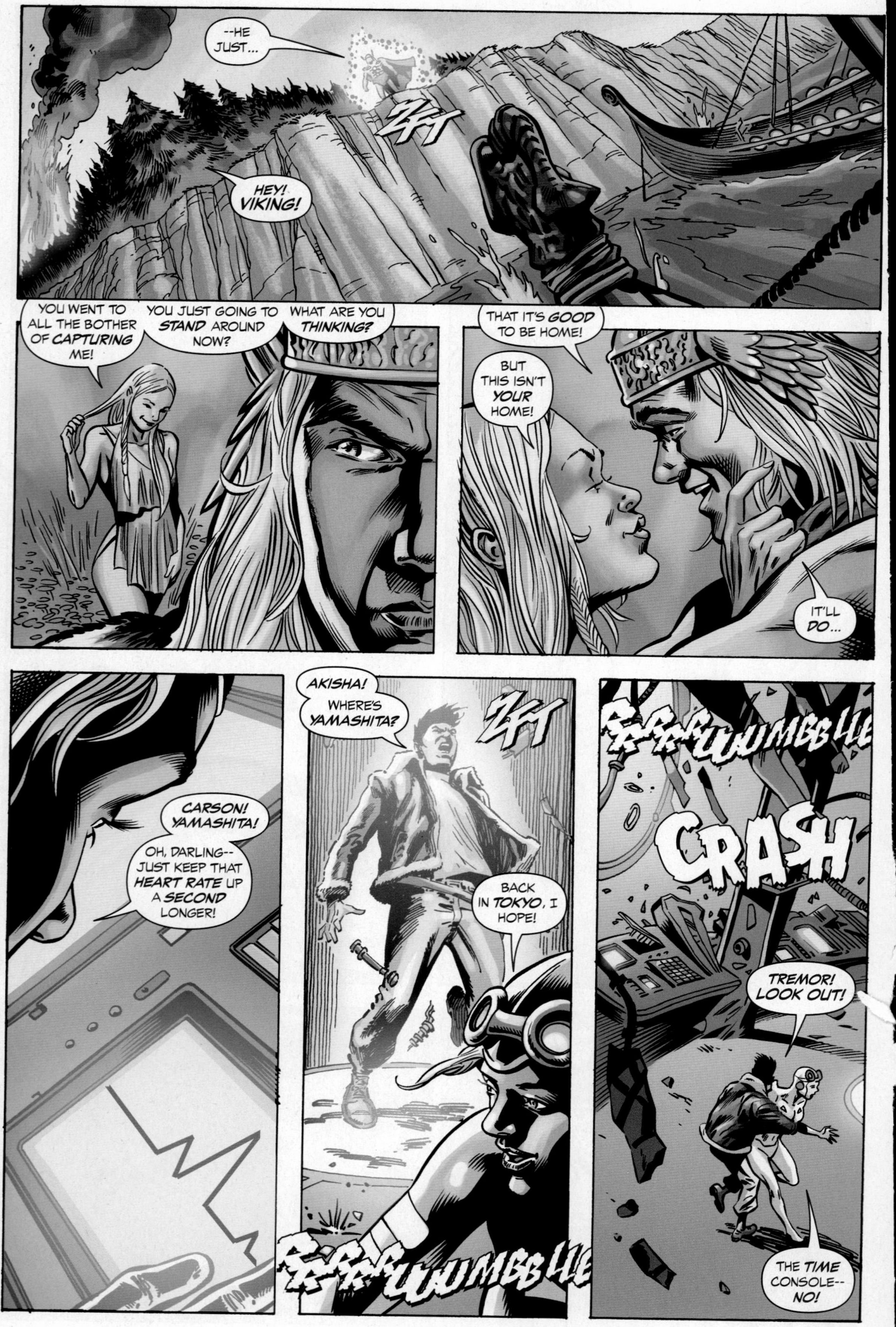
--HE JUST...
ZFT
HEY! VIKING!
YOU WENT TO ALL THE BOTHER OF CAPTURING ME!
YOU JUST GOING TO STAND AROUND NOW?
WHAT ARE YOU THINKING?
THAT IT'S GOOD TO BE HOME!
BUT THIS ISN'T YOUR HOME!
IT'LL DO...
CARSON! YAMASHITA!
OH, DARLING-- JUST KEEP THAT HEART RATE UP A SECOND LONGER!
AKISHA! WHERE'S YAMASHITA?
ZFT
BACK IN TOKYO, I HOPE!
RRRRUUUMBBLLE
RRRRUUUMBBLLE
CRASH
TREMOR! LOOK OUT!
THE TIME CONSOLE-- NO!

THAT DOES IT FOR *US!*

CRASH CRUNCH

MAROONED ON A *SINKING* ISLAND!

MAYBE *NOT!* THIS WAY!

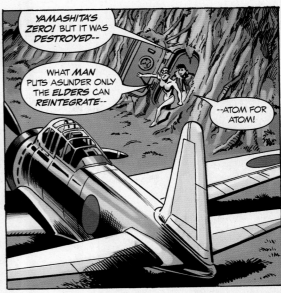

YAMASHITA'S ZERO! BUT IT WAS *DESTROYED*--

WHAT *MAN* PUTS ASUNDER ONLY THE *ELDERS* CAN REINTEGRATE--

--ATOM FOR *ATOM!*

YOU, UH...*CAN* FLY IT, RIGHT?

HOW HARD CAN IT BE?

WHAMM

WRRROOM

WHAT WAS *THAT?*

THAT WAS THE TRANSPORTER *IMPLODING* UNDER IMPACT!

CARSON, FLY *INTO* THE VORTEX!

INTO THE *WHAT?*

IT'S THE *ONLY* WAY, CARSON--

--TO GET *OUT* OF THIS TIME PLANE!

IF *YOU* SAY SO...

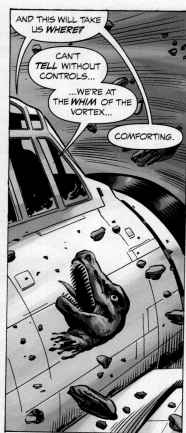

AND THIS WILL TAKE US *WHERE?*

CAN'T *TELL* WITHOUT CONTROLS...

...WE'RE AT THE *WHIM* OF THE VORTEX...

COMFORTING.

THAT'S BETTER! *BLUE* SKIES!

CARSON-- WHAT'S THAT *BELOW* US?

LOOKS LIKE *PEARL HARBOR!*

UNDER JAPANESE ATTACK!

SPRAOW POK POK POK POK

THEY'RE NOT THE *ONLY* ONES!

THAT'S ONE OF OUR *CURTIS P-40'S*-- --I'M BEING *ATTACKED* BY MY *OWN* PEOPLE!

THERE'S A *LESSON* HERE SOME-WHERE!

BRATTA

BRATTA BRATTA BRATTA

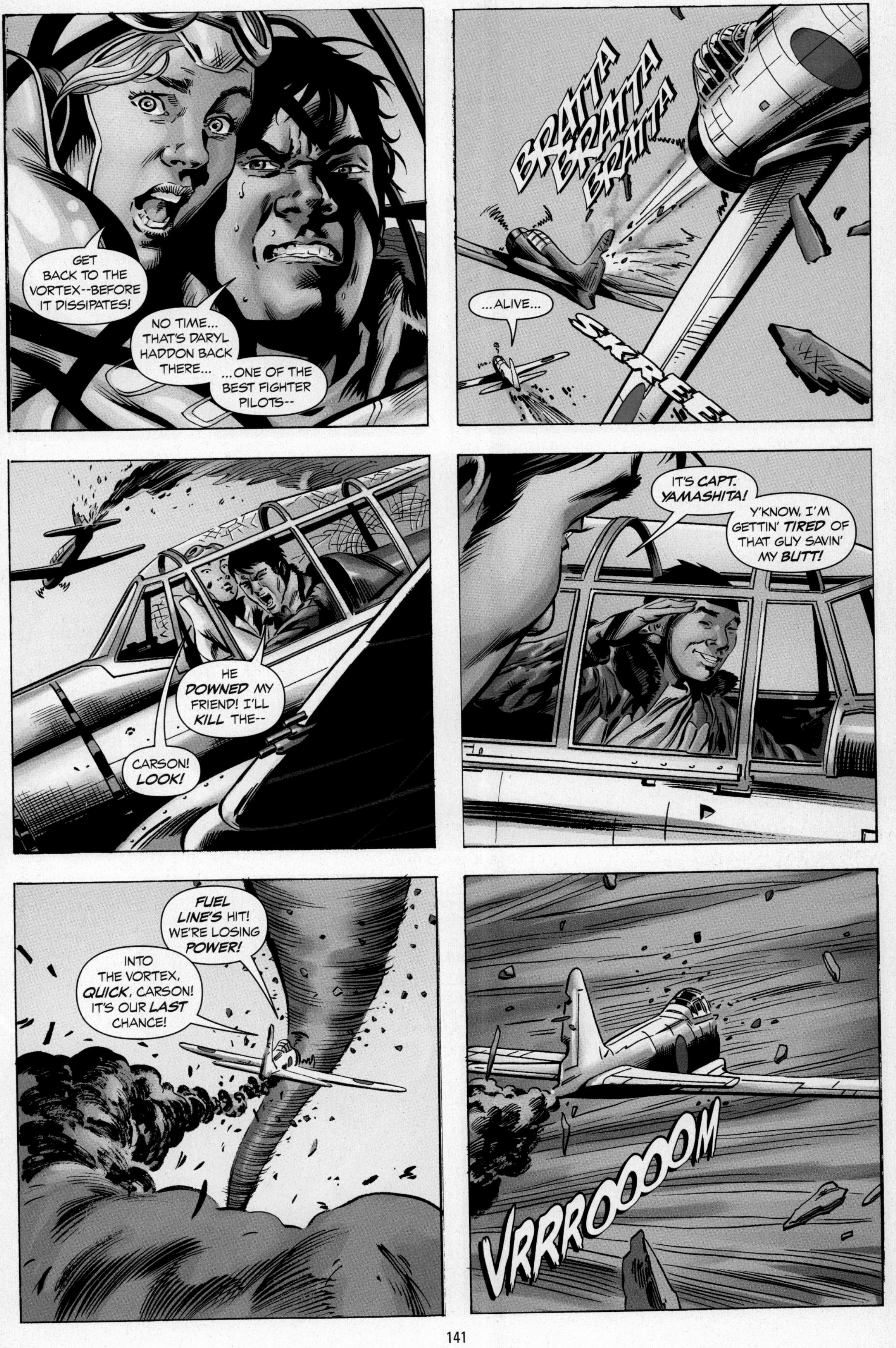
GET BACK TO THE VORTEX--BEFORE IT DISSIPATES!
NO TIME... THAT'S DARYL HADDON BACK THERE...
...ONE OF THE BEST FIGHTER PILOTS--
BRATTTA BRATTTA BRATTTA
...ALIVE...
SKREEE
HE DOWNED MY FRIEND! I'LL KILL THE--
CARSON! LOOK!
IT'S CAPT. YAMASHITA!
Y'KNOW, I'M GETTIN' TIRED OF THAT GUY SAVIN' MY BUTT!
FUEL LINE'S HIT! WE'RE LOSING POWER!
INTO THE VORTEX, QUICK, CARSON! IT'S OUR LAST CHANCE!
VRRROOOOOM

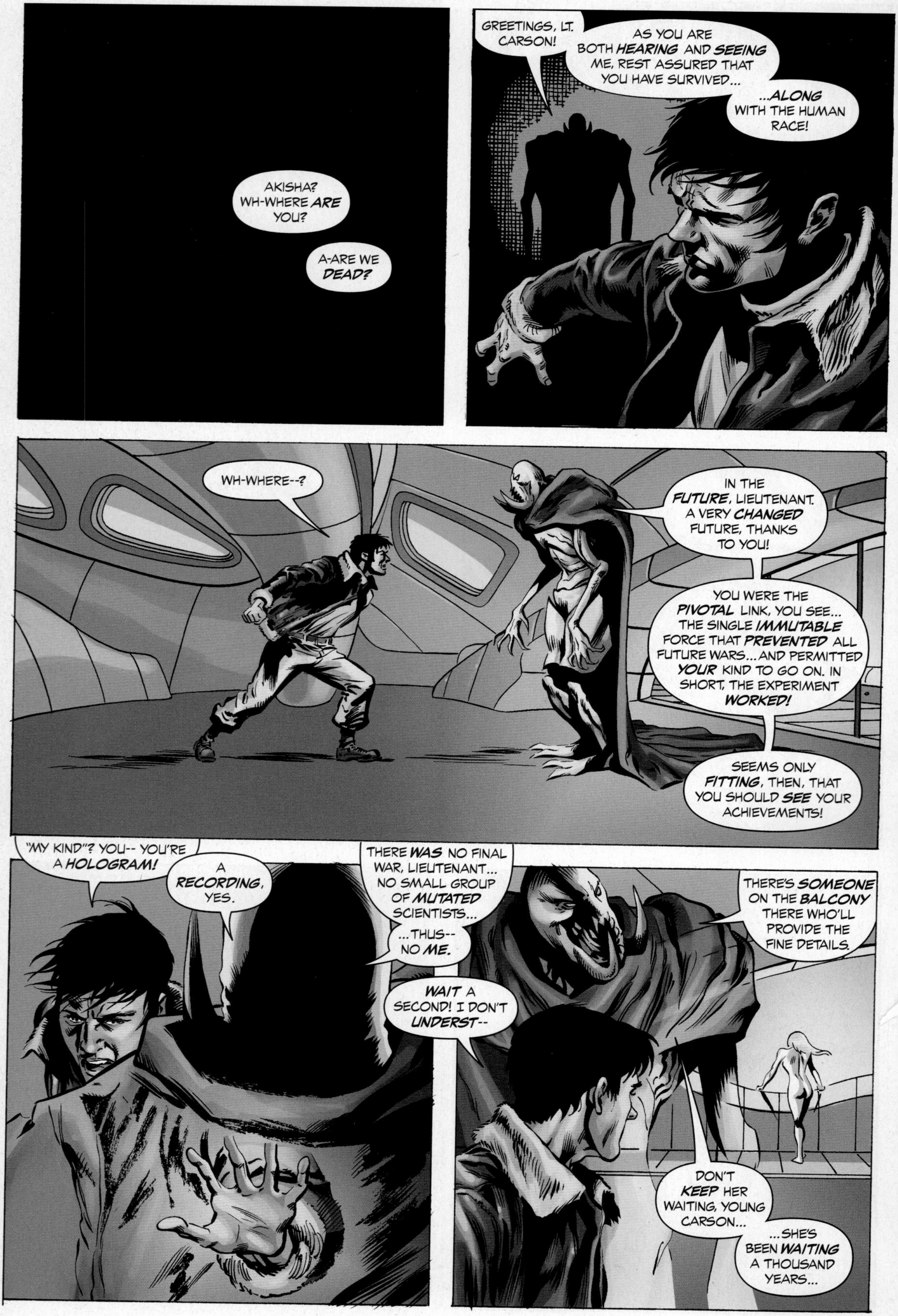

AKISHA? WH-WHERE ARE YOU?
A-ARE WE DEAD?
GREETINGS, LT. CARSON!
AS YOU ARE BOTH HEARING AND SEEING ME, REST ASSURED THAT YOU HAVE SURVIVED...
...ALONG WITH THE HUMAN RACE!
WH-WHERE--?
IN THE FUTURE, LIEUTENANT. A VERY CHANGED FUTURE, THANKS TO YOU!
YOU WERE THE PIVOTAL LINK, YOU SEE... THE SINGLE IMMUTABLE FORCE THAT PREVENTED ALL FUTURE WARS...AND PERMITTED YOUR KIND TO GO ON. IN SHORT, THE EXPERIMENT WORKED!
SEEMS ONLY FITTING, THEN, THAT YOU SHOULD SEE YOUR ACHIEVEMENTS!
"MY KIND"? YOU-- YOU'RE A HOLOGRAM!
A RECORDING, YES.
THERE WAS NO FINAL WAR, LIEUTENANT... NO SMALL GROUP OF MUTATED SCIENTISTS...
...THUS-- NO ME.
WAIT A SECOND! I DON'T UNDERST--
THERE'S SOMEONE ON THE BALCONY THERE WHO'LL PROVIDE THE FINE DETAILS.
DON'T KEEP HER WAITING, YOUNG CARSON...
...SHE'S BEEN WAITING A THOUSAND YEARS...

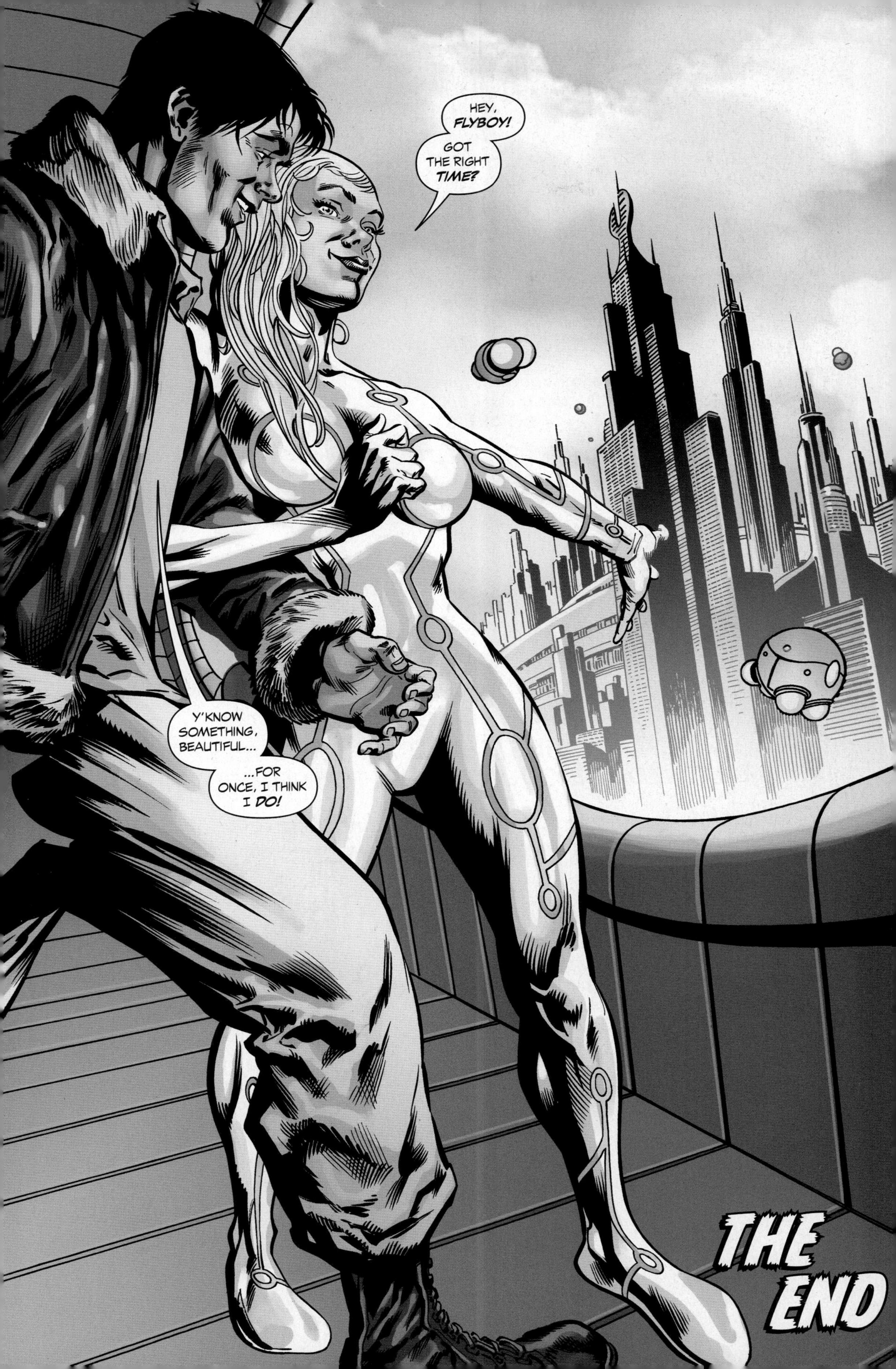
HEY, FLYBOY!
GOT THE RIGHT TIME?
Y'KNOW SOMETHING, BEAUTIFUL...
...FOR ONCE, I THINK I DO!
THE END

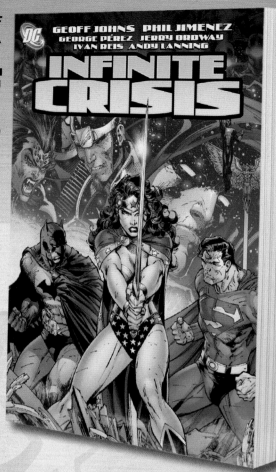